AMBASSADORS OF WAR

The Dynamics of Diplomacy and Armed Conflict

ERIC GUSTAFSON

Copyright © 2010 Eric Gustafson
All rights reserved.

ISBN: 1453668349
ISBN-13: 9781453668344

TABLE OF CONTENTS

Preface iii

Origins of the First World War 1

Origins of the Second World War 33

Anglo-American Diplomacy, 1939-45 56

The Algerian War 77

The Suez Crisis 107

The Vietnam War 137

The Falklands/Malvinas War 173

The Kosovo War 195

Origins of the Iraq War 221

Conclusion 239

Notes 243

PREFACE

Alongside war there has always been diplomacy; alongside the warlord, the diplomat seeking a nonmilitary solution. Some of our worst wars have been abbreviated through diplomatic efforts, while others have continued and worsened in spite of them. This theme is avidly studied in educational and research institutions worldwide, considered by political and military strategists, and watched over by everyone with an interest in international affairs.

This volume is intended for those described above and uses various case studies and assessments. It leads the reader through the evolution of conflict prevention or reduction. It takes into account not only the changing philosophies among the participants – politicians, diplomats, and the military – but also the outside influences that may have changed the nature, and even the purpose, of peacekeeping and conflict-resolution work over the past century.

Nowadays, the military threat can be applied without recourse to the deployment of vast armies, and this threat can be reduced by the involvement of international organizations rather than single warlords. So public awareness of war and military threat is now broadcast to a worldwide audience, instantaneously and without fear or favor, along with shrill calls for diplomatic intervention. In respect of the media and military affairs, certain evidence shows that the metaphoric "pen" can be mightier than the sword.

This collection seeks to provide a rounded examination of where political negotiation has had influence over military intentions or actions. It concentrates on how the diplomatic and military requirements are established for each potential or actual conflict, the technological trends, and how they have influenced diplomatic theory and practice. Taken in its entirety, the book allows readers to see various themes of how the military-diplomatic relationship works in both peace and war, while it also provides key insights into aspects of leadership, command, management, and prioritization of strategic options in both of those conditions.

Today, the major political factor influencing diplomacy is the relative decline of the role of national governments, as they increasingly face stern competition from other actors. The private sector, religious groups, immigrants, media, and other entities of civil society are demanding from the government that their interests be taken into consideration and that they have a say in making and implementing foreign policy. These case studies will allude to past interactions of such groups in the making of diplomacy, suggesting that such a condition is not as new as some might claim. Here also the importance of economics and its relations to diplomacy, along with such topics as intelligence, civil-military relations, and world views – all being integrated into the diplomatic process – highlight the need for a comprehensive approach to the creation of any successful diplomatic effort. For readers wishing for insights that may help in the shaping of today's diplomatic endeavors, the absolute differences between those working in a bilateral environment versus a coalition or collective environment will be obvious.

Finally, *Ambassadors of War* confirms the unavoidable truth that the creation of diplomacy is very much dependent on individuals. The best results have come from a balanced, layered, and questioning system, populated by honest, open, and informed practitioners. People make diplomacy, and that truism should not be forgotten.

———

The author would like to acknowledge and thank the institutions whose grants helped cover expenses of acquiring and translating foreign documents: the Goethe-Institut; the Fund for Central and East European Book Projects; the National Endowment for the Humanities; and the Office of Cultural Services at the French Embassy in the United States.

ORIGINS OF THE FIRST WORLD WAR

At the end of June 1914, a young Oxford historian named E.L. Woodward was spending part of his summer vacation in a Black Forest spa town. In the late afternoon of Sunday, June 28, the polite tinkling of cosmopolitan teacups on the long terrace of the Badenweiler spa hotel was interrupted by some startling news. The Archduke Franz Ferdinand, heir to the Habsburg throne and future ruler of some 45 million people in Central and Southeastern Europe, had been assassinated in Sarajevo. The hotel crowd excitedly dispersed and formed separate groups according to nationality. "I knew that something very grave had happened," Woodward reflected years later.[1]

That morning, Franz Ferdinand had paid his long-planned visit to Sarajevo, capital of the Austrian-administered province of Bosnia-Herzegovina. Military intelligence had warned the archduke not to go or, at any rate, not to visit the city on that particular day. That Sunday was a special day in the political calendar of Serb nationalism. It marked Vidovdan, the anniversary of the historic defeat of Tsar Lazar at the hands of the encroaching Ottomans at the Battle of Kosovo in 1389. The event had acquired a quasi-mythical importance to Serb identity, and it was central to the nationalist revival in Serbia in the second half of the nineteenth century. The visit of the future ruler of the

Habsburg Empire, much maligned by Balkan nationalists as "the prison of the nationalities," was therefore likely to be resented. The fact that that Sunday in 1914 marked the 525th anniversary of the Battle of Kosovo added further piquancy to the archduke's visit.

Franz Ferdinand ignored the advice of his intelligence service. His visit went ahead as scheduled. Having inspected Austrian troop maneuvers near the Bosnian spa town of Ilidža on June 26 and 27, the archduke and his wife, Sophie, Duchess von Hohenberg, set off for Sarajevo the following morning. There the Hapsburg heir's stubborn refusal to heed advice was compounded by official blunders. The route the archducal couple would take in the Bosnian capital had been well advertised, yet security precautions in the city were practically nonexistent. The local police was scarcely sufficient for traffic duties. And while the Sarajevo garrison stayed in its maneuver encampment, the one remaining infantry battalion in the capital had been stood down and was confined to barracks. As the archduke's motorcade headed down Appel Quay, Sarajevo's principal boulevard along the Miljacka River, a bomb was thrown at his car. It bounced off and exploded in the street, injuring the driver and passengers of the following vehicle. The archducal party nevertheless continued its procession to the city hall. Suggestions to bring up the garrison troops from their maneuver camp to secure the streets of the capital were dismissed by the provincial governor, General Oskar Potiorek. The troops, after all, were not kitted out in the full-dress uniform required for official functions involving members of the imperial family.

Before the imperial visitors set off for a luncheon party at the Konak, the governor's official residence, it was decided to change the advertised route. It seemed advisable to stay on the broad Appel Quay rather than to drive through the old city's picturesque but narrow streets. In the febrile atmosphere after the first attack, no one had thought of informing the official drivers about the alterations to the route. Thus, on reaching the Latin Bridge (*Latinska ćuprija*), the lead car turned off Appel Quay, as originally planned. The driver of Franz Ferdinand's vehicle followed suit. General Potiorek realized the mistake and ordered the driver to stay on the quay. The driver braked and threw the car into reverse. As the car came to a standstill, a man stepped forward and fired two shots from a semiautomatic pistol, hitting Franz Ferdinand in the neck and the duchess in the abdomen. As the assassin was wrestled to the ground, the archducal car sped toward the Konak. But it was too late for medical assistance. By 11:00 a.m. the heir to the oldest dynastic throne in Europe was dead.[2]

The archduke's violent death appalled all of Europe. This, after all, was a civilized age. Europe's monarchs died peacefully in their beds; they were not gunned down in the street. The European public's initial sympathies lay with Austria-Hungary. Suspicions of Belgrade's involvement soon hardened into evidence of a plot, aided and abetted by elements in the Serbian military-intelligence service.

As it turned out, the assassin, Gavrilo Prinčip, and the unsuccessful bomb thrower, Nedeljko Čabrinović, were part of a seven-member group affiliated with and trained and equipped by Black Hand (Црна рука), a Serb nationalist terrorist organization. The group's guiding spirit was Colonel Dragutin Dimitrijević, the charismatic and ruthless chief of the Intelligence Department in the Serbian government with the unique nickname of Apis (the Bee). The plot to kill the archduke was his. In fact, Apis was experienced in killing royalty. In 1903 he had taken a leading part in the bloody *coup d'état* by nationalist army officers against the autocratic and unpopular Austro-Hungarian client-king Aleksander Obrenović. The decision to kill Franz Ferdinand, meanwhile, was rooted in fear. Apis and others around him anticipated that the federal reform scheme that the archduke was rumored to favor might solve the multiethnic Habsburg Empire's nationality problems. In such an event, nationalist dreams of a Yugoslav kingdom centered on Serbia would never materialize.[3]

In light of the assassination's enormity, and given the increasingly apparent Serbian connection, the public reaction in Europe was somewhat muted. Austria-Hungary, it was generally agreed, was entitled to some form of retribution. There was some apprehension of international complications, not least because the Balkans had been a source of international tensions in recent years. Few people, however, expected a continental war to erupt. Indeed, as late as July 20, the permanent head of the British Foreign Office was confident that "matters will not be pushed to extremes."[4] And yet, within two weeks, by August 3-4, all of the Great Powers of Europe (with the exception of Italy) were plunged into war.

To appreciate Europe's path to war, it is necessary to distinguish between short-term and longer-term causes. Sarajevo was the trigger event, but it was not the conflict's cause. At the root of the war's origins was a mixture of individual decisions and "structural" forces that shaped the world in which the statesmen of 1914 had to act.

Nationalism – "a state of mind, in which the supreme loyalty of the individual is felt to be due to the nation-state"[5] – had established itself as a potent political force in Europe under the impact of the French Revolution. The restoration of 1815 delayed, but could not prevent, the further spread of nationalist ideals across the continent. By mid-century nationalism had transformed the map of Western and Central Europe. An independent Belgian nation-state emerged in 1831. Three decades later much of the Italian peninsula was united. And in 1871 thirty-eight German states, principalities, statelets, and city-states were united as the German Empire. War had made both unifications possible.

Eventually, national movements gained strength in every part of Europe. Serious diplomatic crises produced by the various "national questions" established nationalism as a profound influence on Great Power relations. European governments supported national independence movements with varying degrees of commitment and success. For the most part, the Great Powers sought to contain and control the forces of nationalism, especially so at the interface of the Ottoman and Habsburg worlds in the Balkans. The Congress of Berlin in 1878 preserved Turkey's fragile rule in Southeastern Europe for the next thirty years. At the same time, partial autonomy for Bulgaria provided a safety valve for nationalist aspirations in the region. The Powers frequently intervened on behalf of the Christian population in the Ottoman dominions. Toward the end of the nineteenth century, preserving the Balkans' stability was dependent principally on diplomatic cooperation between Vienna and St. Petersburg. The 1897 Austro-Russian Balkan entente, extended in 1903, provided for the coordination of efforts in Macedonia to which Bulgars, Greeks, and Serbs alike laid claim. The unraveling of the Austro-Russian entente in 1908, as will be seen later in the chapter, magnified the disruptive potential of Balkan nationalism. Until then, the Powers had acquiesced in the gradual decline of Ottoman authority in Turkey-in-Europe and had sought to manage this process. Internal reforms in Turkey, autonomy, or independence were meant to diffuse nationalism and to protect the Powers' interests. After 1908, managed nationalism was no longer in effect.[6]

Indeed, in the decade before 1914 nationalism became more explosive. The overall effect of nationalism's growth was ambiguous. It presented opportunities for political leaders: the urban masses could be manipulated and mobilized for a large national cause, so helping to stabilize potentially volatile societies. But it also entailed risks, for nationalist public opinion had the potential to develop a dynamic of its own and to interfere with foreign policy making. The nature of nationalism, moreover, had been transformed. If it espoused the rights of nationalities and demands for popular representation in the early nineteenth century, it lost much of this democratic impulse later on. Suffused with Social Darwinian ideas, it had come to revolve around notions of national exclusivity and racial superiority.

The growth of this new type of nationalism affected much of Europe. In France and Britain, nationalism's effect was deeply divisive. By 1914 the revived Irish "Home Rule" question threatened to drag Britain to the brink of civil war. In the seemingly secular French republic, the Dreyfus scandal had revealed the ugly truth that Jews and Protestants were not regarded as real Frenchmen.

In the Eastern European military monarchies, governments tended to use nationalism to buttress the existing regimes. Already under German Chancellor Otto von Bismarck, nationalist campaigns (orchestrated by government offices) had been used to push armaments programs through the Reichstag. Official patronage of pan-German and other extreme nationalist groups increased. Indeed, Berlin relied on such groups for its vigorous Germanization policy in the Eastern provinces. The Navy Office even created and financed its own navalist pressure group and propaganda organization to drum up support for the creation of a powerful High Seas Battle Fleet.

Even an autocracy like tsarist Russia was not immune to nationalist public opinion. Faced with proto-revolutionary pressures from below and with centrifugal tendencies in its Polish, Finnish, and Baltic provinces, the Russian government resorted to Russification measures. Building on the intimate connection between tsardom and the Orthodox Church, the latter's wealth and authority were increased throughout the empire. State authorities and right-wing groups viewed Russification as an efficacious means of stabilizing the existing regime. But right-wing publicists and many army officers also espoused the cause of pan-Slavism. This was a somewhat amorphous phenomenon, a mixture of Western-style racialist nationalism and Eastern Orthodox mysticism. It was based on assumptions of a Slavic fraternity and ascribed to "Mother Russia" the role of protector of the smaller Slavic peoples. Pan-Slavism had been a factor in Russian politics since the 1870s. In the last years of peace before 1914, however, the government in St. Petersburg found it increasingly difficult to ignore such currents of opinion.

The impact of nationalism on the multiethnic Austro-Hungarian dual monarchy was twofold. The rise of nationalist sentiments among the various subject nationalities posed an existential threat to the empire's survival. This threat, of course, could not be countered through some form of generic Habsburg nationalism, since the monarchy's whole *raison d'etre* was dynastic and supranational. In this respect Austria-Hungary was placed in a unique position. There was, however, one form of nationalism that enjoyed a privileged position. Under the 1867 constitutional compromise between the dynasty and the Hungarian nobility, the latter had won the right to govern the monarchy's eastern half from Budapest, though foreign and defense matters were left in the hands of a common government. Crucially, since the 1890s the Austro-German and Magyar governments pursued increasingly divergent strategies in the nationality question. Vienna sought to accommodate the national aspirations of its non-German subjects, especially the Czechs, within the existing framework. The authorities in Budapest, by contrast, pursued a ruthless Magyarization policy in the Hungarian half of the dual monarchy. What both governments agreed on, however, was that the rise of Slavic nationalism within the empire and without was best countered by reasserting Austria-Hungary's authority in the Balkans.[7]

Another significant structural force that shaped pre-1914 international politics was the combined effect of the industrial and demographic revolutions. Technological progress and the increased production capacities of the advanced industrial nations also enhanced the Great Powers' war-fighting capabilities. The mass production of modern weaponry of uniform quality made warfare more effective. Metallurgical advances allowed for the production of more durable and larger-caliber artillery pieces. These not only had a much longer range than the bronze cannon of

Napoleon's day, but thanks to increasingly sophisticated range-finding technology, they were also more precise. The development of chrome-tipped steel shells, meanwhile, made these long-range guns even more devastating weapons. Already the Franco-Prussian War of 1870 had demonstrated the fortress-busting power of modern Krupp or Schneider-Creuzot guns that had ranges of twenty to thirty miles. In the 1890s, advances in chemical engineering allowed for the production of more efficient gunpowder that combusted without leaving dangerous residue and was "smokeless". Better concealment of artillery positions and advancing infantry – the inevitable results of such inventions – further increased the destructive potential of nineteenth-century warfare.[8]

The demographic explosion in Europe magnified the impact of the Industrial Revolution. With the notable exception of France, where the population was relatively stagnant at an increase of a mere 2.3 million between 1876 and 1906, the population of Europe grew from some 283 million to 392 million, an increase of 38.5 percent. Such growth was particularly pronounced in the more advanced industrial nations. In Britain, the population rose from some 27.5 million in 1850 to just over 46 million by 1914, an increase of 67.2 percent. Population growth in Germany followed a similarly exponential curve, rising from a little over 41 million in 1871 to 64.9 million in 1910, a rise by 58.2 percent. Indeed, even in the economically backward Russian Empire the population doubled, from an estimated 74 million in 1859 to about 149.3 million in 1906. In the Habsburg lands the population growth was less pronounced but still amounted to a 10 percent increase between 1890 and

1900 alone.[9] As all the major nations of Europe, except for Britain, had instituted systems of universal conscription, the demographic explosion resulted in larger armies, which Europe's expanding industries could keep supplied. In 1900 the five Great Powers were in a position to mobilize 10 million men among them.

The advent of steam-powered locomotion reinforced these trends. Railways had demonstrated their revolutionary military potential in the American Civil War and, more especially, in Prussia's wars of the 1860s. The growth of strategic railway networks across Europe fundamentally altered the nature of warfare. The railroads expedited the process of mobilizing troops and allowed for the transport of increasing numbers of soldiers. While on average no more than 80,000 soldiers were committed to battle during the Napoleonic Wars, railways allowed the Prussian general staff to deploy 1.2 million troops to the battle zone in 1870. By 1914, this figure had risen to 3.4 million.

Railways placed a premium on speed of mobilization and deployment. Crucially they blurred the difference between these two. Mobilization, in effect, became deployment. Given the prevailing emphasis on speed of mobilization, political crisis management was more difficult once mobilization had been ordered. Finally, railways connected the theaters of war to the industrial centers in the interior. They now formed a steady supply line and so increased the capacity of the Powers to sustain their war efforts for a prolonged period. Mobilizing the logistics skills available in the European railways and harnessing them to the strategic requirements of warfare therefore placed war on a quasi-industrial basis.[10]

In part, these developments also influenced the much more competitive international environment of the two decades before 1914. European imperialism, the competition for overseas colonial possessions, reflected some of these pressures. However, the industrial economies did not need to secure foreign markets for surplus goods or surplus investment capital. Indeed, the overseas possessions the Great Powers had acquired since the mid-1880s absorbed only limited amounts of capital. And these colonies did not produce the economic benefits that contemporary colonial agitators and later theorists have claimed. European colonial expansion was not the product of carefully calibrated economic strategies. Rather, it was the result of a mixture of strategic calculations and domestic political pressures. Crises along the periphery of the existing informal spheres of empire and local initiatives by the "men on the spot" played a far greater role in imperial expansion than centrally crafted and executed policies. Rounding off existing colonial possessions was dictated more by questions of military strategy than by expectations of economic gains. The growing concern of British governments in the 1890s with securing the Upper Nile Valley against French encroachments, for instance, underlined this trend.[11]

Domestic considerations undoubtedly fueled European imperialism. Germany's pursuit of *Weltpolitik* was to no small degree driven by such calculations. Rallying pro-regime parties around a populist, though ill-defined, policy of overseas expansion would stabilize the political and social status quo, the Kaiser and his entourage reasoned. In a similar manner, Russian expansionism in Central Asia and the Far East and, after 1905, Russia's more overt support for the smaller

Slavic nations in the Balkans were also attempts to divert domestic attention to foreign-affairs issues and to buttress autocracy.

Colonial lobby groups and Christian missionary societies were also capable of generating pressure on the governments. The *parti colonial* in the French chamber, though informal, had the power to make or break governments and ministerial careers. In Britain, the cross-party "Pig-tail Committee," representing largely Chinese commercial interests, was well established in the House of Commons and dominated parliamentary debates on Far Eastern affairs. The German Kolonial-Verein was large and funded well enough to embarrass the government from the right. Finally, Social Darwinism had gained intellectual currency in Europe since the 1890s. Although it is difficult to quantify the impact of ideas on practical politics, there can be little doubt that demands for greater national efficiency and for firmer government action to safeguard national security shaped public political discourse in the decade before 1914. On the whole, the governments of Europe were more cautious. Yet, if they understood the potentially deleterious impact of war on Europe's growing prosperity, which was dependent on financial and commercial expansion, they were not altogether immune against the pressures from below.[12]

The harsher international environment and the growth in Europe's armed forces led to a creeping militarization of Great Power diplomacy. The mass conscript armies that the Powers commanded and the vast military bureaucracies that supported these armies influenced political thinking. The unceasing advance of weapons technology and the more competitive international climate made constant modernization of the existing armed forces a strategic imperative. In turn, this generated arms races on land and at sea. The inherent logic of the arms-race dynamic began to influence international politics. Questions of armaments programs had acquired the potential of becoming questions of international diplomacy.

A side effect of the growth in armaments was the Powers' growing temptation to resort to saber-rattling to intimidate potential enemies. It would be wrong, however, to argue that armaments alone destabilized international politics. As will be seen below, the growing incidence of such international bullying after 1905 reflected shifts in the global balance of power. Indeed, for the most part, the Powers' armaments programs had a deterrent effect. Since armies were so much larger and so much better equipped, and could so much more easily be kept supplied, war, once started, threatened to turn into a prolonged conflict. The likely enormous financial, material, and human costs of a prolonged war, and the social disruptions such a conflict would cause, were a powerful constraint on governments in this period and provided an incentive to accommodate the interests of other Powers. Conversely, the same development also provided an incentive for launching a preemptive war with the aim of eliminating an actual or perceived potential enemy before he was strong enough to launch an attack on his part.[13]

None of these background influences made war inevitable. But they shaped the environment in which the statesmen of the period had to operate.

The arms race that captured contemporary imagination as much as that of later historians was that at sea. Great Powers and smaller nations alike accepted the precepts of "navalism," a doctrine first propounded by the American naval officer and historian Captain Alfred Thayer Mahan. His writings were based on the historical insight that all empires in history had been sea-based. Mahan, therefore, stipulated that world power rested on sea power. Sea power, in turn, required command of the sea, and that was not to be had without capital ships. A Great Power without a sufficiently strong navy, then, could never aspire to acquire world power.

All the major powers of the period expended substantial sums on naval armaments programs, and even such smaller nations as Greece and Brazil sought to acquire dreadnought-type battleships, the latest fashion in naval technology after 1906. To an extent capital ships were prestige objects, the floating equivalent of the world exhibitions so popular during this period. They advertised a nation's technological sophistication, industrial capacity, and financial prowess as well as its ability to project its naval power on a global scale.[14]

The most intense naval competition, and the one that has attracted the most attention among historians, was that between Britain and Germany. The German challenge to Britain, the preeminent naval power of the period, evolved gradually. It was the brainchild of Grand Admiral Alfred von Tirpitz, the head of the German Navy Office. The naval program's anticipated domestic stabilizing function aside, strategically it was directed against Britain from the outset. The German Navy Laws of 1898 and 1900, and the further naval expansion under the 1908 *Novelle*, or amendment, to the 1900 law, aimed at creating a force that could effectively rival the Royal Navy. By 1918 the Imperial High

Seas Battle Fleet was planned to have reached about two-thirds of the numerical strength of Britain's navy. The 2:3 ratio was crucial, for contemporary naval warfighting doctrine suggested that such a ratio gave the weaker side a realistic chance of victory in a surprise naval attack.

The German naval buildup did not go unnoticed in Britain, where it was rightly seen as a threat. As Winston Churchill, first lord of the Admiralty between 1911 and 1915, observed, a large fleet was a luxury to primarily land-based Germany but a vital necessity to Britain and her empire. Tirpitz and the German leadership calculated that, in light of competing domestic demands for social welfare legislation, the British government could not afford a major new naval building program and would lack the political will to increase the tax burden in order to meet the German challenge. At least in its original conception, the German program was also based on the assumption that the antagonism between Britain and her two traditional imperial rivals, France and Russia, would continue unabated.

The Germans miscalculated on both counts. Parallel to the growing Anglo-German naval rivalry, but quite independent of it, British diplomacy succeeded in mending relations with France and Russia in the agreements of 1904 and 1907. These agreements were colonial and imperial in nature and scope and were not at all aimed at containing Germany in Europe. Still, the subsequent improvement in relations with these two erstwhile rivals, combined with the fact that the destruction of the Russian fleet in the Russo-Japanese War had eliminated Russia as a naval power, allowed Britain to concentrate its naval efforts on Germany. In consequence, German assumptions that Britain would not be able to mobilize the necessary financial resources in order to meet the German challenge at sea were misplaced. From 1906, Germany and Britain were locked in a naval arms race. For as long as Germany kept laying down battleships, the race continued.

By 1913, however, the naval race was effectively over. It ended like all previous naval arms races: the color of British money had won. Faced with an intensified Franco-Russian military buildup on land, the Berlin government saw itself forced to channel the bulk of its defense spending back to the army again. Thus, by the time war broke out in 1914, the Anglo-German naval race no longer mattered. But it had soured relations between the countries. Attempts by both sides to improve relations through cooperation in the Balkans or in colonial questions in Africa could not overcome the bitter legacy of mutual suspicion.[15]

Anglo-German cooperation, then, could not easily be obtained. Other developments also made for greater inflexibility in Great Power politics. One was the initiation, in 1894, of the Franco-Russian alliance, very much a triumph of the national interest over the deep ideological fissures between the secular republic and tsarist autocracy. The *Franco-Russe* was poised against Germany and the German-led Triple Alliance with Italy and Austria-Hungary. Its existence meant that any conflict in Europe involving either France or Russia and Germany or her allies had the potential of escalating into a full continental war. One, no doubt unintended, side effect of the Franco-Russian alliance was a deterioration in Britain's relations with Germany. Faced by France in the West and Russia in the East, Germany had to go overseas in pursuit of her *Weltpolitik* ambitions, and there she was liable to clash with Britain.[16]

The rigidity of the two opposing alliances grew in reaction to a series of international crises. Most of these were prototypes of the July crisis of 1914. For the purposes of this survey it will suffice to focus on two of them in more detail: the First Moroccan Crisis of 1905-06 and the Bosnian Annexation Crisis of 1908-09.

At its core, the First Moroccan Crisis was a Franco-German confrontation about the future of the northwestern African country. Its origins and its impact, however, went well beyond the region and beyond relations between the two traditional enemies. In deciding to challenge France over Morocco, German leadership was guided by concerns about national defense rather than by ambitions for colonial expansion. Two factors were central to German calculations.

The first of these was the Russo-Japanese War. By the time the Moroccan Crisis began in March 1905, Russia's admission of defeat in the Far Eastern conflict was only a matter of time. The impending defeat at the hands of the rising, non-European nation was not only a serious blow to Russia's international prestige. The war had also overstretched its military resources, depleted its financial reserves, and plunged the empire into its most serious domestic crisis yet. The "Bloody Sunday" demonstration on January 9, and the industrial strikes, unrest at the universities, and disturbances in the Baltic provinces and in Poland that followed, were storm petrels of the constitutional crisis that was to shake a panic-stricken tsarist regime in September and October 1905. Faced with defeat on the battlefield, financial exhaustion, and domestic turmoil, the Russian government required a period of international calm to restore Russia's position abroad and to consolidate the tsar's rule at home. Indeed, most contemporary intelligence estimates calculated that Russia would not be in a position to sustain a major military campaign, let alone one involving another Great Power, until around 1916 or 1917.

Russia's current and medium-term weakness had significant international ramifications. Its most immediate effect was on France, for the outcome of the Russo-Japanese War effectively disabled the Franco-Russian alliance. The combination with Russia had been the cornerstone of French security strategy. Since 1894 Russian military might had helped to constrain the much-feared neighbor east of the River Rhine. Now, freed from the prospect of having to fight a continental war on two fronts, Germany was in a position to threaten France without fear of Russian intervention.[17]

The second factor that influenced German strategic thinking at the time was the Anglo-French agreement and declaration of April 8, 1904, more commonly known as the Entente. This was not an alliance at all. It did not pertain to European questions either. It was a strictly colonial agreement that settled a number of long-standing colonial disputes between Paris and London. Indeed, its chief attraction for the Marquess of Lansdowne, who, as foreign secretary, had signed the agreement, was its seemingly limited nature. The agreement touched on such diverse matters as fishing rights off Newfoundland, the demarcation of colonial frontiers in West Africa, and the status of Siam and the New Hebrides in the Pacific. At its core, however, was a deal concerning Egypt and Morocco.

In return for France's formal recognition of exclusive British control over Egypt, Britain pledged to lend political support to French ambitions in Morocco. In this way, the dispute over Egypt's future was settled, a dispute that had bedeviled Anglo-French relations since Britain's military occupation of the country in 1882.[18]

This seemingly limited agreement affected Germany on two levels. In diplomatic terms, Anglo-French tensions over Egypt had enabled Germany to play these two powers against each other in the past. By removing this bone of contention from their agenda, Paris and London had now diminished Berlin's ability to manipulate Anglo-French relations. Germany's international position was thus somewhat reduced.

In strategic terms, the German government suspected that there was more to the Entente than a colonial deal. In this, Berlin projected onto Britain and France its own Bismarckian practice of often adding secret military clauses to alliances and other diplomatic agreements. The German leadership resolved to use Morocco to test the Entente's nature and solidity. Thus, when France dispatched a military expedition to Fez, ostensibly to support the beleaguered sultan of Morocco, whose writ no longer ran the whole breadth and length of his realm, Germany decided to act.

The French action was, indeed, problematic. Morocco's independence had been guaranteed by an international treaty, the 1880 Madrid Convention. The dispatch of an imperial policing force could be construed as a breach of that treaty, especially as there was no guarantee that the French force would eventually be withdrawn. There was, therefore, a good legal pretext for German intervention. Its form, however, was dramatic. The German chancellor, Prince Bulow, sent the somewhat reluctant Kaiser to Tangier on Morocco's Mediterranean coast. There he proclaimed Germany's resolve to uphold Morocco's independence and international rights. What had started as a French policing expedition into Morocco's interior had thus been transformed into an international crisis.

A war of nerves ensued. With the Damocles sword of Russian intervention no longer hanging over it, Germany was free to rattle its own powerful saber. Intermittent rumors of German troop concentrations in the West and an imminent invasion heightened the tension. The German general staff, in fact, did consider the option of a preventive war against France. Ultimately, the Kaiser's reluctance to be the man who broke the peace of Europe halted plans for such an action. With hindsight it could be argued that this was a strategic mistake: Germany should have exploited the window of opportunity pushed open by Russia's weakness and gone to war in 1905 rather than later.

Still, the decision against war in 1905 did not stop the saber rattling. As happened so often during the Third Republic, the external crisis pushed the government to the brink of collapse. In July, fearful of a German invasion, his cabinet colleagues forced the resignation of Foreign Minister Théophile Delcassé, whom, as the architect of the Entente, they blamed for the crisis. (The financier-turned-premier Pierre-Maurice Rouvier also blamed his foreign minister for advice that had brought him substantial financial losses as a result of the Russo-Japanese War.) Delcassé's fall was a considerable diplomatic success for Germany. It demonstrated that international questions could not be settled without Germany's consultation. Having decided against war, Berlin should have let the matter rest there. Instead, the German government pressed for an international conference at which it hoped to complete France's humiliation. In this, it overplayed its hand.[19]

The First Moroccan Crisis posed awkward problems for the British government. The rationale of the 1904 agreement had been to improve relations with France by settling colonial disputes. Now, the Egypt-Morocco barter threatened to drag Britain into a continental war between France and Germany. Britain was pledged to give diplomatic support to France. If it failed to do so, the current standoff could end in only one of two ways. There would either be a Franco-German war, which was likely to be a repeat of the events of 1870, or France might yield to German pressure and come to an arrangement with Germany on the latter's terms and, quite possibly, at British expense. In the first eventuality, Germany would emerge as the dominant power in Europe, with Russia eventually gravitating toward it. A Franco-German deal, on the other hand, would kill off the Entente, and Britain's position in Egypt would once more be open to challenges. Finally, if Britain hinted at giving more than diplomatic support, France might be emboldened to provoke Germany into an act of aggression, thereby triggering a war.

In consequence, the Marquess of Lansdowne and, beginning in December 1905, his Liberal successor, Sir Edward Grey, had to perform a careful balancing act. Throughout the crisis, British diplomacy sought to stiffen French resolve in the face of German pressure by giving strong diplomatic support. Any temptation on France's part to convert this into something more tangible was countered by hints that military support could not automatically be relied on. Even so, Grey found it necessary further to reassure the French by permitting the French military attaché in London to continue talks with British staff officers about the eventuality of a continental war. Simultaneously, British diplomacy sought to deter Germany from escalating the crisis through hints that, while the Entente was not aimed against it, any aggression against France was likely to bring Britain into the war on the latter's side.

At the international conference that assembled in the Spanish resort of Algeciras in February 1906, Germany's Moroccan ploy finally unraveled. Confronted by Anglo-French opposition, not even its own allies, Austria-Hungary and Italy, were willing to support it. The conference's final outcome strengthened France's position in the Moroccan question. Germany's hectoring diplomacy had snatched defeat from the jaws of victory.[20]

The consequences of the First Moroccan Crisis went beyond the future of that country. It soured Anglo-German relations and gave rise to a perception of a German threat to European stability. Under the pressure generated by German diplomacy in 1905-06, the Anglo-French entente had hardened into something more than just a colonial agreement. It was still no alliance, nor did it indicate an unconditional British commitment to France. Indeed, already in 1906, the staff talks fell into abeyance. Nevertheless, German bullying had established a nexus between the Entente and European security questions.

Like the Moroccan Crisis, the significance of the so-called 1908-09 Bosnian Annexation Crisis extended beyond its immediate locale. At the Congress of Berlin in 1878, the Great Powers had given Austria-Hungary a mandate to occupy the Turkish province of

Bosnia-Herzegovina. This did not affect the province's legal status. It remained part of the Ottoman Empire, but its administration and policing were transferred to Austria-Hungary. This measure was aimed at increasing Europe's leverage over the sultan at Constantinople so as to force him to introduce the internal reforms that the Powers regarded as necessary to contain the danger of further instability in the Balkans.

For thirty years, the wily Sultan Abdülhamid II had promised such reforms yet evaded carrying them out. In 1908, however, the successful "Young Turk" revolution overthrew his regime. Young Turk plans of a parliamentary constitution for the Empire meant that Vienna might be forced to evacuate Bosnia since Turkey was now serious about reforming her internal political arrangements. This prospect filled the Habsburg government with disquiet.[21]

At the root of the Bosnian crisis was a secret deal struck between the Austro-Hungarian foreign minister, Alois Baron Lexa von Aehrenthal, and his Russia counterpart, Aleksandr Pyotrovich Izvolsky. A mixture of strategic calculations and personal vanity drove the latter. After the humiliation of 1905, Russian diplomacy sought a foreign policy success to reestablish Russia as a major player in international politics. External success, moreover, was also likely to stabilize the Tsar's regime at home. And Izvolsky had convinced himself that he was the man to attain such a foreign policy triumph by securing the opening of the Turkish Straits, which had been closed to Russian warships since 1856. Given the existing Balkans entente with Austria-Hungary, it was natural that he should turn to Vienna, especially since Russia was in no position to run the risk of serious foreign complications.

Aehrenthal, meanwhile, was acutely concerned about newly resurgent Serb nationalism and the growth of Slavic nationalism within the Habsburg realms. Both had the potential to tear apart the multiethnic empire. Such danger could only be checked through the vigorous reassertion of Austro-Hungarian influence in the Balkans. Returning Bosnia to its nominal Turkish overlords, by contrast, would signal Habsburg weakness. However, since Austria-Hungary's occupation of the province rested on the decisions of an international congress, its retention would have to be attained with the other Great Powers' consent. This was unrealistic. Alternatively, the Powers could be bounced into accepting it. And that could be done only with the connivance of Russia.

There was, then, the basis for an Austro-Russian deal. This was finalized at a secret meeting at Buchlau Castle in Bohemia in September 1908. Under its terms, Russia would support Austria's annexation of Bosnia in return for Vienna's backing of her attempt to open the Turkish Straits. The problem was that this was a verbal agreement. This made it easy for Aehrenthal. Almost as soon as the deal was struck, and with Izvolsky sampling the delights of Paris, Vienna announced the annexation of Bosnia in October 1908. To complicate matters further, encouraged by Austria-Hungary, Bulgaria – technically a suzerain part of the Turkish Empire – declared its independence. Russia was left empty-handed. At one stroke, the status quo in the Balkans had been altered and the regional balance of power tilted in Austria's favor.

Izvolsky's personal diplomacy had placed Russia in an invidious position. Russia was still too weak to force Austria-Hungary to stick to its end of the Buchlau bargain. Support from Russia's French ally, however, was largely dependent on British support, and that was not forthcoming. Indeed, Izvolsky's attempts at political blackmail – he threatened the end of the 1907 Anglo-Russian convention – failed to make any impression on London. Izvolsky, therefore, encouraged Serbia to challenge Austria-Hungary and to demand compensation, which would have negated much of the former's gains. Aehrenthal would not be deterred, however, and Europe faced the prospect of an Austro-Serbian war.

With France refusing to moderate Russian policy, only Britain and Germany could ensure a peaceful settlement. The two governments were in full accord as to the need to restrain Vienna and St. Petersburg. But they could not agree on the terms of any joint mediation. Grey wished Germany to restrain Austria-Hungary before British diplomacy sought to moderate Russia's stance. Prince Bulow, though irritated at Aehrenthal's failure to consult him prior to the annexation, insisted that Britain restrain St. Petersburg as a precondition of similar German efforts in Vienna.

The crisis wore on. Only winter militated against its further escalation. In the end, what amounted to a German ultimatum to Russia broke the deadlock at the end of March 1909. Unprepared for war, Russia had to yield. The outcome of the Bosnian crisis was widely regarded as an Austro-German victory. In the longer term, the affair had profound consequences for European politics. It destroyed Austro-Russian co-operation in the Balkans. Both countries were now on a potential collision course in the region. Far from securing Habsburg Empire's southern flank, the annexation encouraged the further growth of anti-Austrian Slav nationalism. Finally, Germany's stance throughout the crisis soured Anglo-German relations. Britain came to conclude that Germany could not be relied on to restrain Austrian behavior. Indeed, in 1909 Austro-German staff talks began. They did not produce joint war plans, but they indicated Germany's strong commitment to her principal ally.[22]

There were other crises before 1914, most notably the Second Moroccan (or Agadir) Crisis in 1911 and the events surrounding the two Balkan wars of 1912 and 1913. Although these crises were resolved, they created a sense of latent hostility. At the end of 1912, German military planners concluded that another continental war was inevitable.[23]

The notion of the "inevitability of war" affected the political and military leaders of much of continental Europe. All the military staffs had worked out offensive plans for a short, sharp, and decisive war. German war preparations were based on the "Schlieffen Plan", named after the head of the general staff between 1891 and 1905, Field Marshal Count Alfred von Schlieffen. Although historians debate the extent to which Schlieffen's ideas constituted a formal "plan", they were fundamental to Germany's preparations for a continental war. The Schlieffen Plan, moreover, played a key part in the events of the summer of 1914.

German planning for a two-front war revolved around the assumption that, given her vast expanse and limited rail network, Russia would be slow to mobilize. The Schlieffen Plan, therefore, envisaged concentrating seven-eighths of the German army in the West. The massed German forces would then wheel through the Low Countries (later narrowed down to Belgium) in a massive encircling movement with the aim of forcing the French army to fight a "battle without a tomorrow." Once the French had been annihilated, the German army could then be turned eastward. Most likely, Russia would not continue the war once her Western ally had been forced out of it. The plan was based on the assumption that, under modern industrial conditions, a long war was impossible. Germany had to gain the initiative from the outset so as to be able to strike first. This strategic decision placed a premium on the speed of mobilization.

This plan had two fundamental problems. First, Belgian neutrality had been guaranteed by all of the Great Powers, including Germany. The invasion of Belgium, therefore, entailed the risk of other Powers, especially Britain, intervening. And second, the Schlieffen Plan was dictated by railway timetables. It meant the abdication of civilian political control once the decision to mobilize was made. Mobilization meant war. Time, for Germany, was of the essence. Therefore it was imperative that Germany strike first and ensure that the initiative was taken and held. There could be no halt, no delay, not even a change of plan. All of this added to the rigidity of German policy in 1914.[24]

Thus, when Prinčip's fatal bullet struck Franz Ferdinand, the event came against the backdrop of a decade or so of heightened tensions, hypernationalism, arms races, and suspicions among the Great Powers. A major war of either the Ottoman or Habsburg succession had been widely anticipated. In the end, Sarajevo triggered a war crisis at the interface of the Ottoman and Habsburg worlds.

Austria-Hungary immediately resolved on a war against Serbia to reduce its threat to the monarchy. Ironically, the archduke's assassination had also removed the one man who had previously restrained the "war party" around Aehrenthal's successor, Count Leopold von Berchtold, and the chief of the general staff, Field Marshal Franz Graf Conrad von Hötzendorf. To them, the assassination had demonstrated that, in a crisis that threatened the vital interests of the Habsburg monarchy, they could rely on German support. To some extent, it seems that Vienna and Berlin may have hoped that Russia could be forced to yield once more. This time, however, both Austria-Hungary and Germany were willing to risk a continental war. Already before the events in Sarajevo, Schlieffen's successor as chief of the German General Staff, Helmuth von Moltke the Younger, had come to the conclusion that, in light of Russia's ongoing rearmament efforts, Germany would have to go to war sooner rather than later.

Such calculations help to explain Germany's issuing of the so-called blank check to Austria-Hungary on July 5. Absolute German support for Austria, whatever the consequences, effectively robbed Berlin of its ability to influence and restrain Austria. The difficulties of reconciling the plans of the government in Vienna with the wishes of the Magyar government in Budapest caused considerable delay in Habsburg policymaking. Another factor that made for delay was the fact that the French president, Raymond Poincaré, and his foreign minister, René Viviani, were on a state visit to St. Petersburg. An escalation of the crisis, therefore, had to wait until the two Frenchmen left Russia on July 23 so as to prevent close coordination of French and Russian policy. Indeed, the Germans jammed wireless traffic between Paris and the French warship that carried Poincaré and Viviani back to France. Not until

July 25, therefore, did Austria-Hungary issue a ten-point ultimatum to Serbia.[25]

The document, if accepted by Belgrade, would have reduced Serbia to an Austrian satellite. It was designed to be rejected. Regardless, the Serb government accepted nine of the ten points, and half conceded the other. It was to no avail. On July 28, 1914, Austria-Hungary declared war on Serbia, and on the following day commenced military operations against Belgrade.

In the meantime, on July 26, in response to the Austrian ultimatum, the Russian government ordered a "partial" mobilization. Russian incompetence complicated matters, for it was by no means clear what precisely partial mobilization was meant to be. German military intelligence, however, had picked up evidence of Russian troop movements. Germany now faced a problem. The Schlieffen Plan was predicated on speedy German mobilization. Russia's early mobilization meant that Germany might lose the initiative in any war. It now risked being invaded in the East before victory in the West could be accomplished.[26]

The clock was now ticking. The German chancellor, Theobald von Bethmann-Hollweg, was a well-meaning if ineffectual politician. A trained bureaucrat, he willingly bowed to military expertise. On July 29, Germany demanded the immediate cessation of Russian mobilization. This served only to confirm St. Petersburg's suspicions that Austria-Hungary and Germany had colluded from the beginning. Foreign Minister Sergei Dimitrievich Sazonov refused, and the government ordered general mobilization on July 30. In the Russian case, this did not necessarily mean war for, unlike the

German army, Russia's troops could be stood down again.

In response, on July 31, Germany declared *Kriegsgefahrzustand* (the state of imminent danger of war), the step immediately prior to general mobilization. When on August 1 Russia had not revoked her mobilization order (the chief of the Russian General Staff, General N.N. Yanushkevich, had smashed his telephone to prevent the Tsar from countermanding the order once again), Berlin ordered full mobilization and declared war on Russia. This triggered the Franco-Russian alliance, and France immediately began to mobilize its armed forces.

French mobilization trapped Germany in its own military planning. Germany had declared war on Russia because Russian mobilization threatened to derail its operations. But its only war plan required a massive thrust against France first, and French mobilization now threatened to derail that, too. In response to French mobilization, Germany declared war on France on August 3. During the night of August 3-4, German troops began to pour into Belgium and Luxembourg.[27]

At that moment, earlier British efforts to mediate came to an end. At midnight, Berlin time, on August 4, 1914, a British ultimatum calling on Germany to halt operations in the West expired. For the first time since Napoleon's defeat in 1815, all of the Great Powers of Europe were at war. Ninety-nine years of practically uninterrupted peace had come to an end. Thus commenced the "seminal catastrophe" of the twentieth century. The self-destruction of Europe as the epicenter of world politics had begun.

The assassination at Sarajevo triggered a sequence of events that ended in world war. Longer-term factors provided the general framework within which the decision makers acted, but it was individual decisions that put Europe on the path to war. Political leaders, especially in Germany and Russia, abdicated control over political decisions to the military. Combined, it was a recipe for disaster.

ORIGINS OF THE SECOND WORLD WAR

The topic of the origins of the Second World War is one surrounded by difficulties. Not the least of these is the simple question: Which war? Conventionally, the Second World War is considered to have begun with the German invasion of Poland in September 1939, but such a view is not universal. For Italy, the war's beginning was delayed by a period of Italian "nonbelligerency" (the term preferred over neutrality by the Italian dictator, Benito Mussolini) until June 1940. For Soviet Russia, the Great Patriotic War began with the German invasion of June 22, 1941. For the United States, World War II started with the Japanese attack on Pearl Harbor. For Japan there was an expanding conflict, starting with the Japanese action in Manchuria in 1931 (commencing the so-called Fifteen Years War), moving to the formal declaration of war between Japan and China in 1937 and culminating with Pearl Harbor (beginning the Pacific War).

For the most part, these difficulties have been either ignored or glossed over in standard works dealing generally with the war's origins. The most common approach has been to focus on the war that began in 1939 and to relegate the events in the Far East to a token chapter or two. A second method is to deal with the two topics separately and explicitly.[1] Another avenue is to consider the war's origins in a broader sense, with each of the powers involved being treated individually and wider, contributory themes (such as economics and arms competition) dealt with separately.[2] All these approaches have their strengths and weaknesses and reflect the fact that a comprehensive explanation for such a complex historical event is at best difficult and perhaps impossible.

Another difficulty that complicates matters is the notion of what is to be discussed. With respect to the First World War, F.H. Hinsley made the powerful point that what "occasions" wars is not the same as what "causes" them.[3] This distinction between the long-term and short-term – that is, between the individual act that led immediately to war and the circumstances that both permitted that act and its consequences – is particularly apt with respect to the Second World War's origins. For those who seek deeper causes, the war is often thought to derive from the failures implicit in the Versailles settlement at the end of the First World War.[4] An even longer-term argument was made by A.J.P. Taylor, who contended that the Second World War was merely a continuation of the First, with Adolf Hitler as a statesman (while certainly unique in his ideological predilections) only continuing the German attempt to achieve hegemony on the European continent.[5] If the focus is on what "occasions" war, there is less range of debate, at least with respect to the war's outbreak in 1939. However, the events surrounding the invasion of Soviet Russia in 1941 (Operation Barbarossa) and Pearl Harbor are hotbeds of historical controversy. With respect to the former, there is a debate as to whether Barbarossa forestalled a Soviet attack on Germany. The latter is enshrouded in arguments as to whether the American president, Franklin Roosevelt, was aware of Japan's intentions and allowed the attack to occur as a means of bringing the United States into the war.[6]

These, then, are some of the problems inherent in the topic. However, there is a means of looking at it that allows some of these difficulties to be overcome. The interwar period was a time of flux in international relations in which the methods of the nineteenth century – the Concert of Europe, alliances, and the balance of power – were no longer acceptable, as they were widely believed to have caused the First World War.[7] Instead, the new world order created at the Paris Peace Conference was to be maintained by the liberal international means – sanctions and guarantees – embodied in the League of Nations, while nations gradually disarmed. This new world order was not universally accepted. Not only were many of the major powers – notably the United States and Soviet Russia – outside the League, but also a number of states – the "revisionist" powers (Soviet Russia, Fascist Italy, Nazi Germany, and Imperial Japan) – were ideologically opposed to the entire underpinnings of the new international system.[8] By considering how this system was developed and maintained by those nations who created it (the "status quo" powers), we can better determine both what "caused" the Second World War and what "occasioned" it.

A key point to remember is that the interwar period was not all of a piece. In fact, it splits nicely into two parts: from 1919 to 1933 and from 1933 to the war's outbreak.[9] In the first part, the status quo powers were strong enough to defend the peace settlement by the means permitted in the new world order. The new order also allowed them to begin to take action on one of the pillars on which that order was based. Naval disarmament had the best results, successively at conferences held in Washington in 1922, Geneva in 1927, and London in 1930.[10] General disarmament had less success. Each of the powers was reluctant to give up the arms that it considered necessary for its own security, and by 1932 the entire process was grinding to a halt just as the Geneva Disarmament Conference opened.

Some progress was also made on the linked issues of security guarantees and international financial stability. The Locarno settlement of 1925, in which among other things Britain and Italy guaranteed Germany's western borders with France and Belgium, both eased France's concerns about security and brought Germany back into the comity of nations.[11] The Dawes and Young plans, respectively in 1924 and 1929, equally eased the tensions over reparations, but the intertwined issue of war debts remained unsolved, ensuring that American relations with Britain remained uneasy.[12] Nonetheless, by 1929 the international order seemed stable and the specter of war remote.

This changed dramatically in the next four years. In 1931 the Japanese army began an assault on Manchuria. China's appeal to the League of Nations yielded condemnation but no collective action either in the form of military action or economic sanctions.[13] Japan's response was to withdraw, not from Manchuria but from the League itself. A second blow to the status quo was the rise to power in Germany of Adolf Hitler and the Nazi Party. This was triggered by global financial and economic instability.[14] The Nazis quickly put an end to all of those things that they opposed ideologically: in

October 1933, Germany left both the League and the Disarmament Conference at Geneva; in March 1935, Hitler formally repudiated the disarmament clauses of the Treaty of Versailles and Germany began to rearm openly.

This change of weather prompted a response from the status quo powers. Britain, despite concerns that to do so would pander to the armaments firms – those "merchants of death" who had helped cause the First World War – began to rearm, calling into session a Defence Rearmaments Committee to assess the country's defense deficiencies.[15] Others began to consider collective security and the possibilities of alliances. In September 1934 Soviet Russia entered the League, and on May 2, 1935, a Franco-Soviet defensive alliance was concluded. Several weeks earlier, representatives of Britain, France, and Italy met at Stresa (in northern Italy) to establish a common response to Hitler's intention to rearm. This "Stresa front" did not last long. In June 1935 Britain signed a naval agreement with Germany, in which the latter agreed to limit its building to 35 percent of the British total. This was meant by London to prevent a naval arms race of the pre-1914 variety and to maintain British naval superiority in the light of the collapse of naval arms control talks at the London Naval Conference of 1934. Its effect, however, was to reveal just how tenuous the links between the Stresa powers were.[16]

This point was made manifest at the beginning of October 1935, when Italy invaded Abyssinia[17] It was a measure of the League's failing authority that its condemnation of the Italian move was ignored by Rome. Instead, the British foreign secretary, Sir Samuel Hoare, and his French counterpart, Pierre Laval, attempted in December to bring a negotiated end to the invasion by forcing Abyssinia to cede nearly two-thirds of its territory to Italy. This unsavory solution was leaked to the public, resulting in universal condemnation and Hoare being forced from office. His removal did not reverse the situation in Abyssinia, and on May 9, 1936, Mussolini announced that the country had been annexed by Italy.

Between Abyssinia's annexation and the Hoare-Laval plan, another event further eroded the existing order. On March 7, Hitler announced the rearmament of the Rhineland, something the Treaty of Versailles specifically forbade. While this led Britain to reaffirm its Locarno obligations to France at the beginning of April, neither country took any concrete steps to oppose the German action. The pace of disorder grew. On July 18 the Spanish army, under the governor of the Canary Islands, General Francisco Franco, began a revolt against the socialist and anti-clerical Republican government. The Spanish Civil War was a microcosm of the tensions in Europe.[18] Franco's forces soon came to receive direct support from the Fascist and Nazi regimes, both proclaiming ideological solidarity with Franco against what they falsely termed the Bolshevik menace. Giving plausibility to their contention, Soviet Russia provided matériel support to the Republican government.

The British and French faced a conundrum. They preferred a victory by neither side, since a Spain allied with Fascist Italy and Nazi Germany would mean that France was surrounded by forces of the Right, while a victory for the "Red" Republicans would provide support for France's own leftists. In this situation, London and Paris opted for nonintervention and called on the other states to do the same. Their fond hope was that the Spanish alone would settle the Spanish issue. Instead, the Spanish Civil War became both a symbol of and a focus for the ideological split in Europe.

As the war in Spain intensified, the ideological split grew wider and assumed a global dimension. On October 25, the Rome-Berlin Axis was formed, in which the two countries agreed to coordinate their policies with respect to Spain and Southeastern Europe. A month later, Japan and Germany signed the Anti-Comintern Pact, affirming their mutual opposition to communism and raising the fear for Britain of having to deal with the two revisionist powers in widely separated areas.[19] The British response was to attempt to break the growing solidarity among the revisionist powers. In January 1937, Britain signed an arrangement – the misnamed "Gentleman's Agreement" – with Italy, both sides agreeing to maintain the status quo in the Mediterranean.[20] The motivations for each country were completely different: Rome anticipated that the signing would ease the way for a British recognition of the conquest of Abyssinia and drive a wedge between France (which adamantly opposed all Italian aspirations in the Mediterranean) and Britain; London hoped that the threat to its maritime lines of communication to the Far East would disappear and the fate of Abyssinia and Spain could be resolved diplomatically.

The policy of trying to split the revisionist powers grew stronger in 1937, when Neville Chamberlain became prime minister on May 28.[21] Chamberlain wished to pursue a foreign policy quite distinct from what had gone before. While realizing that lip service had still to be paid to the League's tenets, he wished to follow a dual course of rearmament and reducing the number of potential enemies that Britain faced. This was sound policy if it could be achieved. But Chamberlain was both ill-fitted to pursue the delicate diplomacy that such a policy would require and quite ignorant of the difficulties involved in doing so.[22] His task did not become easier when, on July 7, full-scale war was declared between Japan and China.

Chamberlain's new policy was already going badly when, in late July 1937, the Italian ambassador to London, Dino Grandi, misled him into beginning futile talks with Mussolini. Chamberlain participated in a September conference at Nyon, Switzerland, to deal with Italian submarine activity in the Spanish Civil War. The need was becoming even more pressing because of events in the Far East. In the fall of 1937, Japan's offensive in China was becoming increasingly violent. While Roosevelt gave a speech on November 5 calling on the nations of the world to "quarantine" what he called the "gangster powers," it was clear that the United States would not take action to prevent Japan's depredations, something underlined by the stance that Washington took at the Brussels Conference held in November to discuss the Far East situation. To make matters worse, Italy joined the Anti-Comintern Pact on the November 6 and followed this by withdrawing from the League of Nations on December 11. And an attempt in November to improve Anglo-German relations by means of a high-level visit by British statesman Lord Halifax to Berlin only underlined how little the two states had in common.

The deterioration of the international situation and the failure of the mechanisms created after the First World War to provide any effective barrier to aggression led to several innovative attempts to curb the escalation of lawlessness. In January 1938 Roosevelt called for an international conference to discuss matters. This met with stony silence from the revisionist powers, and Chamberlain, much to the chagrin of his foreign secretary, Anthony Eden (who favored taking up Roosevelt's offer), offered only a noncommittal reply, as he believed that the United States would do nothing concrete to improve the situation.[23] This added to the existing strain between Chamberlain and Eden over the issue of recognizing Italy's conquest of Abyssinia (something which Eden strongly opposed). The result was Eden's resignation in February and his replacement by Lord Halifax.

Chamberlain's policy of trying to reach accommodations with the revisionist powers – what is disparagingly termed "appeasement" – continued after Eden's departure with an offer of colonial concessions to Germany at the beginning of March.[24] This gesture met with no positive response. Instead, on March 13, the German army marched into Austria and an *Anschluss* (union) of the two countries was confirmed by plebiscite on April 10. This action, another contravention of the Treaty of Versailles, increased German strength in an area where Italy had aspirations to be powerful, and thus encouraged the British to think again that the Rome-Berlin Axis might be broken. The result was the Anglo-Italian Easter Accord of April 16, 1938. While the British believed that this agreement – by which the British tacitly agreed to recognize Italy's conquest of Abyssinia in exchange for a phased withdrawal of Italian troops from Spain – would lessen their military difficulties by eliminating the Mediterranean as an area of contention and thus make Britain's lines of communication with the Far East secure, this was not the case. Italy's objective in signing the accord was to weaken Anglo-French ties further and to improve Italy's position in the Balkans. The gap between Britain's desire to maintain the status quo (or, at least, ensure that it changed only by agreement) and Italy's widespread ambitions remained.[25]

In May 1938 another legacy of the Versailles settlement threatened peace. Hitler demanded that the Sudeten Germans, an ethnic minority in Czechoslovakia, be allowed to join the Reich. War was averted in this "May crisis," but it was clear that the respite was only temporary. In the fall of that year, the issue was raised again in a more virulent form. This raised the overarching question of how to oppose any threat by force to the status quo. Neither Britain nor France wished to go to war over Czechoslovakia. Chamberlain opposed war generally, and, in any case, Britain's rearmament program was not yet far enough advanced to make war seem possible. Misled by exaggerated reports of Germany's aerial strength, the British were concerned about the impact that war would have on Britain itself. The French, without some firm guarantee of British support, also preached caution, despite their treaty obligations to Czechoslovakia. Soviet offers of support were neither trusted nor believed to be of any value. This feeling was owing to the fact that the Red Army had been purged of its leading figures in mid-1937, and military opinion in Britain and France was that Soviet strength had been dramatically reduced as a consequence.

In these circumstances, Chamberlain decided to negotiate.[26] He twice flew to Germany during September, and each time conceded more to Hitler at Czechoslovakia's expense. The final result – the so-called Munich Settlement – effectively dismembered Czechoslovakia. The German-speaking frontier areas were joined to the Reich, and Poland and Hungary took part in the despoiling, each taking a piece of the remaining "rump state" of Czechoslovakia. The settlement, which Chamberlain famously proclaimed provided "peace in our time," has had a varying reception.[27] At the time of its signing, it was widely hailed as preventing war. When war ensued in a year's time, Chamberlain was widely denounced, and "Munich" and "appeasement" became bywords for cowardice and vacillation. This state of affairs lasted until the late 1970s when new research suggested that Chamberlain's choice was an unpalatable one forced on him by general British unpreparedness for war. In the 1990s the balance swung back toward a condemnation of Chamberlain, as historians argued that British strength had been sufficient to have allowed other choices than those taken at Munich. Most historians today would say that Chamberlain's actions were misguided.

The perceived weakness of Britain and France in the face of German aggression soon had its effect. In the wake of its continued military successes in China, on November 5 the Japanese government announced that there was to be a "New Order in East Asia," one in which the Western Powers were to play at best a diminished role. A few days later, Jewish homes and offices were smashed in Germany as the Nazi regime made clear that there were few limits to the violence it was willing to permit against the racial groups that it had targeted and that it feared no international condemnation. However, the close avoidance of war had a salutary effect on France.[28] The political paralysis that had been such a feature of governments in the 1930s was overcome and a massive rearmament program was launched. In addition, France rejected any British suggestion of reaching a compromise with Italy over their North African disagreements. But Chamberlain did not give up his grand plan to detach Italy from its alignment with Germany. On November 16 the British Parliament ratified the Easter Accord, and in January 1939 Chamberlain traveled to Rome in the hope that this personal intervention might lead to warmer Anglo-Italian relations. He was disappointed, and the two countries continued to eye each other warily in the Mediterranean.

On March 15-16, 1939, German forces occupied the rump state of Czechoslovakia. This brought an end to Chamberlain's hopes that accommodating German interests could resolve outstanding difficulties. With the League completely discredited, what means was left to prevent the Versailles order from falling completely to the ground? As an interim measure, amid fears that Germany might strike quickly against Poland, on March 31 Britain and France unilaterally guaranteed its security. A week later, on April 7, Mussolini took advantage of the situation to begin an Italian advance against Albania. In the face of such action, the British and French extended their unilateral guarantee to include Romania and Greece on April 13 and, a day later, began negotiations with Soviet Russia for a triple alliance to curb the revisionist powers' actions.

This negotiation lasted until August 1939 and reflected a number of things.[29] First, it meant the final abandonment of the belief that alliances were in and of themselves an evil that had caused the First World

War. It was now clear that the means provided by the new world order created at Versailles were inadequate to the task of dealing with aggressive states. Second, it meant that the ideological dislike of Soviet Russia in Britain and France had to be suspended in the face of the greater peril that was embodied in Nazi Germany. But it was the ideological gulf between the two Western states and Soviet Russia that ensured that the negotiations came to naught. What Soviet Russia insisted on throughout the talks was that Britain and France agree to recognize the principle of "indirect aggression" and allow Moscow to take appropriate action when it occurred – that is, that Soviet Russia might occupy Poland or the Baltic states if the latter seemed likely to succumb to German pressure. The British and French refused, as none of the states named would accept the idea that Soviet Russia might violate their sovereignty on the pretext of defending it. The result was stalemate.

Meanwhile events had not stood still. On May 22, Germany and Italy signed the "Pact of Steel," which virtually committed Italy to go to war alongside Germany, although Mussolini made it clear that Italy would be unprepared to join in hostilities until 1943. Just as disconcerting was the emergence of an increasing threat in the Far East. In mid-June, four Chinese citizens sought refuge from the Japanese authorities in the British Concession at Tientsin. Suddenly, in the midst of the delicate negotiations with Soviet Russia and with Germany continuing to threaten Poland over the fate of Danzig (Gdansk), there emerged the unwelcome possibility of Japanese aggression against British and French possessions in East Asia. As the British felt themselves unable to contemplate the possibility of two simultaneous wars, they entered into negotiations with the Japanese that resulted in a lessening of tension between the two countries by the end of July. However, the interlinked nature of the European and Imperial spheres had been underlined.[30]

A bold step by Hitler ended the deadlock in the negotiations with Soviet Russia on August 23. Anxious to avoid a two-front war in the fashion of the First World War, the Führer decided to jettison temporarily his ideological antipathy to communism and conclude an agreement with Moscow. The result was the Nazi-Soviet Pact of August 23, 1939, which publicly pledged the two states to nonaggression toward each other and secretly divided Poland and the Baltic states between them. Hitler now turned his undivided attention toward Poland. On September 1, 1939, German forces invaded Poland. Two days later, Britain and France declared war on Germany and the Second World War in Europe had begun.

But this declaration of war, while it spelled an end to the settlements reached after the First World War, did not bring about a global, or even a pan-European war. In Europe, Italy promptly declared itself a "nonbelligerent," a new appellation in international affairs that emphasized its solidarity with Nazi Germany and at the same time proclaimed its neutrality. In addition, there existed a host of neutrals, each of which had to consider its interests carefully.[31] Of particular significance was Soviet Russia. For Moscow, the Nazi-Soviet Pact was a temporary expedient, designed to buy time while rearmament progressed. Its first move was, on September 17, to invade Poland from the east, ensuring that it obtained its share. Further, inspired by fears resulting from the events of the civil war of 1918-20, Soviet Russia also was concerned about its northern and southern maritime approaches in the Baltic and Black Seas. And, despite the thorough defeat that Soviet forces had administered to Japan in the border clashes at Nomonhan from May to September 1939, Tokyo still threatened Soviet Russia's position in the Far East.[32] Indeed, Tokyo's activities also were now a heightened threat to a Britain at war and raised the worry of a two-front war for London.

Soviet Russia moved swiftly to attempt to shore up her exposed flanks. Negotiations with Turkey over the future of the Dardanelles and Bosphorus Straits were inconclusive, but discussions with Finland for an exchange of territory and the lease of the Finnish naval base at Hanko (both of which were designed to enhance Soviet security) turned sour in November 1939. The result was a Soviet assault on Finland on November 30, beginning the Winter War, an action that turned any public sympathy Soviet Russia had earned through its anti-fascist rhetoric of the 1930s into widespread dislike. It also made official opinion in both France and Britain turn toward another possibility: declaring war on Moscow.[33] The reasoning behind this was straightforward. The Allies planned to win the war against Germany utilizing the weapon of blockade that had been so successful in the First World War. Soviet Russia's neutrality not only put a hole in the British blockade, but also her supplying of vital war matériel, particularly oil, ensured that the Nazi war economy would not be hit by crippling shortages. With Soviet Russia viewed as a belligerent in all but name, it was only the end of the Winter War on March 12, 1940, that prevented an Anglo-French force from sailing to Finland's aid and initiating a state of war with Moscow.

Hitler moved rapidly to forestall any attempt to shore up the blockade and to create a possible threat to his northern flank. On April 9, Germany invaded Denmark and Norway. British assistance to Norway proved futile, and the country was quickly overrun. A month later, on May 10, Germany unleashed its armies against France and the Low Countries. Utilizing the mechanized warfare that it had pioneered in the late 1930s and honed in the Polish campaign, the Wehrmacht quickly defeated the French, with the British Expeditionary Force making a rapid and haphazard retreat from the continent at Dunkirk, leaving the bulk of its heavy equipment behind. On June 10, Italy abandoned its equivocal position and entered the war, invading France. France's capitulation occurred on June 22, and a peace settlement was signed on June 28, a date chosen to emphasize the fact that the Versailles diktat was no more.

At this point the war in Europe, as it had been planned for and envisioned since the end of the First World War, was over. The situation was reminiscent of the position after the Treaty of Tilsit of 1807 when Alexander I of Russia and Napoleon Bonaparte had divided Europe between them. However, the Second World War's global nature had not yet begun. This expansion took a variety of forms. Japan was quick to take advantage of the situation. During the French collapse, Tokyo demanded that Britain close the Burma Road, the supply line that led from British India to those parts of China still resisting Japan. Britain, under threat of invasion and with the Luftwaffe poised to attack, agreed to cease sending supplies for a limited period. The United States, warily observing the situation, decided to back the British by trading American destroyers for British naval bases in the Western Hemisphere – the Destroyers for Bases Agreement – on September 3. On September 14, Italy expanded the war to the African continent by invading Egypt. The connections between the aggressive powers was underlined on September 27, when Germany, Italy, and Japan signed the Tripartite Pact by which the three countries agreed to assist each other should any of them be attacked by a country not yet in the war.[34] This was both anti-American and anti-Soviet, and many of the Balkan neutrals joined this alliance to protect their own territories should a German-Soviet war ensue.

Tensions continued to escalate through the fall of 1940. Italy added to its fronts by attacking Greece on October 28, while in December the United States proclaimed an embargo on sales of scrap iron and war matériel to Japan. The U.S. continued to move away from strict neutrality in the New Year, signing a Lend-Lease agreement with Britain on March 11, 1941, something that relieved the pressure on Britain's strained financial resources.

In Europe the war continued to expand. Hitler was set on an attack on Soviet Russia but first wished to end the ongoing struggles in the Balkans, where his Italian ally was bogged down. On April 6, German forces invaded Yugoslavia and Greece, rapidly overrunning the two countries. Seeing this, both Soviet Russia and Japan, each for its own reasons, decided to simplify their own strategic situations. On April 11 a nonaggression pact was signed between the two states, allowing Moscow to concentrate its attention in the West against Germany and permitting Tokyo to focus on its ambitions for southward expansion without concern about Soviet actions in the north.

On June 22, the Germans invaded Soviet Russia. This reopened the European phase of the war by providing an active front against the Nazis. The British response was to affirm its support for Soviet Russia and to promise as much material aid as possible in the Russian struggle against Hitler. The invasion also had immediate repercussions in the Far East. On July 2 Japan decided to advance against French Indochina.[35] Washington's increasing tilt toward Britain was underlined when Churchill and Roosevelt met at Placentia Bay (in Newfoundland) from August 9 to 12 and signed the Atlantic Charter, a document stating the two countries' opposition to territorial changes imposed by force and asserting the right of people to live free from fear or want. While this had no immediate practical value, it underlined the continuity of interests and principles between the two countries.

In the fall of 1941, tensions in the Far East continued to build. As the German advance into Russia proceeded rapidly and the final collapse of Soviet Russia seemed increasingly inevitable, the Japanese government decided to widen the war. Unable to obtain any Western acceptance of its territorial acquisitions in China and increasingly affected by the economic blockade, the Japanese government felt that Japan's future lay with the creation in the Far East of an economically self-sufficient region – the Greater East Asian Co-Prosperity Sphere. This could only be achieved by eliminating British and American power in the region. Thus, the peace proposals put forward on November 26 by the American secretary of state, Cordell Hull, were deemed unacceptable, as they called for Japan to give up its advances on the Asian mainland. Instead, the Imperial Japanese Navy was instructed to cripple American naval strength in the Pacific by means of a strike against Pearl Harbor, while the Imperial Japanese Army was tasked with capturing the British naval base at Singapore, thus ending the threat that the Royal Navy posed to Japanese lines of communication. These two actions began on December 7, with the attack on Pearl Harbor by Japanese carrier-based aircraft and the rapid attacks by the army and air force on Hong Kong, the Philippines, and Malaya. The American and British declarations of war on Japan were joined on December 11 by declarations of war against the two North Atlantic states by Italy and Germany. The Second World War had taken on its final form.

How did the peace of 1919 turn into the wars that began in 1939-41? The causes of war stem from the unfinished nature of the transformation of the international order that occurred during the First World War. Not only was the existing European order shattered by the demise of the Ottoman, Austro-Hungarian, Russian, and German empires, but also the global system had changed with the rise of two powerful extra-European states, the United States and Japan. How these two would fit into the new world order created at Paris in 1919 was unknown. Unknown, too, was whether the new circumstances and structures – the League of Nations, disarmament, and the renunciation of the balance of power – would prove capable of maintaining the peace.

The unwillingness of various states – Nazi Germany, Fascist Italy, Soviet Russia, and Imperial Japan – to accept the changed circumstances of the postwar world and their willingness to challenge them by force of arms meant that there were only two possible courses of action. The status quo powers could accommodate – appease – the revisionist states' demands, or they could resist them by force of arms. The vacillation between these two responses was the stuff of international politics in the interwar period.

Thus, the deeper causes of the Second World War are clear. The clash of irreconcilable aspirations made war inevitable. The ideological requirements of the Nazi, Fascist, and Imperial Japanese regimes (while the latter was dominated by its military elites) could not be satisfied within bounds acceptable to the status quo powers. While Soviet Russia's long-term goals were also incompatible with the Versailles order, its timeframe for achieving them was much longer and, thus, Soviet Russia was not necessarily a regime whose very existence carried with it the likelihood of war.

As to what occasioned the Second World War, much depended on politics and particular circumstances. It is conceivable that the German invasion of Poland could have been treated by Britain and France in the same fashion as had the German action against Czechoslovakia a year earlier. However, British and French opinion, both public and among the elites, was that Hitler could not be satisfied and that a recourse to war was necessary. The expansion of the war proceeded willy-nilly. Soviet Russia's war with Finland resulted from the latter's unwillingness to accept Soviet assertions about security; the German extension of the war into Scandinavia resulted from memories stemming from the British blockade in the First World War. Fascist Italy's entrance into the war came about as a result of Mussolini's ideological dreams of Italian glory, and it occurred when it did as a result of Germany's rapid success against France. The German invasion of Soviet Russia flowed naturally from Nazi ideology. A dislike of communism blended nicely with the requirements of *Lebensraum* (living space) and Nazi racial theories to make a Nazi invasion inevitable. The only unknown was the timing. As to the Far East, Japan's unwillingness to give up its acquisitions in China and the equal unwillingness of Britain and the United States to accept them meant that war with Britain and America was always likely. Only a change of heart in Tokyo, London, and Washington could have prevented war. In the existing circumstances, the single unknown was when such a clash would occur. Again, military actions pushed events. The Nazi successes against Russia (with the implications for Britain) combined nicely with internal Japanese politics to yield a decision for war. What had begun as a war in Eastern Europe of limited scope had become a war that affected the entire globe. The Second European War had become the Second World War.[36]

ANGLO-AMERICAN DIPLOMACY, 1939-45

During the Second World War, the most important element in the strategic relationship between Great Britain and the United States was their sophisticated, layered, multidimensional, and relatively open form of diplomatic processes. The strategy-forming element of diplomacy during the war can be classified as war diplomacy, because its main concerns were directed toward how, why, when, where, and by whom military operations would take place. Often, historians of Anglo-American wartime diplomacy forget, however, that almost as much time and effort in the diplomatic arena was given over to the need to shape the peace and, most importantly, safeguard each nation's national interests within that new framework. Here, the diplomacy of various groups such as each nation's treasury, banks, business leaders, and scientists all fed into the war-planning, as well as peace-planning, process. Also, defense diplomacy, the ongoing relationship between the various militaries, was an important part of the overall diplomatic relationship. Generals and admirals had as important a role in the shaping of strategic diplomatic relations as ambassadors, foreign secretaries, presidents, and prime ministers.

This chapter is based on a number of pre-1939 lenses through which the growth of that strategic relationship during the years of global crisis must be viewed. The first important perspective is that both nations had a similar worldview, largely derived from affairs linked to Far Eastern security and containment issues. This parallel but not joint approach to affairs in the Far East was tempered by a mutual suspicion and distrust of each other's strategic motives and aspirations in Europe throughout the 1930s. Another key lens is that the two English-speaking nations were the world's most dominant maritime and economic powers. In merchant shipping strength, naval combat power, and intrinsic industrial and economic strength that was created and focused on the production of maritime power, both the United States and the British Empire required control of the seas for any successful prosecution of a global war strategy.[1] Given these prewar aspects of the Anglo-American strategic relationship, it is no surprise that the three main areas of importance with regard to diplomatic activities during the war were agreeing where to fight, agreeing how to allocate vast resources and supplies to those chosen theaters of operations to ensure operational success, and, once victory appeared assured (roughly in the fall of 1943), agreeing what shape the new world would take once peace was declared.

One of the major areas where cooperation and diplomacy was necessary, if the Anglo-American strategic relationship was going to be successful in harnessing maritime power in a war-winning effort, was that of allocating vital shipping resources to the various theaters of operations. While at first glance such an allocation would appear to be a simple logistics matter, one that qualified military or civilian administrators could adjudicate, such a perception would be incorrect. The determination of the uses of scarce shipping resources and landing craft were two of the most important parts of the Anglo-America military relationship. Where those resources went, so too did the main war effort. All of the major diplomatic discussions at the various high-level strategic conferences held throughout the war dealt with these two items. How much of each resource was given to the Far East, the Mediterranean, the Atlantic, or the Soviet dimensions of the global war was a question that had to be arrived at through the diplomatic process or the alliance. Sometimes this was done at the highest level through the conference or envoy system. Often, however, it was done more regularly on a day-to-day basis through an elaborate system that combined civilian and military representatives.[2]

Four main factors governed Anglo-American wartime logistics diplomacy. The first of these was the British dependence on the United States for the necessary tonnage of merchant shipping required for sustaining its war effort. Even before formal U.S. participation in the war, British planning required a degree of certainty about the use of American merchant shipping being provided for necessary key resources and finished products.[3] Though Britain had maintained the world's largest merchant fleet throughout the interwar period and still possessed the world's largest shipping fleet in 1940, the pace of military operations and production, combined with losses to the German and Italian fleets, meant that Britain was dependent on the United States for overcoming any shortcomings in tonnage.[4] Such a situation struck a deep resonance within the British policymaking elite, who remembered the loss of key shipping routes and markets to the Americans after the First World War as a result of having to allow American shipping contributions to supplant the British during the latter larger war effort. Throughout the Second World War, Winston Churchill and his cabinet, as well as his chiefs of staff, were always aware of what a growing dependence on the Americans for shipping would mean. Not only would it give the Americans a bigger voice in deciding what strategic decisions were made – the timing and place of Operation Overlord, for instance – but it would also mean that in the postwar period Britain would once more have lost key shipping routes and an even greater share of the world merchant shipping market to the United States.

This last point, especially with regard to the Far Eastern parts of the British Empire, meant that the United States represented a possible threat to Britain's imperial coherence. If British shipping after the war was unable to compete fiscally and economically with a faster, larger, and more powerful American merchant fleet, Australian, New Zealand, Chinese, and other Asian markets and producers would give preferential treatment to the Americans. British ship owners and the Bank of England, along with other manufacturers and businesses with interests in that region, lobbied the British government long and hard not to sell out the imperial interests in pursuit of a war-winning strategy.[5] Churchill, as well, was determined that the British Empire would return to the Far East and erase the embarrassment of Singapore. Lord Halifax, the British ambassador to the United States, also was conscious at all times of the risk the postwar British strategic position ran if the Americans became "too Pacific minded."[6] American policymakers, such as the head of the U.S. Army, General George Marshall, presidential adviser Harry Hopkins, and Secretary of War Henry Stimson, were determined to see that the British Empire did not prosper from American actions in the fighting of the war. To that end, economic dominance and control in the region, underpinned by complete naval and maritime control of the Pacific (especially the commercial aspects of that maritime power) were items that the Americans were not willing to negotiate away in any diplomatic process during the war.[7]

This matter of the maintenance of Britain's overall strategic position within the partnership and postwar period is linked to the second element in the Anglo-American logistics diplomacy: the avoidance of a Second Front for as long as possible. Much has been written of the compromise that was Operation Torch, the invasion of North Africa, leading to continued operations in the Mediterranean theater through to Operation Husky and the post-Sicilian invasion operations against the Italian mainland itself. All of this was seen as a sideshow by the American chiefs of staff, in particular Marshall, whose Clausewitzian appreciation of the center of gravity for the entire global war was the quick and final elimination of the main military threat: Nazi Germany. To Marshall, any operations that did not aim at putting ground forces in Europe, where those forces could then exert direct and decisive pressure on the German war effort and occupy key industrial centers, were a waste of time and resources.[8] These tensions in strategic direction during Operation Bolero, the buildup of American forces in England, were a source of constant diplomatic attentions, at both the political and military levels. Marshall's diplomatic role during the course of the war was that of the professional military officer: adviser and defender. He advised both Franklin Roosevelt and other Allied leaders and their military staffs on the American views as to which war-winning strategy was most appropriate. His style of defense diplomacy was blunt and direct, a characteristic appreciated by his military counterparts, such as the British General Alanbrooke. Marshall's bluntness, as well as that of the American naval representative to the U.S. chiefs of staff, Admiral Ernest King, often created difficult questions and bad blood. However, their directness and ability to speak their minds forced others to do likewise, a condition that allowed negotiations and agreements to be reached in an open and honest atmosphere of defense diplomacy, as well as political diplomacy, an important aspect of the Allied war-winning formula.[9]

For most commentators on the function of military leaders and the strategic direction of the war effort prior to Overlord, it is generally recognized that General Dwight Eisenhower's main role was that of supreme military diplomat. His experience in the Mediterranean operations and his personal contacts and knowledge of the key British military commanders, as well as his status with various British political leaders, including Churchill, made Eisenhower the ideal man for the job of supreme allied commander of forces in Europe. That role was as much about diplomacy, the massaging of various military egos, and political goose chases as it was about the selection and maintenance of strategic direction.[10] Eisenhower's effective dealing with American dissent over the decisions reached at the January 1943 Casablanca Conference indicated he was suited for the position. Brigadier

General Albert Wedemeyer, a U.S. Army officer commanding in the Middle East, was not alone in believing that the British had hoodwinked an ill-prepared and naïve American delegation over such factors as the issue of unconditional surrender and the delaying of a major cross-channel crossing into France in favor of operations aimed at Sicily and Italy. That conference highlighted the need for American delegations in the future to prepare and plan in order to counter the British diplomatic efforts to create and dominate the direction of the war strategy. Eisenhower took that lesson to heart but also did not allow bitterness or anger to cloud his focus. He remained committed to the concept that such differences of opinion and/or any feeling of suspicion by American military commanders had to be overcome by diplomatic efforts by those officers themselves. To his mind, the trust and integrity of the Anglo-American military relationship was the key to any success. If that failed to become a reality, any plan, no matter how brilliant or how well provided with resources, would fail as well.

A key element in the diplomatic relationship surrounding the strategic direction of the Anglo-American war effort was the creation and usage of intelligence. The Anglo-American strategic relationship between diplomacy and intelligence had its roots in cooperation and coordination long before Eisenhower became the supreme commander. One of the first key diplomatic intelligence relationships was that forged by Colonel Raymond Lee, the American military attaché to London. Even before American entry into the war, Lee's efforts to obtain information for the American military and other policymaking organizations, as well as his role as interpreter of American intentions and military capability, made him as much a diplomatic envoy as a military observer. In the face of an ineffectual and unsatisfactory American ambassadorial presence (ie. Joseph Kennedy), Lee's importance was magnified to a great extent.[11] Indeed, he often acted as a personal conduit of information between Churchill and Roosevelt, and certainly he was the man whom all roving American representatives, such as Harry Hopkins or Sumner Welles, met first before going off to see the British about any issues. Even when a new American ambassador, Gilbert Winant, replaced Kennedy, Lee maintained his preferred position as the confidant of and conduit to the highest levels of British military planning and decision making. Indeed, Winant was happy to accept this relationship, preferring to concentrate on the more exclusively foreign-policy issues and leave the war effort and military appreciation to Lee's expertise.[12]

In Washington, Lee's role of observer was duplicated not just by one man, but by a series of missions to the United States. In a replay of the British First World War experience, a flood of officials, businessmen, and minor functionaries invaded America in an attempt to oversee the acquisition of vital war supplies and materials and to try and put forward the British case for greater American involvement in the war in Europe. The efforts to achieve the latter met with limited success. But over the question of getting America to safeguard Britain's position in the Far East and to act as the main strategic deterrent to Japan's aggressive posture, the British efforts were more fruitful.[13] Under the untried but flamboyant guidance of British ambassador Philip Lothian, and then, on Lothian's death in the late fall of 1940, the more solid and measured approach of Lord Halifax (former secretary of state for foreign affairs and viceroy of India), British diplomatic efforts were normalized in their procedures. This was in stark contrast, as both British representatives testified, to the more chaotic and personalized processes of decision-making found in the Roosevelt-dominated American system. Both Lothian and Halifax followed a tried-and-true formula for ambassadorial procedures in America, laid down by Ronald Lindsay during his nine-year stint as Britain's eyes and ears in America during the 1930s. The principles were simple and straightforward: never be seen to be practicing propaganda or influencing American politics; give honest and open answers when you can and say nothing when you cannot; and constantly hammer home to Whitehall the fact that the United States was not a cousin, or any other sort of relative, but a distinct and separate nation that held agendas and desires of its own.[14] And, while the role of the two wartime ambassadors in the process of diplomacy has often been overlooked in the maintenance of the Anglo-American wartime relationship, it was the various committees and boards that sprang up in Washington following the attack on Pearl Harbor – or their offspring which changed along with shifts in need and focus – that did the bulk of the mundane and routine daily grind of alliance diplomacy that was the mainstay of those effective and good relations.

The first momentous Anglo-American diplomatic success was the passing of the Lend-Lease Act of January 1941. For two years, British diplomatic pressure, from traditional sources, economic sources, military sources, and public opinion, all concentrated on trying to get the American people to agree that the Roosevelt administration's desire to allow Britain the necessary tools to prosecute a successful war was morally and strategically the right thing to do. France's collapse drove home to the American people the reality of war: Britain stood alone in the spring of 1940. Churchill and Roosevelt's "special" relationship is often thought to have started here, as Britain waited for munificent aid from America. While the Destroyers for Bases Agreement of September 1940 was one such product of Churchill's personal appeal to the American president, by the end of 1941 Britain faced an economic and fiscal crisis that could be solved only if America acted in a non-neutral fashion. Following Harry Hopkins's fact-finding mission to Britain to ascertain if the British were really in as desperate a plight as they continued to plead (and following Roosevelt's reelection for a third term), Roosevelt sent the Lend-Lease Bill to Congress in January. It was passed through that body in the face of severe opposition by March 1941. This "most unsordid act" was an enormous boost to the British war effort, but it was not an act of unrestricted kindness from one brother nation to another.[15] In fact, it was the beginning of a continuous process of strategic diplomacy that would see the two nations continuously negotiating America's support and supply of the British war effort and the British attempting to use negotiations over those supplies to shape the war effort to the empire's best advantage. Through such machinations, both nations always had one eye firmly on the peace.

The American war effort prior to Pearl Harbor, in terms of the mobilization of industry and the economy, was seen from the British perspective as being far from that which was necessary to fight a modern, industrial, total war.[16] Various economic, financial, and defense missions were sent from London to Washington in attempts to drive home to the Roosevelt administration the need for greater action.[17] The growing dependence of the British war effort on American money and resources, such as shipbuilding and repair facilities, made it imperative that continued access was assured. These various special missions not only lobbied the American officials responsible to the House and Senate committees that would ensure such access but also performed important lobbying among American special interest groups such as heavy industry, bankers, and even church groups. Fears of charges of waste and incompetence were rife among not only British policymakers but American officials as well. These were the sort of incidents that needed constant attention from both parties, and this was why, wherever possible, the pre-1942 British efforts to sway the American public and officialdom to the British cause were pursued with such vigor. Seen as the best way to aid a favorably disposed Rooseveltian government in making the case with the American public, British public diplomacy, through the propaganda opportunities generated by these various missions, did a great deal to ingratiate both official and public American opinion to the "realities" of British needs.[18] However, it took the Japanese attack on Pearl Harbor to create the full wartime conditions for the ongoing diplomacy of such missions during a time of war. The attack was the ultimate persuasive tool. Then teams of British representatives from the Treasury, Bank of England, businesses, and industries, all intent on obtaining, directing, and explaining British resource needs, became an occupying force in Washington. There, for the next three years, daily acts of personal and institutional diplomacy ensured that the necessary coordination and administration of the largest combined war effort the world had ever seen was a success.

Once America was in the war, the informal diplomacy at all levels could cease and open alliance diplomacy could begin. Nowhere was this open atmosphere more welcome than in the military-to-military relationship. The secret discussions of the pre-Pearl Harbor era, such as those held in Placentia Bay between Roosevelt and Churchill in August 1941, gave way immediately to the shift of assumptions as espoused in such plans as Rainbow, Dog, and ABC-1. The Newfoundland talks had committed Britain and the United States to such Wilsonian notions as no territorial advantages to be incurred by the powers due to the war; the territorial integrity of other nations being inviolate; national self-determination and self-government a fundamental right; free trade; future economic collaboration to ensure world economic stability; disarmament of aggressive nations; and the replacement of the League of Nations with some suitable international body.[19] The Arcadia Conference, held in Washington from December 22, 1941, until January 13, 1942, signified the solidification or, sometimes, the rejection of the various Placentia Bay ideals. With America now actually in the war, the relationship was that of formal allies. And, most important, Roosevelt's pre-Pearl Harbor agreement with Churchill that America would also pursue a Germany-first policy of prosecuting the war would be upheld.[20] However, one of the first Anglo-American defense diplomacy decisions would be enacted in the Pacific.

Field Marshal Sir Archibald Wavell's appointment to the post of Allied commander for the Australian,

British, Dutch, and American forces in the Pacific (known as ABDA command) was a clear indication of the American, and in particular General Marshall's, willingness to ensure that not just cooperation and coordination took place between the two nations, but that the absolute integration of commands would cement the Anglo-American war effort into one. This gesture, in the face of heavy support for General Douglas MacArthur to be given the post, illustrated the high level of importance put on the issue of unity of command.[21] Along with this military appointment, two Pacific War Councils were set up to help direct the course of the war in that region. The first was established in early February 1942 in London in the hope that the creation of such a council would mollify growing Australian cries of dissatisfaction over the British conduct of the war in the Pacific. That goal was never achieved, and the council was of little importance as an effective tool of imperial diplomacy and coordination. However, Australian pressure for a greater American role in the direction of Pacific affairs led to the establishment of a second Pacific War Council in Washington, in April of the same year. Roosevelt chaired the council, and representatives (usually the ambassador or equivalent officer to the United States already present in Washington) from China, Great Britain, the Netherlands, Australia, New Zealand, and Canada were all members.

This was a large step forward for the British Dominions, especially in terms of their links and dependency on Great Britain for war leadership. It also highlighted the layer of diplomacy that the United States was not encumbered by in its wartime relations, but which Great Britain always had to be aware of and manage: imperial diplomatic relations. While the council was a good propaganda and diplomatic tool as far as face-saving, image, and public relations for each member, the reality was that this council did not exert any substantial strategic influence on direct war planning for the Far East.

The operational concession to Wavell's appointment was only a part, however, of the larger strategic defense diplomacy that was put in motion immediately on the American entry into the war. The decision to establish a continuously sitting Combined Anglo-American Chiefs of Staff (CCS) in Washington, made up of British and American air force, army, and navy chiefs, was the most important part of the defense diplomacy aspect.[22] For the Americans, this concession was a victory in the overall running of the war, as the committee was something that both Roosevelt and Marshall desired. The price of success, however, meant that the United States would have to reconstruct its entire higher command structure to conform to the British model in order to make the system work. From this process the American Joint Chiefs of Staff system was born.

Accompanying the establishment of the CCS, diplomatic negotiations between political and military representatives divided the world into various theaters of operations, with each nation having overall command authority within that region. The Americans were in charge of the Pacific and British India, the Middle East, and southern Asia, while European considerations would be a shared process. In India and southern Asia, Anglo-American conflict over strategic direction, particularly the attitude to take toward China and levels of aid to give its war effort, as well as the best means of attacking the Japanese in southern Asia, required both political and defense diplomacy to iron out awkward divergences between the Allied visions. The reality throughout the war in the Pacific, however, was that the British were constantly fighting to retain the status quo, while the American, Chinese, and even Australian and New Zealand efforts at negotiation and diplomacy were often working to erode the British position in the Far East. The lack of a single command for the European theater also spread into the Atlantic Ocean. As a result, the American and British efforts in the Battle of the Atlantic were never as coordinated or as effective as could have been expected.[23]

Since the European theater was the most important as far as alliance relations and the need to keep Russia in the war were concerned, it is no surprise that the diplomatic issues were given primacy over military effectiveness and expedience. Also, the idea that America, because of its larger army forces, would lead not only on land but also usurp the Royal Navy's traditional dominance over European waters, was a step too far for any diplomacy to overcome. Yet these awkward divisions in the overall unity of the Anglo-American command relationship paled in significance in comparison to the total lack of Axis diplomatic and command coordination.[24] Once Allied victories – Alamein, Stalingrad, Guadalcanal, and Torch – began to occur by the end of 1943, the Anglo-American leaders could begin to realistically look to the victorious future. The combination of a lack of fully developed American combat power, in particular adequately equipped U.S. Army divisions with sufficient armor and firepower for the modern European battlefield, along with the continued reluctance by the British to risk the casualties believed to be possible in a full-fledged invasion of the French mainland, created a constellation of strategic pressures. In the spring of 1943 the Trident Conference was held in Washington to deal with them, along with others.

Political and military diplomacy at all levels was required to keep serious breaches from being created as the two sides argued over the higher direction of the war. Churchill and his chiefs of staff wanted to invade Sicily and then Italy, in an attempt to isolate Germany. Roosevelt, and in particular Marshall, wanted to get to grips with the German army on the mainland. Both sides recognized the need to continue operations in order to keep Soviet suspicions of Western foot-dragging to a minimum. These discussions and diplomatic maneuvers resulted in the Americans agreeing to the invasion of Italy in what remained of 1943, but the British were forced to commit to an invasion of mainland Europe in the spring of 1944. Fed up with watching Roosevelt being swayed by British strategic arguments based on piles of figures, papers, studies, and data, the American chiefs of staff had laid their groundwork well. They met every British argument and volley of information with their own barrage of statistics and strategic logic. In the end, late-night talks, luncheons, and behind-closed-doors diplomacy saw Roosevelt finally support his own military advisers against Churchill's oration. The military path for the future conduct of the war was now set.[25] However, and particularly as the American war effort grew larger in relation to that of the British, diplomacy at all levels was called into greatest need for the achievement of an agreed on and decisive victory, as well as a lasting, suitable peace.

In 1943 the first administrative organs of the Anglo-American peace-building process were put in place. By May the Allies had concluded a preliminary agreement that would establish the United Nations Relief and Rehabilitation Administration (UNRRA). That organization was approved by September of the same year and began to operate an international administrative body to distribute relief supplies in the postwar period. Economic issues were included in this organization, as well, but would not be resolved until well after the war.[26] At the same time, the European Advisory Commission was set up in London in November 1943. This body was responsible for coordinating the surrender terms for Germany and its allies. And while other UN-sponsored bodies began to appear after this period in anticipation of the peace that was to come, it was in the areas of influence and control that Anglo-American wartime diplomacy began to play a bigger role. Who would control operations in the Pacific after the war? Who would be the stronger nation in China? What would the alliance relationship be in Germany's reconstruction? Who had greater interests in remaining the major power broker in the Middle East?

Some of these questions were answered by discussions that took place at Cairo in November 1943. Roosevelt pushed the American agenda for the postwar Pacific circumstance, helping Chiang Kai-Shek to obtain the Cairo Declaration. That statement promised that Japan would lose all territories conquered by her since 1914, China would be fully restored, Korea would become an independent state, and plans for the invasion of Japan were begun. This planning, and American insistence on taking primacy of place in Pacific affairs in general, caused hard feelings among the British military, but mostly among the Treasury, Foreign Office, and Cabinet members who were linked to the British negotiations. They rightly saw that the British dominance of that region was now over and that the United States would be the future guarantor of security in the Far East. The Tehran Conference in November 1943 only further highlighted how the growth of American military capability was now translating into diplomatic leverage during these negotiations over the war's strategic direction. Such was the state of affairs that Churchill himself was the butt of Roosevelt's teasing manner at the conference, as the president worked to coerce Soviet leader Joseph Stalin into a shared camaraderie through both men poking fun at the prime minister.[27]

However, all of the powers came together in the summer of 1944, after the successful beginning of Allied operations in Western Europe, for the Bretton Woods Conference. This gathering was held to ensure that postwar economic and monetary policies allowed for the most efficient and expedient reconstruction of a world suffering its second international war in thirty years. This economic and monetary diplomacy would result in the creation of the International Monetary Fund and an International Bank for Reconstruction and Development. The latter would eventually be called the World Bank. Both were established to guarantee economic stability, primarily through ensuring the solvency of postwar currencies, avoiding restrictive trade practices, and providing affordable credit for reconstruction. At almost the same time, thirty-nine nations (either fighting with or favorable to the Allies) convened at the Dumbarton Oaks mansion in Washington to discuss what shape the replacement organization for the failed League of Nations would take. Those diplomatic efforts resulted in the structure and powers incorporated into the United Nations. In all cases, political, economic, and military representatives, as well as banking, industrial, and public groups, were involved in the formulation of proposals, structures, and powers.[28] The diplomatic efforts required, in order to produce any coherent and functioning direction from these processes, was a testament to the desire on the part of all participants to establish bodies that would truly be able to avoid global warfare in the future.

The Yalta and Potsdam conferences, the last of the big wartime gatherings designed to prepare for the postwar period, hammered out the final areas of U.S. and British responsibility and interest. Exhausted by the war, facing a new America, one that was operating the world's most powerful armed forces (backed up by the newly emerging atomic bomb technology), as well as possessing the world's most powerful economy, the British diplomatic efforts in the war's final stages were concentrated on protecting British interests around the world to as great an extent as possible. The return of Hong Kong and Singapore were of a vital importance, as were other parts of the overrun British Far Eastern Empire. The Far East was now America's area of responsibility, and, if Britain was to remain a viable power in Europe, then having America's support was a paramount requirement as a balance to the overwhelming Soviet position. War-torn Europe could not be rebuilt by Britain and the reclaimed European nations, especially with the economic heart of Europe – Germany and France – devastated by the war.[29] The enormous diplomatic effort that had been an ongoing element of all levels of administration and coordination for the Anglo-American alliance would have to continue on into the peace of the postwar world.

Anglo-American diplomacy during the war was a complex, dynamic, and constantly challenging reality. There was no certainty that things would work smoothly, that egos at various military and political levels would tolerate insult and challenges to their own perceptions and interpretations of strategic conditions and events. Money – the lifeblood of both capitalist nations – and how it was translated into military power, as well as how it was distributed not only between the two English-speaking nations but how it was given over to other Allies, always threatened to create a major disruption of the alliance's smooth running. At the economic, fiscal, military, political, business, and public levels, various forms of diplomacy were constantly in motion, creating the environment for the greatest modern military alliance the world had yet seen create a war-winning effort. Without the diplomatic grease to lubricate that alliance machinery, failure was always a real possibility. The actuality was, however, that in the European theater (largely defined to include North Africa), the armies of both nations fought as one. In the Far East, the Americans dominated all affairs related to the war effort's strategic direction. And diplomacy was such a necessary part of the Anglo-American wartime experience from 1939 to 1945 because of the transitional state of that relationship, a shifting from the British Empire to the United States as the world's most powerful capitalist democracy.

Without astute diplomacy at all levels, the relationship between the two nations could have been impossible to manage, in terms of arriving at a commonly agreed on strategic direction for the war, as well as the peace. That impossibility could easily have been a result of the fact that the war was weakening the British Empire, accelerating a prewar condition, in comparison to the United States, as a truly dominant global power. Frictions that arose over the initial U.S. steps to fill the international vacuum created by a diminished Britain held great dangers for cohesion within the Anglo-American relationship if sound diplomacy failed. Negotiations over basing, loans, troop deployments, arms acquisition, the use of raw materials, and relations with various nations were all combining, in the Far East in particular, to shift the power relationship between the two. Diplomacy at all levels of government and the state found ways for this awkward transition to be managed in a cooperative and coordinated fashion, while permitting at the same time a major global war to be fought. In that environment, the British Empire's survival rested on U.S. decisions and actions. In all deliberations of international relations and military policy, the United States was now *the* primary consideration for British strategic foreign policymakers.

Diplomacy, therefore, with regard to the Anglo-American relationship during the Second World War, is most remarkable for fashioning that circumstance in the face of so many pitfalls on which those good relations could have floundered. Diplomacy on both sides of the Atlantic was hard-nosed and bloody-minded with regard to the protection of each nation's own national security interests. And yet, a certain element of accommodation and patience permeated many of what could have been catastrophic exchanges over the timing, direction, and aim of the joint war effort.

No longer the world's economic leader, the supreme maritime power, the provider of security for Australia, New Zealand, or Canada, or the globe's greatest trading nation, Great Britain used effective diplomacy to continue to provide support to its weakening position. Indeed, without such subtle and practiced diplomatic means, it is easy to believe that the American demands on the British Empire during the war would have been guaranteed to ensure that the empire would not survive. Such was not the case. Anglo-American diplomacy at all levels, even when the two nations passionately disagreed, remained focused first on ensuring that the war was fought. Future studies would do well to investigate in greater detail and depth the level of tensions, agreement, and options that American and British policymakers were faced with, in order to better understand the environment in which this wartime diplomacy operated.

THE ALGERIAN WAR

France's most searing colonial conflict exercises historians and media commentators to a greater extent than any other postwar-era French decolonization. Over its eight-year course from November 1954 until a final anarchic withdrawal in July 1962, the Algerian War exemplified all that was worst about colonialism: racial exclusion, intercommunal antagonism, and a final orgy of protracted, often fratricidal, violence between the colonial state and its nationalist opponents. Estimates of the final death toll remain hotly disputed, but a combination of demographic statistics and various other contemporary records point to a figure in excess of 300,000 and perhaps many more. The great majority of these were Algerian civilians. For most observers, specialist or otherwise, this is reason enough to accord Algeria a unique place in recent colonial history. Yet for others, French Algeria was very different, something whose passing might even be lamented as a uniquely Mediterranean society forged, for better or worse, by European settlers and North African populations of Arabs, Berbers, and Jews.

As these opposing views suggest, the Algerian War is a story of contested memories. For Algerians, it was a struggle that had to be fought. For the French, the rationale for the conflict seems less obvious as the imperialist sentiments of old become ever more outdated and indefensible.[1] Yet there is some consensus within the historical writing on the subject. Most acknowledge that the conflict originated in French dispossession of the Muslim majority and in the resultant emergence of a popular nationalism that saw no alternative to armed struggle and the overthrow of a settler order that denied Muslims economic opportunity or a political voice. Both in its origins and its bloody course, this was a colonial conflict whose bitterness mirrored the ethnic discrimination and acute economic imbalance between rich and poor intrinsic to settler dominance. However, to leave matters here would be to miss an essential dimension of decolonization. In addition to the colonies' internal dynamics, the end of European empires had obvious international dimensions, and Algeria was no exception. It is widely recognized that the Algerian War was also a diplomatic contest between the colonial power and its nationalist rivals, but the multifaceted nature of this diplomacy is less well understood.

At least four distinct strands made up the diplomacy of Algeria's struggle for independence from colonial rule. Of these, the bilateral relationship between the conflict's principal antagonists – the French state and the Algerian nationalist Front de Libération Nationale (FLN) – was, in some ways, the least significant and the slowest to develop. From the war's ostensible beginnings in November 1954 until the first in a series of Gaullist negotiation proposals in late 1958, dialogue between the FLN and the colonial state was nugatory. High-level talks between Charles de Gaulle's government and the FLN leadership, by then organized into a provisional government-in-exile, did not begin in earnest until 1960 and faltered several times thereafter before culminating in the Evian peace talks that secured a definitive ceasefire in March 1962.[2]

Perhaps inevitably, historical attention has focused on these exchanges as the Algerian War's definitive diplomatic endgame. This chapter suggests that this assumption is at best questionable and at worst misleading, in light of the three other strands to the diplomacy of the Algerian conflict. All of these were multilateral, not bilateral, and by focusing on them, we place the war squarely in the context of a Cold War international system convulsed by two related pressures: the gathering pace of European decolonization and the consolidation of a non-aligned movement led by a bloc of Asian and African states. The first of these three diplomatic interactions is that between France and its major Western allies in NATO, the European Economic Community, and the United Nations. The second is a mirror image of the first, namely, the increasingly formal diplomatic ties between the FLN, fellow Arab nationalist movements, supportive neighbor states, key backers in the communist world, and members of the non-aligned movement of neutral states, most of them former colonial dependencies. The final diplomatic strand excludes France and its Algerian opponents entirely. It covers the discussions between major powers on both sides of the Cold War divide over the war's impact on the long-term future of the North African Maghreb. This was a more or less constant process of discussion. Sometimes it was informal and conducted among politicians, diplomats, military attachés, and other specialist officials. Occasionally, it was formal and took place within the framework of intergovernmental conferences, joint staff talks, security service meetings, and other major international gatherings. Whichever the case, these exchanges generally turned on questions of national and alliance interest. What would the war do to Western standing in the developing world or the Middle East? How important were Algeria's economic resources and ultimate political alignment? What would be the strategic significance of an independent Algeria, and with whom was it most likely to align?

At the risk of confusing the reader, it should also be acknowledged that international diplomacy alone cannot explain the Algerian War's course or its outcome. Indeed, one could contend that domestic dialogues within France and Algeria were far more crucial to the end of French colonialism in North Africa. In other words, public disenchantment with the war in France and the FLN's ultimate imposition of its undisputed authority as the sole voice of integral Algerian nationalism, both products of internal conflict and debate, represented more important discursive processes than those conducted at the interstate level through the medium of diplomacy.

Differing analytical approaches to France's late colonial crises in North Africa are themselves the product of unique national perceptions. Maghrebi historians naturally set decolonization in the context of nation-building, the reassertion of Algeria's Muslim cultural integrity, and a heroic fight against racial oppression. Conversely, French historians tend to interpret their country's contested withdrawal from North Africa as primarily a national crisis, secondarily a colonial one, and only marginally an international one. This propensity to privilege the local and national over the international diplomatic arena makes good sense. After all, the human tragedy of violent decolonization touched colonial and French lives far more closely than the war's international dimension. That said, the concern here is with international politics and so the four diplomatic strands identified above provide the framework for what follows.

As external actors with discrete interests, France's major Western allies – the United States, Britain, and West Germany – usually assessed its colonial problems in terms of their wider strategic, political, and economic consequences. By 1950 regional instability in the Maghreb was rarely analyzed from a purely regional perspective. Conflicts of decolonization in North Africa impacted on NATO planning and affected global trade patterns. Colonial conflicts were a constant preoccupation in UN politics and stymied Western efforts to conciliate the emerging non-aligned movement. Nothing damaged the image of the capitalist West in non-Western societies more fundamentally than long-standing associations with a colonial past. In this sense, internationalization of the colonial breakdown in North Africa, as elsewhere, was both unavoidable and critically important.[3]

Wars of decolonization were asymmetrical conflicts. With only rare exceptions, they pitted well-armed professional forces against nationalist insurgents who launched raids and urban attacks while seeking to avoid encounter battles with imperial troops. Imperial authorities responded with strategies of containment, isolation, and eventual eradication of their opponents, just as nationalist forces sought to attenuate and expand the conflict, sapping the colonial power's will to remain. As a result, anti-colonial insurgencies after 1945 shared a common dynamic: an escalator effect in which the conflict was gradually internationalized despite the best efforts of the imperial power to prevent just such an outcome. If it served the imperial powers' interest to prevent international scrutiny and external support for "rebel" forces, so it was vital for the insurgents to offset their military inferiority by mobilizing sympathetic international opinion. This war of opinion was often paralleled by a material contest over military supplies, as insurgents struggled to obtain arms and colonial security forces tried to prevent them doing so. As Matthew Connelly has made clear in his book, *A Diplomatic Revolution*, Algerian nationalists faced with overwhelming French military preponderance recognized that their wisest strategic gambit was to bring the injustice of colonial rule to international attention. Their efforts to do so had a dual focus: on one hand, a "soft diplomacy" that vied for the sympathies of the publics and governments of Western nations and UN member states, and, on the other, a "hard diplomacy" that sought arms, money, and technical support from potential allies within the Arab world and the communist bloc.[4]

It cannot be said that colonial Algeria was ever a society at peace with itself. Even by the standards of European colonial violence, it stood apart, distinguished by the scale of European dispossession of its indigenous populations, by the intensity of Muslim resistance to this colonization, and by the enduring suspicions between the colony's haves and have-nots. Even so, the colonial administration in Algiers and the provisional government in liberated France were taken aback by the events of VE Day on May 7, 1945. It was then that several towns and outlying settlements in the Sétif region in eastern Algeria descended into an intercommunal bloodbath. After the French army's murderous repression of this Sétif uprising, the operational commander, General Raymond Duval, advised his political masters that the security forces had ensured a decade of peace. The politicians were now responsible for transforming colonial Algeria to prevent further rebellion.[5] Duval, who was the divisional commander in Constantine, was wide of the mark. The Sétif uprising marked only the beginning of the Algerian rebellion, the radicalization of a new generation of nationalist militants, and a more profound alienation between the European and Muslim communities in the colony.

The FLN, the organization that would mount a violent challenge to French authority from 1954 onward, was characterized by its youthful membership. Few activists had direct links with the foremost existing nationalist organization of the preceding decade, Messali Hadj's Parti Populaire Algérien (PPA). The emergence of a new generation of nationalist militants was evident in the FLN's forerunner, the Organisation Spéciale (OS), developed in the late 1940s as the PPA's paramilitary wing. In 1949 the average age of OS "general staff" members was only twenty-seven.[6] The army and police cracked down hard against the OS from 1950 onwards, but the FLN would prove a different proposition. On November 1, 1954, FLN militants launched a series of coordinated bomb attacks across Algeria, targeting public buildings and security force installations. The armed struggle for independence had begun in earnest. Part ruthless terrorist group, part socialist front, part defender of Muslim rights, and – albeit only in the latter stages of the Algerian War – a genuine mass movement, the FLN was in rapid evolution. The French authorities never bested it.[7] They were nonetheless adamant that the Algerian "rebels" be defeated militarily and discredited diplomatically.

It was several months before the severity of the Algerian disorders and the FLN's directing hand struck home to the politicians and public in France.[8] But this period of uncertainty did not last long. The nature and scale of the Algerian War was utterly transformed between August 1955 and October 1957. On August 20, 1955, FLN commanders in eastern Algeria ordered their Armée de Libération Nationale (ALN) cadres to impose a reign of terror in the Constantine and Philippeville regions. Seventy-one settlers and at least sixty-one Muslims suspected of loyalty to the French were butchered, sometimes in front of former workmates, farmhands, and other bystanders. Many were mutilated, and there was widespread evidence that female victims were raped before they were killed. Horrified by the massacres, the security forces went on a rampage of retributive violence comparable to that which had followed the nearby Sétif massacres a decade earlier. The colonial government admitted to 1,273 Muslims killed; the FLN claimed upward of 12,000. It was the first decisive escalation of the war and the clearest indication of the FLN's unswerving commitment to the terrorist methods of revolutionary warfare.[9] The terrible events of August 1955 also signified another landmark. As both sides crossed the nebulous boundary between warfare and murder, so Algeria's "dirty war" began.

After the summer's killings, state-of-emergency measures were brought into operation region by region. Troop reinforcements, already announced by Edgar Faure's French government in April and May 1955, were also rushed through the National

Assembly.[10] Yet the most critical decisions – to send conscripts to the war and to use no-holds-barred, inhumane tactics to dismantle the FLN-ALN command structure – were still to come. Both occurred during a period of center-left Republican Front administration from February 1956 to June 1957. The irony was that this left-leaning coalition, headed by Socialist Party leader Guy Mollet, was elected on a platform of bold administrative reform in Algeria.[11] The Mollet government's turnaround – from liberal reformers to protagonists of a massive war effort – was fatal to France's future in Algeria, and during this period the critical shift in the balance of power between civilian government in Paris and military leadership in Algiers took place. The introduction of special powers legislation in March 1956 extended the state's capacity to wage war against the FLN, most importantly by designating French national servicemen to serve in the conflict, something hitherto precluded. An opinion poll conducted in the aftermath of this vote recorded that 63 percent of the French public now estimated Algeria to be France's gravest problem.[12]

Conscripts poured into Algeria during the latter half of 1956. By the time France and Britain embarked on their disastrous Suez intervention in October, French forces in Algeria stood at 476,279.[13] The failure to oust Nasser's regime in Egypt, always the FLN's preeminent Arab supporter, only increased French military resolve to smash the Algerian rebellion. Senior French commanders now had the resources both to drive the FLN from its rural hideouts and to strike at its urban underground support networks. The paradox was that in doing so they lost two other, more important struggles: for Algerian hearts and minds and for international support of their actions. As a result, the French population, too, gradually turned away from the war, its costs, and those who fought it. Why was this so?

One reason was that the greater availability of conscripts (as well as helicopter transport) released professional troops to conduct more ambitious operations: search-and-destroy missions in the hilly upcountry and along Algeria's land frontiers and, more famously, an aggressive counterterror campaign against the FLN's support network in Algiers. These actions had devastating social consequences. Military success was achieved by "dirty war" practices, so much so that army actions are remembered for the methods employed, not for the objectives sought. During 1957 and afterwards, executions without trial, torture of suspects, and maltreatment of civilians became the markers of the French army in Algeria, despite the sustained efforts of some, such as the doctors, administrators, engineers, and Arab specialists of the army's Sections Administratives Spécialisées, to improve the lives of Algerian Muslims.[14] The French army, whose resurrection after the 1940 defeat was rooted in the struggle against Nazi tyranny, was now an occupying force whose elite units employed similar methods of torture and reprisal. Even the French legal system was tainted, and some fifteen hundred nationalists were condemned to death (of whom almost two hundred were executed).[15]

Another new development from 1957 onward was the greater stress placed on depriving ALN bands of essential weapons, supplies, and reinforcements. This was to be achieved by constructing a network of barbed-wire fences, minefields, and observation towers along Algeria's frontiers with Morocco and Tunisia. Sensible in theory and, again, militarily effective, the frontier fortification scheme must be counted a failure because of its human costs – in this case, the forcible relocation of tens of thousands of Algerians from border regions and other known ALN hotspots to the infamous *camps de regroupement*, holding centers reminiscent of the squalid British "concentration camps" of the Second Boer War. Eviction, incarceration, and refugee hardship were persuasive recruiters for the FLN.[16]

Two further results followed from this dichotomy between the army's apparent success in sapping ALN military capacity inside Algeria and the Muslim antagonism provoked by the army methods. First was the FLN's greater concentration on the international stage, the best arena in which to fight a propaganda war against French colonialism. Second was the deepening alienation of French professional soldiery in Algeria from its political masters in Paris and from a wider French public increasingly appalled by the army's behavior. Meanwhile, the war's financial costs spiraled out of control, imperiling France's surging economic growth. War costs, in turn, threatened Gaullist projects to enhance French international influence and construct an independent nuclear deterrent.[17] The combination of all of these factors, more than farsightedness or generosity, impelled General de Gaulle to contemplate French withdrawal.

France's NATO allies were all signatory to a treaty that explicitly committed the alliance to collective defense of "the Algerian departments of France." Yet those same allies, the United States and Britain foremost among them, increasingly derided French Algeria as a colonial anachronism that was bound to collapse. Successive French governments alleged in the years 1954 to 1958 that indissoluble links existed between the FLN, Nasserite pan-Arabism, and the Soviets' plans to draw the Arab world into their strategic orbit. If this were indeed the case, then the French army was not only fighting to defend a colony but also to uphold Western interests. Yet few policymakers in Washington, London, or NATO's Brussels headquarters accepted that the French war effort in Algeria contributed in any way to Western security; quite the reverse: the Algerian quagmire undermined the major Western powers' standing throughout the Middle East and the developing world. Because the FLN was neither communist nor strongly pan-Arabist in orientation, France's dirty war could be only counterproductive, stirring hatred of Western imperialism throughout the Middle East and antagonizing otherwise moderate states in the developing world. The logical conclusion was that France should be made to see sense and accept the inevitability of a negotiated withdrawal.

There were, however, other countervailing pressures to take into account, particularly in the United States. American interest in the restoration of a stable and prosperous France made President Harry Truman's administration reluctant to oppose French colonial rule with Rooseveltian enthusiasm. As it was, by mid-1954 the Fourth Republic was reeling from the loss of Indochina and its governing parties were wary of the growing appeal of a Gaullist right determined to overhaul the constitutional system erected in the Second World War's aftermath. No Fourth Republic government coalition, regardless of its precise interparty complexion, could risk the accusations of weakness and abandonment of essential French interests bound to follow any announcement of talks with the FLN. Put simply, in the French political environment of the mid-1950s it was politically suicidal to espouse the merits of a diplomatic solution that would legitimate the FLN as Algeria's rulers in waiting. Truman and Eisenhower's America, Adenauer's West Germany, and Macmillan's Britain all knew this and tempered their criticism of French actions as a result.

Soviet identification with colonial liberation movements against the capitalistic West also confronted Western governments with a difficult choice between democratic principles and strategic interest. They tried to balance the requirements of alliance diplomacy and regional strategy with the conciliation of moderate colonial nationalism. These contradictory objectives proved impossible to reconcile in the case of Algeria and the Arab world more generally. Although Dwight Eisenhower's Republican administration was immediately engaged by North African problems, it struggled to find the middle ground between strategic cooperation with European allies and theoretical support for colonial self-determination. As in the Middle East, the means, if not the ends, of a more interventionist U.S. policy were poorly defined. The search for compromise based around an Arab nationalism reconciled to Western hegemony was futile. It rested on the fallacy that dependent territories should achieve national independence at a moment appropriate to their socioeconomic and cultural development. The "appropriate" moment was to be defined by the colonial powers and their Western partners rather than by the colonized peoples themselves.[18]

Whether the American government perceived North African events through a "Cold War lens" or dwelt on the consequences of alienating the rising third-world nations of Africa and Asia, the result was a growing impatience with French colonial interests. Africa was emerging as a key Cold War battlefield. The United States could not win the resultant ideological contest if it were tainted by support for a dying colonialism, a fact that North African nationalists did their best to exploit by cultivating ties with State Department officials, Washington lobbying groups, and the New York media. Washington feared that the colonial conflict unleashed in November 1954 would be interpreted as a race war between white Europeans and oppressed Africans. The Eisenhower administration felt bound to distance itself from the French cause. The more French government statements stigmatized the FLN as religiously fanatical, illiberal, and anti-Western, the more Washington recoiled from involvement in a conflict spiraling beyond control.[19]

State Department Africanists rejected French stereotyping of FLN terrorism. This was symptomatic of a more profound attitudinal shift. During Eisenhower's first term, the growing cadre of African specialists broke down the entrenched Europeanism of State Department policy formulation on imperial matters. It nonetheless accepted an unspoken Washington consensus that the political upheaval and regional instability engendered by colonial war favored communist penetration of the African continent. African-affairs advisers dismissed French allegations of Moroccan or Algerian nationalist crypto-communism as patently absurd. They did, however, concede that the violent endgames of European colonial control facilitated the penetration of the communist bloc's arms, money, and influence. They further agreed that the key objective of U.S. diplomacy in Algeria was to combat any such Soviet, Chinese, or Yugoslav maneuvers.

In this regard, the U.S. was broadly in step with other leading Western states – Britain, West Germany, Italy, Canada, and the Benelux countries (Belgium, the Netherlands, and Luxembourg). The Algerian situation was raised informally time and again in exchanges between Western foreign ministries, embassy staffs, NATO planners, and visiting parliamentarians whenever France, the Mediterranean theater, or Arab world problems figured in discussions. In this background noise of workaday international diplomacy, concern over communist subversion of the FLN's anti-colonial nationalism weighed more heavily than any residual fears about the loss of Algeria as a strategic rampart in the defense of Southern Europe and the Mediterranean basin. After all, in any hot war between NATO and the Warsaw Pact, whether conventional or nuclear, it was difficult to see what difference Algeria's air and naval bases could make. If Soviet forces marched against Western Europe, the presence of a large part of the French army in Algeria could only be a disadvantage. If war began with a limited nuclear exchange, something considered a viable option after 1957, NATO missiles could be fired from plenty of sites other than the Oran submarine base. Add to this de Gaulle's mounting hostility to NATO's entire structure and it was little wonder that the alliance's European command was, by late 1958, dismissive of Algeria's importance to the organization. Far better to end the war as quickly as possible, both to release French forces for NATO service and to remove what was widely perceived to be an underlying cause of French truculence in dealings with its Western allies.[20]

The United Nations' role in decolonization was set to increase markedly over the course of the Algerian War. While the organization helped supervise transitions to national independence in the former colonies of the Italian Empire (Libya above all), France, like Britain, remained profoundly hostile to UN involvement in its colonial affairs. This French position would remain fundamentally unaltered from 1954 to 1962. That said, a combination of extraneous events and the increasing effectiveness of FLN and Arab League lobbying, plus a shift in the balance of power between the West-dominated UN Security Council and an enlarging General Assembly, would, on occasion, force the French hand. As a result, a distinct diplomacy of decolonization developed at the UN in regard to Algeria and, indeed, numerous other contemporaneous instances of European decolonization, from Cyprus to Malaysia.

Faced with mounting criticism of military practices, sluggish reform, and colonial iniquity more generally, the French delegation in New York set out to contain UN criticism, not to satisfy it. Open debate of the Algerian crisis was scrupulously avoided. Indeed, the primary objective of French UN policy from 1955 onward was to prevent inscription of Algerian questions onto the agenda of annual General Assembly sessions, a position justified on the dubious grounds that Algeria was not really a colonial matter at all as the territory was constitutionally integrated into France. When these French efforts failed, the French response was obstructionist: it either refused to accept UN competence and boycotted the discussion (as in

1955), staged a vigorous defense of French actions (as in 1957-58), or cultivated a studied indifference (as in 1959).

Whichever tactic adopted, French standing at the UN declined proportionately as the FLN's star rose. Once Morocco and Tunisia achieved full independence in early 1956, FLN representatives were quick to make the most of their neighbors' sympathy for their cause. Much the same applied in regard to the Arab League, Nasser's Egypt, and the major powers of the non-aligned movement, all of which were vocal supporters of Algerian nationalism on the floor of the General Assembly. Within the Security Council, the USSR, though supportive of the Algerian case, stopped short of risking an open breach with France, a fellow Security Council member and, as recently as 1949, a nominal ally. The Americans were similarly caught between indulgence toward a key European ally and awareness of African and Asian resentment at such Machiavellian calculation of Cold War strategic interest. Between 1960 and 1962, a chorus of new Asian and African member states, most of them former European colonies, added their voices to General Assembly condemnations of French actions. While de Gaulle's administration gave little ground, it was, by then, apparent that France had lost the diplomatic war at the UN and its affiliate organizations. FLN success in drawing attention to Algeria's plight did more to legitimize the movement and, in particular, its provisional government-in-exile than any number of local military operations. One could go further: by the time the Fourth Republic was nearing collapse in early 1958, the FLN had utterly discredited France's Algerian policy in the court of international opinion.[21]

General de Gaulle's return to power as French premier at the end of May 1958 was the direct result of a military coup triggered by the Algerian War. Within six months the Fourth Republic had been replaced by a new constitutional settlement that vested supreme power in an executive presidency and severely restricted the National Assembly's autonomy and powers of scrutiny. De Gaulle's immense personal popularity, his legendary reputation, and divisions within the republican left made all of this possible. So, too, did national fatigue with the unending Algerian conflict. In addition, the crisis of May 1958 had four quite specific short-term triggers. The first of these fired on February 8, 1958, when French air force jets bombarded Sakiet Sidi Youssef, a Tunisian village near the Algerian border. The villagers' "crime" was to have housed a major FLN base from which numerous cross-border incursions had been launched. The attack revealed a contemptuous disregard for Tunisian national sovereignty, but its human cost was far worse. French bombs killed scores of Tunisian civilians, many of them pupils at a primary school. The resultant international outcry spread to the UN and drove Eisenhower's government to force the French authorities to admit culpability.[22]

This brings us to the second short-term factor. Once Prime Minister Félix Gaillard accepted the need to admit French guilt in mid-April, his government fell. A lengthy cabinet crisis ensued as no stable ministry could be formed with broad cross-party support. The U.S. government meanwhile continued to flex its diplomatic muscle in Paris. Loan funding was withheld in a bid to secure sweeping changes at the top.

This pressure paralleled the third and perhaps best known catalyst to change. In Algeria, Gaullist envoys led by Léon Delbeque worked covertly with leading army generals to discuss ways and means to engineer de Gaulle's return to power in a new, more disciplined regime. When Pierre Pflimlin, leader of France's Christian Democrats, managed to form a cabinet in the second week of May 1958 and seemed set to enter negotiations with the FLN, the Algiers generals and their Gaullist supporters struck. Their decision to act was the fourth and final trigger for the May Crisis. On May 13 a Committee of Public Safety led by the army commander in Algeria, General Raoul Salan, was formed in Algiers. It immediately pressed for de Gaulle's assumption of power and threatened to oust Pflimlin's government by force if necessary. This was no empty threat. Parachute regiments loyal to Salan seized control of Corsica on May 17 in an obvious show of strength. De Gaulle, still at home in Haute-Marne, conspicuously refused to condemn these military actions, although he claimed to have had no part in provoking them. By late May it seemed that the only means to ensure a quick, nonviolent end to the crisis was to issue a formal government appeal for de Gaulle's return to politics. Once President René Coty did so on May 27, de Gaulle's accession was assured. The general initially took office as acting prime minister but immediately sought parliamentary approval for his declared objective: rewriting the French constitution.

Between June and December 1958, the terms of the new Fifth Republic were finalized, although they had taken shape in de Gaulle's mind over the twelve years since he had last resigned from government in January 1946. De Gaulle's principal lieutenant, soon to be his first prime minister, Michel Debré, not only helped reorganize the old Gaullist Rassemblement du

Peuple Français (RPF) into a more coherent and modernistic party, the Union pour la Nouvelle République (UNR), but also helped devise the legal framework for the decisive shift in political power from parliament to president. Under the new constitution, parliamentary sessions were limited, deputies had less opportunity to unseat a sitting government, and the Fourth Republic system of proportional representation that ensured multiparty government was replaced by a return to a single name ballot in which electors chose representatives over two electoral rounds. The relationship between president and prime minister was left deliberately ambiguous, allowing de Gaulle to accrue power to himself, particularly during his first term in office with Debré as his junior.

However, the old republican parties were unable either to unite in opposition to the new system or to propose a more viable alternative to it that ensured the Fifth Republic would enjoy more stability and powerful leadership than the Fourth Republic. Most of the Socialist Party under Guy Mollet backed de Gaulle's return to power, both to end the May Crisis and to hasten a negotiated settlement in Algeria. Republican Socialist diehards led by Daniel Meyer, Edouard Depreux, and Michel Rocard broke away to form a new center-left grouping – the Union des Forces Démocratiques (UFD) – with Méndesiste Radicals and supporters of François Mitterand. Yet, despite its impressive leadership, the UFD failed to excite much public interest. The Communists, too, were increasingly divided. Some saw in de Gaulle the only means to limit army power in Algeria, and they welcomed the general's willingness to challenge American global hegemony. Others, increasingly identifiable with Trotskyism and what would soon crystallize into the "New Left" student politics of the 1960s, considered the Fifth Republic little more than an authoritarian regime hidden behind the mask of a presidential democracy. As a consequence, the extreme and mainstream lefts would remain split in the years ahead.

The general public was for more united. The constitutional referendum on September 28, 1958, registered over 85 percent support for the Fifth Republic system. In the subsequent general elections in November, the Gaullist UNR romped to victory, leaving the UFD, the Communists, and the Socialists woefully outnumbered. A month later, on December 21 an electoral college elected de Gaulle president. The institutions of the Fifth Republic were in place, and their Gaullist political course was charted.

From the outset, de Gaulle's authority stemmed primarily from his unique popularity among the French people, something that transcended party loyalties. He was a skilled television performer, his statesmanlike gravitas heightened by his sonorous voice, extravagant hand gestures, and thick-rimmed glasses. His inspirational public appeals to put country above factional party or class interest struck a chord with domestic viewers and impressed countless foreign diplomats and dignitaries. Both audiences concurred that de Gaulle was uniquely qualified to end the Algerian conflict, a factor that only enhanced his majestic authority during his first presidential terms from 1958 to 1963. It was no coincidence that France's leading satirical magazine, *Le canard enchaîné*, ran a weekly column depicting de Gaulle as Louis XIV and comparing his presidential power base at the Elysée Palace to a royal chateau.

However, it is too readily assumed that de Gaulle's return to power heralded the beginning of the end of the Algerian crisis. The fact that the first official, though abortive, offer of negotiations with the FLN – de Gaulle's so-called "peace of the brave" – followed in October 1958 has strengthened this impression. Removing the Algerian problem was the essential prerequisite to progress in foreign affairs, defense policy, and economic modernization. It is doubtful, nonetheless, that de Gaulle was keenly aware of the need to concede Algerian independence. And de Gaulle's initial initiatives in Algeria combined a reorganization of the rebellious officer corps with renewed government support for wider military operations against the FLN. The general, it seemed, still wanted to win the war rather than abandon it, if at all possible. Furthermore, in 1959 de Gaulle's initial offers of compromise talks with the FLN leadership and long-term French economic investment in Algeria posited nothing more than autonomy for Algeria – home rule, not independence. De Gaulle's willingness to stand up to reactionary army officers and the French Algerian settler community rather than any farsighted acceptance of decolonization's inevitability cemented his reputation as a visionary leader. The same army officers who had supported his return to power in May 1958 conspired to overthrow him in separate coup attempts in January 1960 and March 1961 before launching a counter-terrorist organization, the Organisation de l'Armée Secrète (OAS), which murdered politicians and civilians willing to contemplate a French withdrawal.

Too Gaullist a view of the last years of the Algerian War underplays the extent to which the FLN seized the diplomatic, if not the military, initiative. Building on its existing political bases in Tunis and Cairo, on September 19, 1958, the party announced the creation of a provisional government-in-exile with functioning ministries and accredited overseas representatives. The FLN had found a new way to fight a war of decolonization beyond the colonial power's reaches. Its internationalization of the conflict exploited Cold War divisions and the non-aligned movement's anti-imperialism, leaving France evermore exposed as one colony after another achieved full independence in the years 1958 to 1962.[23] Finally, to regard the May Crisis as the start of the homestretch toward the finishing post of Algerian decolonization is to ignore two uncomfortable facts: the war had longer to run after May 1958 than before, and at a cost of even more Algerian and French lives in these last four years of struggle than in the three and a half that preceded de Gaulle's return.

So what did mark out these last four years of the Algerian War? There is much to be said for Raymond Betts's succinct appraisal in the book, *France and Decolonization, 1900-1960*. He notes the mounting distrust between settlers and French army commanders immediately before May 1958. Yet the settlers and commanders were united by a common fear: that Paris officialdom, alarmed by events running out of control in Algiers, would cave in to FLN demands. After May 1958 these tensions between Algiers and Paris persisted but in different form. During 1959-60 the French armed forces, led by de Gaulle's appointee, Air Force General Maurice Challe, struck hardest at the ALN and came closest to winning the war on the ground. But, in the same period, de Gaulle's administration edged toward negotiated withdrawal as the sole solution to the crisis.[24] Another irony: the refusal of army "ultras" and settler diehards to accept this turn in government policy only deepened state attachment to it. With the Muslim majority by now lost to the French cause, the key constituency of undecided opinion was in France. In this sense, de Gaulle's greatest contribution to ending the Algerian War was as a media performer, a reassuring presence who persuaded fellow politicians, serving conscripts, and the general public in landmark television and radio addresses that the wisest course of action was to leave the quest for a negotiated settlement in his hands. Seen in this light, the war's last two years were as much a Franco-French war as a French-Algerian one.

After the military victories of the "Challe Plan," de Gaulle's public endorsement of Algerian self-determination in September 1959 came as a bitter shock to the elite units, mainly parachute and other specialist colonial regiments, that led the fighting against ALN bands. Hardened campaigners isolated from mainstream civilian society in France, this warrior caste initiated rebellion against state policy and OAS counterterrorism.[25] On January 24, 1960, some of these ultras and their settler sympathizers erected street barricades in Algiers in open defiance of government policy. Defiance turned to violence when troops shot dead fourteen of the gendarmes sent to clear the streets. "Barricades week" ended after de Gaulle renewed his commitment to Algerian self-government in a famous television address on January 29. But the whiff of army revolt was never far away. Anti-government plotting, some of it involving the French intelligence services, became endemic. The government countered with special powers legislation in late February, a purge of dissentient officers, and the disbandment of the psychological warfare bureau, the "brains" of army militancy.

Meanwhile, preparations for negotiations with the FLN continued, although senior party leaders, including Ahmed Ben Bella, held in detention since October 1956, were not released. Not surprisingly, the first direct exchanges between the French government and FLN representatives, held at Melun near Paris in late June 1960, were largely unproductive. At a deeper level, however, the momentum for withdrawal increased. De Gaulle referred to his expectation of an Algerian Republic in another television address on November 4. The raft of new African states that joined the UN in 1960 and the prospect of an incoming Kennedy presidency in Washington committed to faster reform added to the international pressure for an end to the war. Most important, in a referendum on January 8, 1961, 75 percent of French voters endorsed de Gaulle's proposal for Algerian self-determination.[26]

The ultras' response was twofold: the abortive generals' putsch of April 22-25, 1961, led by four erstwhile commanders in Algiers – Maurice Challe, André Zeller, Edmond Jouhaud, and Raoul Salan – and, once that coup attempt collapsed, the intensification of the OAS campaign of murder and intimidation against supporters of a pullout.[27] Discredited and desperate, OAS violence was always counterproductive. It cemented French public support for the resumption of talks with the FLN, and it strengthened the FLN's provisional government-in-exile as the legitimate voice of Algerian opinion. Yet, in another ironic twist, as the French state and the FLN returned to the negotiating table, first at the spa town of Evian from May 20 to June 13, 1961, and then at Lugrin from June 20 to

July 3, the killing in Algeria and in mainland France increased. The final months of the conflict witnessed a further intensification of violence at the moment that the French administration and the FLN's government-in-exile in Tunis edged toward agreement. FLN leaders sought to maximize the pressure on the French security forces to strengthen their hand in final negotiations over independence. Meanwhile, in Paris, long-standing police persecution of the North African immigrant community descended into savage repression and arbitrary killing.[28]

What is remarkable is not how much French public reaction there was to this violence but rather how little. It is at least questionable whether the majority of the French population willed an end to the war out of principle rather than fatigue or even boredom.[29] Even in these later stages, the conflict's brutality was not always apparent to the voting public back home. For many, this must surely have been deliberate – a tuning out. Jim House and Neil MacMaster, co-authors of *Paris 1961*, have highlighted the extent to which police beatings and murders of Algerians suspected of FLN activism became part of a pattern of "routinized state violence" in France in the war's latter stages, particularly in Paris whose infamous police chief, Maurice Papon, orchestrated much of the repression. Few Parisians seem to have been especially animated by police killings of well over a hundred Algerian immigrant protestors during a night of bloody demonstrations in the capital on October 17, 1961. A large proportion were murdered by killing squads of the *companies d'intervention* riot police, many of them hardened ex-servicemen.[30] Only in the 1980s and 1990s did the "Paris massacre" resurface in public debate as a criminal cover-up, a national shame, and a pivotal moment in the racialization of France's North African community.[31] At the time many Parisians were astonished that the FLN "enemy" had the audacity to show itself in public. Most were inclined to forgive any police "excesses".[32]

Not everyone was so blinkered. Some French people were so bitterly opposed to the war that they were willing to go beyond legal protest. A small minority lent active support to the FLN by, for example, encouraging conscripts to desert, raising funds, and distributing pro-FLN literature. This amounted to what may be identified as a resistance movement. The best-known such group was the Jeanson Network, twenty-three of whose members were put on trial for treason amid media frenzy on September 5, 1960.[33]

Meanwhile, high-level talks resumed in May 1961, this time in Evian. Again, progress was slow. Only after the French government yielded in October over the retention of mineral-rich Saharan territories (by then, France's favorite nuclear test site) did later negotiations, first at Les Rousses and later back at Evian, make real progress toward a final agreement. In the last week of the war prior to the signing of the Evian accords on March 18, 1962, the ALN launched a general offensive against the eastern frontier barrage, pounding French army emplacements with Soviet-made artillery.[34] It was final proof of FLN resilience, of the extent of the party's international connections, and a warning that the months following the March 1962 ceasefire would be fraught with danger.

On first reading, the Evian Accords seemed a triumph of compromise, with provision made for an orderly transfer of power and a transitional French administration prior to a final Algerian referendum on independence. French strategic and commercial privileges remained, as did guarantees for settler life and property.[35] In practice, Evian was overtaken by events. The FLN rode to power on a wave of popular enthusiasm. Its retribution against Muslims who had supported or in any way cooperated with the French security forces was savage and swift, running to tens of thousands killed. Not surprisingly, the final declaration of Algerian independence on July 3, 1962, caused a massive human tide in the western Mediterranean as around 650,000 settlers and 130,000 Muslim refugees, most of them linked in some way to the French security forces, flooded into the ports of southern France.[36]

OAS attacks continued in France and Algeria even after the war's formal end. The extreme violence of the OAS mirrored that of the end of the Algerian War as a whole. The negotiated end to the war achieved through the Evian Accords concealed appalling levels of army, FLN, and OAS violence in the last stages of the conflict and the months that followed Algerian independence. On August 22, 1963, the OAS made a final bid to kill de Gaulle, almost succeeding in a machine-gun attack on the presidential cortege in Le Petit-Clamart.

In spite of the war's bitter end, de Gaulle's government considered the Algerian crisis over by late 1962. The dawn of a new era was symbolized by the installation of Prime Minister Georges Pompidou. Another devout Gaullist, Pompidou can hardly be counted a fresh face, but he was certainly a leader determined to turn away from the recent colonial past toward the assertion of Gaullist foreign policy and the quest for unbridled economic growth. His arrival was matched by de Gaulle's further consolidation of his personal authority. On October 28, 1962, the general secured a second presidential term, this time by direct popular vote. For a brief while at least, the war's psychological traumas and human tragedies receded into the background as the FLN concentrated on consolidating its one-party state in Algeria and French attention turned to issues closer to home: leadership in Europe, the development of nuclear capability, and the social upheavals of the 1960s.

A mono-causal explanation of something as complex, as protracted, and as divisive as the Algerian War is clearly impossible. Look, for instance, at two of the conflict's most glaring contradictions. First, the French army virtually eradicated the FLN's military units as an effective fighting force inside Algeria. Yet this counted for nothing both because of FLN success in imposing its will on the Muslim population and thanks to the movement's skilful mobilization of international support for its cause. Second, a war in which the colonial power for years eschewed negotiation was ultimately ended by a lengthy talks process in which France acknowledged the FLN as the only viable Algerian negotiating partner. Yet one thing is clear. Each of these examples points to the central importance of external diplomatic pressure as a determinant of how the war was fought and ended. While it is little exaggeration to say that France won the war militarily, the FLN won it diplomatically. Most important, the latter proved decisive.

One must, however, be careful of undue simplification. Many other crucial factors were at work. Some might be classified as impersonal forces. Among these, perhaps three deserve special mention. For one, rapid economic growth and a new age of consumerism in late 1950s France, each of which diminished state and public interest in holding onto the Algerian colony. For another, the gathering pace of decolonization across Africa after 1957 made the idea of French Algeria appear increasingly anachronistic and untenable. Finally, the advent of the missile age drove the Gaullist Fifth Republic to adopt a nuclear defense system with enormous costs that prohibited the long-term continuation of a massive war effort across the Mediterranean.

To these impersonal forces, one can add the more personal and circumstantial changes that affected the war's course. From the FLN leaders who cultivated working relationships with influential foreign powers including Nasser's Egypt and Maoist China, to the presence of an imperious, single-minded French president in the Elysée Palace, individual political actors clearly mattered. The same held true of countless remarkable individuals in France and Algeria who exposed the realities of dirty war practices, many of them paying with their lives in order to do so. Whether evaluating the deeper economic and geostrategic factors that drove historical change, or the people whose actions made a difference in this process, it is impossible to discount the international sphere. Intervention by foreign states, ranging from diplomatic pressure and forceful condemnation to direct support and monetary aid, was central to this most internationalized of colonial wars.

THE SUEZ CRISIS

As a study in the relationship between diplomacy and war, Suez 1956 remains as fascinating and relevant today as it was over fifty years ago. The fiasco of Anglo-French intervention in Egypt, ostensibly to secure the Suez Canal but implicitly to precipitate President Gamal Abdel Nasser's overthrow, is an object lesson in the necessity for clear political vision as a prerequisite for successful military intervention. Perhaps Britain's most embarrassing diplomatic setback of the second half of the twentieth century, Suez has been held up as the exemplar of exactly how not to do it. It is no coincidence that in the crucial early days of the Falklands Conflict, Margaret Thatcher sought counsel from survivors of Anthony Eden's cabinet and was given the astute advice never to tie military timetables to diplomatic ones but to engineer diplomatic conditions to support military needs. What followed in 1982 was a skilled diplomatic strategy that reinforced Britain's determination to regain the Falklands peaceably if possible but by force if necessary. In 2006, on its fiftieth anniversary, the specter of Suez was raised once again by a deepening political crisis over British intervention in Iraq and its potential consequences for Britain's place in the world.[1] Suez can teach much about the fundamentals of diplomacy and conflict – the immutable rules of international politics – as well as remind us of the additional pressures and complexities that the information age has brought. If Vietnam is remembered as the first war fought in the full glare of the world's media, Suez actually presaged what would come.

To understand Suez's significance, one cannot simply recount the events of 1956. It is not enough to scrutinize the diplomatic and military chronology that eventually led from President Nasser's nationalization of the Suez Canal in July through to the final humiliating withdrawal of British and French forces from Egypt in December and the Eden government's consequent collapse. Suez might have been the immediate catalyst for intervention, but it was not the source of conflict between Britain and Egypt. With the benefit of hindsight, international opprobrium, Soviet threats, and U.S. diplomatic abandonment of its closest ally seem the obvious consequences of British actions, but this was not apparent to key members of Britain's political elite at the time. To grasp these nuances, one needs to look further back.

What really led Britain to Suez? Was it simply the nationalization of the canal, personal distrust of or contempt for Nasser, fear of the rise of pan-Arab nationalism, and/or perhaps even a psychological refusal to accept the inevitability of retreat from empire? The sources of Anglo-Egyptian enmity stretch back at least as far as British occupation of Egypt in 1882, but to reflect on diplomatic lessons with any degree of confidence one can reasonably begin analysis at the end of the Second World War, when traditional British assumptions about its imperial role increasingly ran headlong in the face of changed strategic realities.

Despite the Labour Party's unexpected postwar accession to power, little distinguished the fundamentals of its foreign policy from those of its more conservative predecessors. In marked contrast to a radical domestic agenda, Labour set out to defend British global interests in a familiar manner. Ernest Bevin (foreign secretary, 1945-51) may have recognized Britain's decline relative to the United States but remained determined to retain international influence commensurate with Great Power status – a realistic objective in 1945. Despite the quickening pace of its retreat from a formal empire, Britain's imperial legacy was huge. The nation retained global Great Power status through a remarkable array of diplomatic, economic, and military resources. Over the next decade, Britain's position at the top table became increasingly precarious but only because that was now an exclusive superpower club. When reflecting on Suez and the mistakes made there, one must remember that Britain was still one of the most powerful nations on earth and determined to defend that privileged position. Almost inevitably, Britain was finding the psychological adjustment to new strategic realities problematic and was thus inclined to think and act in tried and tested ways.

Despite a lack of experience in the direction of foreign affairs, Bevin approached the empire's decline with apparent self-assurance, encouraging nations in the process of decolonization to remain closely tied to Britain through various bilateral and multilateral arrangements. The British Commonwealth of Nations, formally established in 1931, was a useful instrument for retaining close relationships and, more important, British strategic leadership, hence the devotion of a "new" government department (the Commonwealth Relations Office) to its expansion in 1947. However, the CRO's eventual incorporation into the Foreign Office in 1968 (creating the Foreign and Commonwealth Office) indicates the organization's natural limitations as an enforcement agent. Suez was an early indicator of this. As Peter Lyon states, "Maybe the Suez episode principally showed that the Commonwealth as a whole was a craft only for collective fair-weather sailing, with little or no capacity to deal decisively with sudden storms and foul weather."[2] Worse, a consequence of Suez was to leave a notable Middle East vacuum in Commonwealth membership.

In fairness, it was never likely that many Middle Eastern states would join the Commonwealth, and neither Bevin nor Eden deluded themselves that this was the solution to the challenges of retaining influence in the region. Instead, Britain continued to exploit regional rivalries, negotiating new alliances and reinforcing existing ones, while simultaneously supporting institutions promoting Arab unity, most notably the Arab League.[3] Interestingly, the two main strands of British Middle East policy – the continuation of large-scale military and economic commitment to the region coupled with the exploitation of awakening Arab nationalism – were at the heart of the problem facing Bevin. Imperial overreach and crippling war debts undermined Britain's capacity to defend its overseas interests physically, while the nature of that physical presence hardened Arab opposition to continued British interference in the region. Widespread British military basing rights together with the disproportionate political and economic power that it wielded fueled incipient Arab nationalism, which in turn made the long-term retention of British influence more problematic. Equally, disengagement was unthinkable: the Middle East was now Britain's primary source of oil as well as a key communications node for its still considerable empire and vital maritime trade routes. The Suez Canal in particular was vital because it was by far the shortest route for oil traveling from the Persian Gulf to the UK. More than 20 million tons – two-thirds of Britain's entire oil supply – was transported annually by this route during the 1950s.[4] Britain maintained one of the largest and most complex military establishments in the world in the Suez Canal's immediate vicinity. Retention of basing rights would not only secure continued British access to the vitally important waterway itself but also guarantee a large-scale British military presence at the gateway between Europe, Africa, and Asia, thus setting in stone Britain's ability to influence Middle Eastern politics by force if necessary. Unsurprisingly, Britain's long-suffering regional "partners," especially Egypt, were resistant to continued British occupation.

When Sir Anthony Eden returned to the office of foreign secretary in 1951, there was little substantive policy shift.[5] The only notable difference was personal: unlike Bevin, Eden was supremely self-confident when it came to foreign policy making. Oxford-educated, with a particular interest in the Middle East (graduating with a First in Oriental Languages), Eden was now confronted with exactly the same challenges that he and Churchill (once again prime minister) had pilloried Clement Attlee's government for failing to address. Post-1945 negotiations to renew and revise the various treaty obligations tying Britain into regional security in return for a preeminent position and largely exclusive privileges stalled on two fronts. While Jordan signed up to a new strategic partnership and Libya drew closer to Britain, neither Egypt nor Iraq updated their existing arrangements, leaving British interests in a precarious position. After Bevin withdrew British forces from their bases in the Nile Delta as a sign of good faith for further negotiations, Egypt ignored the overture and continued to press for the evacuation of British forces from their vital Suez base. In October 1951, during the short tenure of Bevin's immediate successor Herbert Morrison, Egypt unilaterally repudiated the 1936 Anglo-Egyptian Treaty, continuing to insist that all British forces leave Egypt within three years. Thus, Eden reentered the morass of Middle East politics at a time when all attempts to engage Egypt within a new regional security system were likely to be rejected. Though Churchill and Eden viewed much of Britain's Middle Eastern travails as the fault of their immediate predecessors, in truth the geostrategic situation had changed fundamentally since their last tenure in office.

This eventually became apparent as Eden's more nuanced grasp of Middle Eastern politics in general and Arab-Israeli dynamics in particular bore some fruit but ultimately failed to re-secure British regional predominance. First, and most obvious, the creation of a Jewish state in the heart of an overwhelmingly Muslim Arab world was explosive. The first Arab-Israeli War of 1948-49 reinforced Israel's physical position but galvanized pan-Arab hostility, with Egypt in a lead role. Given strong U.S. support for Israel and Britain's undistinguished role in the dissolution of its Palestinian Mandate, it was highly problematic for the Western powers to intervene in the guise of honest peace brokers. Several unsuccessful attempts in the early 1950s should have served as a warning that British influence was in relative decline.

Second, Britain's struggle to retain influence in the Middle East forced it to encourage greater U.S. engagement. This was both a practical necessity and a problematic complication. While increased U.S. involvement was inevitable given the region's geostrategic importance, Britain's need for an ally hastened the transference of influence. U.S. involvement was, of course, vastly preferable to deepening Soviet involvement, but still it created some unexpected tensions. Though broadly compatible, British and U.S. policies diverged in some important respects, reflecting differences in their strategic agendas. Despite valuing Britain as one of its most important allies, the United States was always going to feel uncomfortable with continued British imperial pretensions; anti-colonialism was a core principle of U.S. foreign policy. Equally, U.S. anti-colonialism was never likely to prevent the full exertion of U.S. power – diplomatic and economic by preference, military if necessary – in a region of such vital strategic importance. This assertiveness became more pronounced after the enunciation of the Truman Doctrine, which sought to take the communist challenge head on. In the Middle East, these foreign policy themes manifested through increased American commitment to regional security and the cultivation of its own preferred allies to offset Soviet, and even British, power. The stresses of Suez exposed superficially aligned Anglo-American policies.

Finally, any analysis of the Suez Crisis's origins must acknowledge the significance of decolonization's psychological aspects. From Britain's perspective, coming to grips with the reality of diminished global power was always going to be a painful experience. Though Britain's postwar governments recognized the inevitability of a drawing down of overseas commitments, adjusting an imperial mindset was no easy task. Naturally, all of the major players were products of the system and thus were shaped by it. No matter their diplomatic skills and undoubted intellect, Bevin, Eden, Churchill, Shuckburgh, Macmillan, and so on were almost bound to interpret action and decide reaction in familiar ways. However, the postwar Middle East was not a familiar place. Alongside the obvious geostrategic implications of Israel's creation, the rise of Arab nationalism indicated fundamental change. Britain's instinctive reaction that Arab unity could prove a useful tool for the retention of neocolonial influence missed the point: Arab nationalism, properly galvanized, was a powerful anti-colonial force. All it needed was a credible hero, an iconic figure prepared to take on Israel and challenge Western hegemony.

Colonel Gamal Abdel Nasser first came to prominence as part of the "free officers" military coup that deposed King Farouk in 1952. It rapidly became apparent that Nasser was a prime mover in the Revolutionary Command Council (RCC), and within two years he had effectively assumed Egyptian political primacy. After President Neguib was eased aside, Nasser ascended to the presidency, increasing his personal power in the process. From the outset, Nasser espoused a strong pan-Arab nationalism that ultimately aspired to the strengthening of regional power through concerted, even unified, governance. Though he was subsequently painted an egomaniacal tyrant, many were initially impressed by Nasser's genuine commitment to an idealistic philosophy calling for "dignity" in the Great Powers' treatment of Arab states and, indeed, in Arab states' own self-images.[6] Like several other leaders of the decolonization movement, he was a passionate advocate of the increased influence of the world's so-called smaller states and implored the fierce defense of their political independence from Great Power rivalries. A pragmatist first and an ideologue second, Nasser recognized that what would later become known as the Non-Aligned Movement would wield influence only as long as it remained united and had something that the world's most powerful states needed. In the Middle East, access to oil and control of key trading routes were powerful bargaining chips.

Nasser's policies and political rhetoric during the early years of his presidency were mainly moderate and entirely rational, although his relationship with Israel was highly problematic. In public, he could not be seen to undertake constructive diplomatic relations with Israel, but in private he did not completely reject the possibility of compromise and he kept secret channels open. Likewise, Nasser's refusal to countenance an extension of British basing rights in Suez did not mean he was determined to sever relations and force Britain out of the region. Instead, Nasser saw both Britain and the United States as important allies but in the context of partnership rather than servitude. Certainly, the 1954 Anglo-Egyptian Agreement that finally ended Britain's "occupation" of Egypt did not preclude better relations. In fact, many officials in both the British Foreign Office and the Ministry of Defence welcomed the end of what was now a considerable financial and physical burden on increasingly overextended military resources. The agreement, which promised British withdrawal from the Suez base by 1956 but allowed for the possibility of reentry in the event of attacks on the Arab states or Turkey, would expire permanently in

1961, effectively giving Britain seven years to establish less onerous regional security arrangements. In the circumstances, the Anglo-Egyptian Agreement brought a welcome result all around, but the tense negotiations and deep-seated mutual suspicions that emerged did not augur well for long-term peaceful coexistence in the Middle East.

Nasser's reluctance to enter into disadvantageous security arrangements with the Western powers and his courting of Arab populism made him unpredictable and increasingly untrustworthy in both British and American eyes. Increasing Egyptian sponsorship of clandestine hostilities in Israel during 1955 also complicated relations. In February 1955, an Israeli reprisal raid into Gaza led by a young Ariel Sharon and authorized by the reemergent political power of David Ben-Gurion (first returning as defense minister and later as prime minister) left three Egyptian military camps in ruins and nearly seventy casualties, including thirty-eight dead. Nasser subsequently reinforced Gaza and began formally arming and training refugee Palestinians in specially formed fedayeen units. Gaza confirmed to Nasser that in comparative terms Egypt was militarily weak and needed immediate material support in the shape of arms deals. However, Britain and France continued to drip-feed armaments to Egypt, and the United States refused to hasten the process, much to the frustration of U.S. diplomats dealing with Egypt who saw the issue as central to Middle Eastern politics.[7] Worse, the escalation of tit-for-tat border raiding also entrenched Egyptian and Israeli diplomatic positions, threatening to derail Project Alpha (the Anglo-American top-secret Arab-Israeli peace initiative). Alpha effectively died when Ben-Gurion and

Nasser simultaneously hardened their respective negotiating positions, though it limped on as an ideal of Anglo-American foreign policy for another year.

Britain's increasingly ambiguous regional stance had not helped matters. While the United States viewed the situation with concern and continued to build on its other regional relationships, Britain took more concrete steps to secure its own Middle Eastern position, developing a regional counterweight to both Israel and Egypt in the shape of the Hashemite dynasty in Iraq. With American acquiescence, Britain encouraged the founding of the Baghdad Pact (February 24, 1955), in which Iraq and Turkey entered into a mutual defense agreement that was soon expanded to include Iran, Pakistan, and Britain itself. The speed with which the initial Iraqi-Turkish agreement was signed took Britain by surprise, hence the pact's inauspicious coincidence with worsening Egyptian-Israeli relations and an Anglo-American attempt to act as honest brokers. Nasser naturally concluded that he was being isolated, as did Israel and, to a lesser extent, France, which also felt marginalized. In response, Nasser launched a major propaganda campaign against the pact. Nasser's rhetoric had always been proudly nationalist, but now it became stridently anti-imperialist, marked by thinly veiled attacks on both Britain and the United States. Further, Nasser increased his personal appeal to Arab nationalism by becoming more anti-Israeli. Thus, Middle Eastern politics entered another vicious downward spiral. It was even difficult to discern "sides" in the traditional sense: Britain and the United States were broadly aligned but differed substantially on the potential roles of Iraq and Saudi Arabia; Israel and France drew closer together in response to the

Baghdad Pact; and the Soviet Union looked to exploit the deepening crisis by offering arms to Nasser.

The Soviet (Czech) arms deal of September 26, 1955, dealt a severe blow to Anglo-American Middle East policies, accelerating the deterioration of diplomatic relations all around. Josef Stalin had been looking for opportunities to break into the Western-dominated Middle East for some time and seized the chance to offer Nasser what the West would not. By August, it was apparent that a Soviet arms deal was on the table and, more worrying, that Stalin's negotiators had shrewdly linked it to Nasser's ambitious civil and economic policies by making provisions for payment in a manner that would facilitate the simultaneous building of his cherished Aswan Dam. Nasser announced the arms deal the following day, attempting to mollify Britain and the United States by reiterating his peaceful intent and the fact that no strings were attached. This statement was in response to their charge that the deal would bring him under communist sway, but the implicit accusation that Britain and the United States had attempted to impose conditions that the Soviets had not did not improve relations.[8] A virulent denunciation of Israeli bellicosity further widened the rift. Secretary of State John Foster Dulles and Harold Macmillan, promoted to foreign secretary after Eden's elevation to prime minister in April, papered over the cracks as best they could and argued convincingly for continued engagement with Nasser. Despite personal reservations about the Egyptian leader, Eden saw him as a "better bet" than the alternatives and encouraged President Dwight Eisenhower to enter a joint offer to finance the Aswan Dam as a way of limiting Soviet influence. The offer was made in December and neatly tied Anglo-American government funding to a World Bank loan. The sting in the tail was that financing of the later development stages would be conditional on Western assessments of Egyptian economic strength – serious political leverage.

However, while Britain and the United States continued to woo Nasser, it was increasingly apparent that this was an expedient only in the absence of something better. Fundamentally, neither power trusted Nasser, but they could not afford to alienate him while lacking better alternatives. Though they attempted to resolve the Arab-Israeli dispute during the early part of 1956, the paradoxes in their own policies became more pronounced. Dulles struggled to square the circle of a desire to support peace initiatives with the need in an election year to appease the strong Jewish lobby in Congress. Ben-Gurion, back as Israeli prime minister, was forcefully pleading Israel's case for more arms shipments to counter the danger of the Czech arms deal at the same time Dulles was trying to persuade Nasser to come to the negotiating table with concrete proposals.[9] Similarly, Selwyn Lloyd, Macmillan's replacement as foreign secretary, was trying desperately to initiate a rapprochement with Nasser while also trumpeting the Baghdad Pact. For his part, Nasser was publicly ramping up anti-British, anti-American, anti-Israeli, and anti-Pact propaganda, while privately assuring them all he was still a reasonable man ready to compromise.

In March, Anglo-American patience ran out for different reasons. From the American perspective, Eisenhower and Dulles finally concluded that their peace initiatives were never going to bear fruit. They blamed both parties, but ultimately Israel was the more important ally, and so Nasser bore the brunt of their ire. In Britain, Eden and Lloyd interpreted King Hussein of Jordan's highly provocative dismissal of the British General Sir John Glubb from command of the Arab Legion on March 1 as an act engineered by Nasser. Though plausible in the context of Nasser's other anti-British activities, it is unlikely this was the case, but in the eyes of Lloyd and especially Eden, the two were inextricably linked. Two of the key Foreign Office officials, Anthony Nutting and Evelyn Shuckburgh, recalled numerous violent outbursts from the prime minister who "put all the blame on Nasser and brushed aside every argument that mere personal considerations had in fact influenced Hussein's arbitrary decision. Eden decided that the world wasn't big enough to hold both him and Nasser."[10] On March 8, Shuckburgh, no fan of Nasser but equally aware of Eden's own failings, made a prescient note in his diary: "Today both we and the Americans really gave up hope of Nasser and began to look around for means of destroying him."[11] In Washington and London there was an increasing sense that Nasser's intractability was the major obstacle to progress in the Middle East or, more accurately, to shaping the Middle East in their interest. Anti-Nasser sentiment ran high in both corridors of power: Nasser stood "in the way of Arab-Israeli peace," Nasser was "a communist," Nasser was "the new Mussolini." How much of this sentiment was genuine is debatable, but at the very least it made for a good narrative in the press.

Despite outward appearance of continued constructive dialogue, behind the scenes Britain and America began looking for alternatives to Nasser. With Alpha most definitely dead, new secret plans emerged. Usually collectively known as Project Omega, there were two secret initiatives broadly similar but with a couple of important distinctions. The Omega Memorandum was the blueprint for American Middle East strategy as it mapped the economic and diplomatic means by which a much tougher line against Nasser could bring him around. Significantly, King Saud of Saudi Arabia was the Americans' preferred counterbalance, whereas Britain remained wedded to Iraq and Jordan. The British approach, conceived by Nutting, focused much more heavily on effecting a permanent shift away from Nasser.[12] It is highly probable that it also contained a more menacing covert dimension, given MI6's subsequent activities. Omega also hinted at provision for foul play,[13] although it is apparent from the wealth of official and unofficial correspondence at the time that Eisenhower's personal attitude toward Nasser was considerably more measured than that of his British opposite number.[14] Eden's volatile temper was never more in evidence than when Nasser was the topic of conversation, leaving Shuckburgh with the uneasy feeling that the prime minister was incapable of rational decision-making on the subject.[15] Eden's judgment, and even mental health, became an increasingly prominent concern as the Suez Crisis evolved. Similarly, though the allies coordinated most activities, the difference in emphases became more pronounced as the crisis deepened.[16]

Washington's policy shift manifested in the threatened withdrawal of financial support and tougher regulation of arms sales, as well as even more obvious courting of the Saudis and increased backing of the Baghdad Pact. Britain went further, generally acting in a bullish fashion. This prompted further concern in both Washington and London that Eden's problems with Nasser had become personal and made his decision-making dangerously unpredictable, a feeling not aided by MI6's increasingly desperate attempts to draw the CIA into British conspiracy theories on the subject[17] and Eden's evident willingness to take speculative intelligence claims directly to the president.[18] While Washington was not ill-disposed to MI6's plot to instigate a coup in Syria as an opening gambit ultimately aimed at removing Nasser in Egypt, attempting to secure U.S. support for overthrowing King Saud in Saudi Arabia – whose relationship with Britain had soured over rival claims to oil deposits – along the way was remarkably naïve.[19] On July 19, 1956, after four more months of failed attempts to pressure Nasser into distancing himself from the Soviets and accepting closer ties with Britain and America, the United States decided to take the most direct route and withdrew the offer of financing for the Aswan Dam.

British perspectives on the decision to undermine Nasser by scuppering his treasured Aswan Dam project were ambivalent. Many thought it would force him to the bargaining table or even drive him from power, but other shrewder observers saw the inherent danger of such a high-profile slight to his dignity. British Treasury official Michael Johnston wrote prophetically that Nasser "will seek an occasion to revenge himself. There is not much he can do against the U.S. but a lot he can do against us."[20] Recognizing his weakness vis-à-vis the United States, Nasser looked to an indirect response and reviewed options for retaliation against Britain. Further, like many in London and Washington, his impression of Eden was unflattering:[21] Nasser saw him as weak personally and politically and therefore an easy target. On July 26, 1956, Nasser nationalized the Suez Canal.

The British Cabinet's reaction was no less explosive than that of the press. Military action was a strongly favored option from the start, notionally as a last resort, and Eden wrote to Eisenhower to that effect.[22] Eisenhower's reaction was lukewarm. However, when Eden tasked the military chiefs of staff to come up with a plan that same day (July 27), he was shocked to discover that Britain lacked the military wherewithal to conduct a coup de main. The military option would take weeks to organize. As a result, the mobilization of international opinion through diplomatic activity assumed greater importance, which was problematic because Britain's legal and moral position was not especially strong. A firmer response from Eisenhower on July 31 dealt a body blow to the prospect of conducting even relatively rapid operations. Though friendly in tone, there was no hiding Eisenhower's message: "Until this morning, I was happy to feel that we were approaching decisions along parallel lines. But early this morning I received the messages telling me on a most secret basis of your decision to employ force without any delay or attempting any intermediate and less drastic steps. For my part, I cannot over-emphasize the strength of my conviction that some such method must be attempted before action such as you contemplate should be taken."[23] Eden's war cabinet, the Egypt Committee, was forced to concede the necessity for a diplomatic round of crisis negotiations before military intervention could be justified. The farcical diplomatic slow dance that followed backfired horribly, isolating Britain further and undermining the tenuous legitimacy of a resort to violence.

Open diplomatic activity centered first on the U.S.-backed Suez Canal Users Association (SCUA) initiative and subsequently on the offering of UN Secretary-General Dag Hammarskjöld's "good offices" (or personal intervention). SCUA emerged out of the hastily arranged First and Second London Conferences of Maritime Powers that brought together all of the canal's major users, including the main protagonists: Britain, Egypt, and France. Until now, despite being their cosignatory in the 1950 Tripartite Declaration, which promised unified action to prevent further Arab-Israeli conflicts, Britain and the United States had been singularly dismissive of French interests in the Middle East. In consequence, France had drawn much closer to Israel, a fact that had a major bearing on subsequent events. On the eve of the First London Maritime Conference, August 16-23, it was France's vested interest in the Suez Canal Company that finally drew it into Britain's plans. Unfortunately for Eden, French intrigues proved even more dangerous than his own. Given Nasser's ties to Algerian separatism as well as the canal seizure, the French view of Nasser was even harsher than Britain's, and there was less holding it back from precipitate action: U.S. opinion was not a priority in France in the way it was in Britain. However, at the end of August both Britain and France outwardly pursued the diplomatic route, agreeing to a Second London Conference to develop the SCUA concept.

Perhaps both states still held out some hope for a peaceful solution, but the documentary evidence makes it clear that military planning for Operation Musketeer (originally the Contingency Plan) was their primary focus. Lacking faith in the prospects of SCUA succeeding, Britain and France began scheming to provoke Nasser into making a mistake that would legitimize intervention. To their enormous frustration, Nasser would not be drawn and continued to allow unhindered international access to the canal. British and French shipping was treated like that of every other nation, and, even worse, Egypt was running the canal every bit as well as the Suez Canal Company. With hindsight, the Anglo-French scheme to humiliate the Egyptians by causing a massive traffic jam in the canal, Operation Pile-Up, seems comical but only because the Egyptian pilots achieved a genuinely remarkable feat in getting all the shipping through without a single incident. Only Nasser's apparent intractability at the negotiating table gave Britain and France any hope of a pretext for the use of force. Britain in particular placed much faith in its ability to outmaneuver the Egyptian president diplomatically.

The Second London Maritime Conference (September 19-23) gave substance to SCUA, which had been developed by Dulles out of the first conference's 18 Nation Proposal for the canal dispute's resolution. However, the conference attendees could not agree on the specifics of the canal's international administration. Behind the scenes, Britain was pressing hard for more unequivocal U.S. support and France was growing impatient with the delays that diplomatic wrangling was causing the military timetable. Worryingly, fissures were appearing in the British Cabinet and even within the Egypt Committee. Walter Monckton, secretary of state for defense, and Rab Butler, lord privy seal, were particularly vociferous opponents of proposed military action without stronger justification. Issues of legality and legitimacy weighed heavy on policy deliberations. Lord Kilmuir, the lord chancellor, remained convinced that Britain had international law on its side, citing potential recourse to force over Suez as justified under Article 51 of the UN Charter: right to "self-defense." This was a contentious view even within the British cabinet, but regardless of legal intricacies, it failed to address the key issue of *perception of legitimacy*. One of the most interesting aspects of Suez is how international opinion was central to its outcome. Naturally, U.S. and Soviet influence were paramount but by no means the only reasons for ultimate political failure. British misreading of the level of U.S. support it could expect and aggressive Soviet posturing were only the most high-profile examples of international hostility to Anglo-French military operations. Eventually Britain and France decided to use force anyway, illustrating a fundamental underestimation of the potentially catastrophic consequences of perceived illegitimacy. In the meantime, they decided, largely due to pressure from within the British Cabinet, to take the issue to the UN more in the hope of enhancing their case than resolving the dispute.

By this point, any hope the British and French had of presenting the international community with a fait accompli had receded to the vanishing point. Military planning for the operation had gone through several iterations already,[24] and now diplomatic maneuvering, rather than military operational challenges holding up intervention, was fatally undermining the chances of strategic success. General Sir Charles Keightley, appointed supreme allied commander for the operation in August, and his Anglo-French planning staff were acutely aware of this.[25] Keightley emphasized that time was critical if for no other reason than winter's approach and the consequent degradation of Anglo-

French capabilities. The diplomatic muddle that this lack of decisiveness engendered is best illustrated by the fact that, by early October, Britain and France found themselves simultaneously putting the final touches to the eventual military operations (Musketeer Revise), planning an alternative in the event of further delays (the Winter Plan), conducting negotiations with Egypt within the UN for a peaceful solution, and sealing a secret deal with Israel to manufacture a pretext for intervention.

Far from strengthening the British and French hand, UN negotiations only served to undermine their position further. Lloyd was under strict instructions from Eden not to be separated from his French counterpart, Christian Pineau, but Pineau seemed to be following a completely different agenda from the British throughout. As negotiations moved from the public arena of the Security Council to the private chambers of the Secretary-General, Lloyd became increasingly frustrated with the erratic, contradictory behavior of Pineau, who apparently seemed ambivalent even to the pretence of attempting peaceful resolution.[26]

By contrast, Lloyd began to sense that a diplomatic solution was a genuine possibility. After intense private negotiations with their Egyptian counterpart, Mahmoud Fawzi, the basis for constructive public dialogue was agreed on.[27] Eisenhower was so confident that the crisis was over that he publicly declared that the conflict had been averted.[28] However, the crisis was far from over. Fawzi suspected Anglo-French duplicity and refused to be browbeaten into a precipitate agreement.[29] Soviet support for the Egyptian position ruled out any kind of enforcement resolution in the Security Council. Further, lack of broader support for the British and French meant that even forcing a Soviet veto (which they did) could not be construed as conferring implicit legitimacy. Most damaging of all, the UN negotiations finally exposed the gulf between Britain and the United States over Middle East strategy. Much to Lloyd's infuriation, Dulles committed several diplomatic "howlers" during the course of the discussions that undermined international perception of Anglo-American unity. For his part, Dulles continued to doubt British and French commitment to a diplomatic solution. He correctly interpreted a simultaneous increase in British pressure for firm U.S. support and a decrease in access to privileged information about Anglo-French plans as an attempt to tie the United States into a secret Anglo-French agenda.[30] The two men's personal relationship finally disintegrated over their disagreement about SCUA's purpose. In response to an exchange of letters between Dulles and Lloyd on October 15,[31] a diplomatic telegram from Washington to the U.S. embassy in London neatly summarizes the crux of the issue:

"We are particularly disturbed at the implication of Lloyd's letter that original purposes SCUA have had to be abandoned, in lieu of which he conceives organization as an instrument of coercion. We had thought British and French [UN] resolution was necessarily based upon assumption that SCUA would operate earnestly as instrument to bring about de facto relationship with Egypt which would permit passage of ships through Canal pending final settlement."[32]

Lloyd's frustration at what he saw as American vacillation also found voice in his October 15 letter to Dulles in which he stated, "We are both very conscious of the fact that this is a testing time for Anglo-

American relations. I have done my utmost to prevent exaggeration of our differences. But we must face the fact that revelation of so grave a divergence between us would have serious repercussions in Britain."[33] Eden went further, privately accusing Dulles of misleading Britain.[34] Information-sharing with the United States virtually ceased, leading Washington to conclude that Britain was contemplating something drastic in the Middle East.[35] Meanwhile, intelligence reports indicating unusual Israeli Defense Force (IDF) movements alerted the United States to a more imminent, apparently unrelated, threat to stability in the region.

Superficially Anglo-Israeli collusion was antipathetic to everything Britain stood for in Middle East politics. Britain and Israel were not close allies. In fact, most British contingency planning for intervention in the Middle East was based on the assumption that Israel would be the likely enemy attacking Britain's Arab allies. Alternative scenarios with Israel as either a concerned third party or an ally were barely considered before spring 1956 and not properly developed until well after that.[36] Israel was equally suspicious of Britain. Prime Minister Ben-Gurion in particular harbored a deep-seated conviction that Britain could not be trusted.[37] France, by contrast, had no compunction about approaching Israel as a secret ally and brokered the eventual agreement. The rapid improvement of French relations with Israel after both had been marginalized by Anglo-American policies during 1955 led first to a Franco-Israeli arms deal and subsequently to secret cooperation in the Middle East. For Britain, it opened an interesting but high-risk avenue for justifying intervention: a secret agreement with Israel to attack Egypt as a pretext for Anglo-French "peacekeeping." Unknown to Lloyd in New York but with the full knowledge of Pineau – which explained his seemingly erratic behavior – French Premier Guy Mollet (via a secret visit to Chequers by Pineau's deputy, Albert Gazier, and Major General Maurice Challe of the French General Staff) had presented Eden with an outline plan to bring Israel in on their side.

Both Eden and Ben-Gurion were initially cautious but recognized the potential for such an agreement to serve their purposes. Eden needed an excuse for intervention to secure the canal and topple Nasser, while Ben-Gurion needed support for a preemptive strike against an enemy that he was utterly convinced would, sooner or later, attempt to destroy Israel. The stumbling block was trust. For Israeli aggression to act as the trigger for Anglo-French intervention ostensibly as peacekeepers to separate the warring parties and protect the Suez Canal, Britain and France needed the alliance to remain secret. However, for Ben-Gurion to be certain that a full-fledged IDF attack on Egypt would not leave his forces dangerously exposed, he needed a guarantee that Britain and France would neutralize the Egyptian Air Force (EAF). His instinctive mistrust of Britain meant this would be best achieved through open alliance: "The one thing that Ben-Gurion coveted most was exactly the thing that Eden wanted to grant the least – that Israel would be recognized by the British as a full partner with equal status."[38] Everything hinged on a meeting at Sèvres, a suburb of Paris, on October 22, 1956. Here Ben-Gurion met with Lloyd, who was briefed on the proposal the previous day, and discussed the terms. Neither warmed to the other, probably because both were inherently straightforward individuals uncomfortable with the whole affair,[39] but they did reach tacit agreement on the viability of Challe's plan. Lloyd left with a verbal pledge only, which was Eden's preference, but two days later Ben-Gurion left with a formally ratified agreement, the now infamous secret Protocol of Sèvres.

After over two months of delays to the military timetable, suddenly everything moved into overdrive. Israel began mobilizing immediately, alerting the United States to the fact that something serious was going on. U.S. intelligence agencies speculated about a link with Britain and France, but lacking proof, Eisenhower attempted to intercede with Ben-Gurion by invoking the Tripartite Declaration.[40] At this point, both Britain and France actively deceived the United States, feigning similar concerns over the buildup.[41] It appears Eisenhower was genuinely shocked at the prospect of British collusion in particular. U.S. official records show that in a conversation with Dulles on October 28, Eisenhower "said he just cannot believe Britain would be dragged into this."[42] However, once the IDF launched Operation Kadesh the following day and especially when Britain and France began targeting the EAF on October 31, the deceit was revealed. The problem with the Protocol of Sèvres was that it was at once elegantly simple and ridiculously simplistic: in the highly unlikely event that the international community fell for it, it still didn't legitimize Anglo-French intervention. The requirement for the British and French to keep up the pretense even after Operation Kadesh began meant another few days delay to their landings, thus denying them the possibility of presenting the international community with a fait accompli. Ironically, after all the lengthy postponements to military action imposed by the painful diplomatic farce of the preceding months, this last week's delay finally destroyed any chance of Musketeer Revise resulting in enduring political success. Having thoroughly alienated the United States and antagonized the entire international community, Britain and France found themselves on the receiving end of a wholly predictable diplomatic barrage.

While both France and Israel were prepared to ride out the diplomatic storm, it soon became apparent that Britain was not. Of the three partners, it was actually the main protagonist, Eden, who was in the weakest position to resist international outcry. First, serious division existed within his domestic constituency. Not only were the Labour opposition and nearly half the electorate vehemently opposed to military intervention in Suez,[43] but Eden's own cabinet was split right down the middle. Second, assumptions about the UN's impotence proved entirely incorrect as the Suez Crisis galvanized support for Egypt within the organization. The Soviet Union seized the opportunity to divert attention from its own bloody suppression of the Hungarian Revolution and took the lead condemning the aggressors. On November 5, just as British and French forces began landing, Soviet Premier Nikolai Bulganin sent menacing "private" letters to Eden, Mollet, and Ben-Gurion as well as a devilishly impractical plea to the United States to join forces and stop the fighting.[44] More problematic was a groundswell within the UN to invoke the Uniting for Peace Resolution within the General Assembly to circumvent the Security Council, where both Britain and France had vetoes. Finally, while Britain could probably withstand the various pressures to halt without

U.S. support, it could not do so in the face of active American opposition.

Eisenhower was never going to threaten physical violence against his staunchest ally,[45] but other, equally effective ways to apply pressure were available. With the canal closed and a major oil pipeline through Syria destroyed, Britain was in danger of undergoing a major oil crisis while British shipping rerouted around Africa. Further, British gold and foreign currency reserves plummeted rapidly, threatening an economic collapse that could be staved off only with U.S. support. Macmillan, previously one of the strongest advocates of military action against Egypt, now turned coat and, in his capacity as treasurer, warned that "if sanctions were imposed on us, the country was finished."[46] Eden makes reference to this in a message to Eisenhower dated November 5,[47] and a revealing line in the president's draft reply (which was never sent) hints at U.S. willingness to exploit Britain's economic weakness to force compliance with international pressure for a withdrawal: "As you say, Harold's financial problem is going to be a serious one, and this itself I think would dictate a policy of the least possible provocation."[48] Having been lied to during the presidential-election week, at a time when he was attempting to castigate the Soviet Union for its brutal response to the Hungarian Revolution, Eisenhower was in no mood to support Britain.

Meanwhile, Hammarskjöld's energetic leadership at the UN created conditions for a viable ceasefire arrangement to be overseen by a neutral UN peacekeeping force, the United Nations Emergency Force (UNEF). Despite French and Israeli protests, Eden agreed to the terms of the UN resolution and Anglo-French offensive operations were halted at 2:00 p.m. on November 7, barely two days after they had begun and just as the assault forces were on the verge of securing all of their objectives.[49] Understandably mistrustful of British and French promises, Eisenhower continued to withhold economic assistance from the UK until after UNEF had deployed and the withdrawal was well underway. Eden's fragile health deteriorated once again, and he retired to the Caribbean for some rest and recuperation. By the time he reemerged on the public stage in mid-December, the Anglo-French withdrawal was almost complete,[50] and he was effectively finished as the prime minister. On January 9, 1957, Anthony Eden resigned and was replaced by Harold Macmillan.

Suez is a fascinating insight into the interaction of war and diplomacy for many reasons. Most obviously, the catalyst for the eventual crisis was President Nasser's nationalization of the canal, but to focus solely on the diplomatic machinations that followed this momentous event would tell only a partial story. Where one should really look for lessons from Suez is in the diplomatic morass that preceded the crisis itself. British diplomatic, or more accurately politico-strategic, incompetence in the buildup to intervention was not the long-term cause of subsequent humiliation; rather it was the nadir of contradictory and unrealistic policymaking that had led Britain to that point. With hindsight, it seems incomprehensible that Britain would deliberately mislead its closest ally, and the world's most powerful state, at a time when its own declining power meant it needed U.S. support more then ever. One may also speculate about the special kind of arrogance that encourages a small European nation to assume both the ability and the right to shape Middle Eastern politics through manipulation of regional power balances, encouragement of Arab nationalism, and exploitation of the Arab-Israeli conflict. However, to do so would be to miss the point entirely. Drawing such conclusions would be to impose an inherited wisdom about Cold War strategic realities on a time that was critical to shaping those realities. Regardless of the influence of personality on the crisis – and it was considerable – the basic premise that Britain was still a Great Power that could impose its will on "lesser" states and statesmen had yet to be disproved. Unfortunately for Eden, Suez confirmed that Britain's golden era was not still passing but had passed. What Suez taught Britain was that war without diplomacy, in the sense of intervention without legitimacy, was no longer a genuine policy option.

THE VIETNAM WAR

More than thirty-five years after its close, the Vietnam War still raises problems. Why did the United States fight such a disastrous war, in such a small country, so far from home, so unsuccessfully? Why was the military and diplomatic implementation of U.S. foreign policy so unsuccessful? This chapter addresses these questions by examining the role of broad policy and concepts, namely the containment of communism and the use of coercion, and the difficulty of realizing them through diplomatic and military tools. For the United States as it faced communism, the war was in Vietnam but not about Vietnam; the conflict quickly became about internal and external U.S. credibility. America was unable to reconcile the internal and external demands made on it during the war, let alone match North Vietnam's commitment to victory. By analyzing each administration's approach to Vietnam, one can see that military force could not compensate for a weak and isolated diplomatic position, be it shoring up a new state, coercing the North, or withdrawing and leaving a viable South in place. At each stage, the United States had a weak hand and failed, as the use of military force did not generate sufficient options for the various U.S. administrations.

At its simplest level, the containment policy the United States developed after the Second World War led to the Vietnam War. U.S. foreign policy during the Cold War's initial stages focused on avoiding the weakness of the appeasement policy that Europe had used so unsuccessfully toward Hitler and on developing an approach more stable in the nuclear age than a dangerous preemptive policy. This new policy, termed "containment," aimed to restrict the influence of the Soviet Union and communism until communism collapsed under its own contradictions. George Kennan, the American diplomat who first articulated containment's main features, considered the Atlantic community, the Mediterranean, Japan, and the Philippines to be the key areas of concern for U.S. policy.[1] Vietnam and Southeast Asia were not deemed vital centers of interest. However, the outbreak of the Korean War and the growing tension of the Cold War led to a more rigid reading of containment that saw a militarization of the strategy. This led the United States to begin to view *all* incursions by communism as threats to its national interests, be they in the original centers of interest or not. There was a particular fear that the fall of one country to communism would lead to its neighbors also becoming infected; this was the so-called domino theory.

After the Korean War, the popularity of the domino theory led the United States to consider Indochina (namely Vietnam, Laos, and Cambodia) as vital to its security interests. Vietnam was particularly significant because it was a natural invasion route into the "rice bowl" of Southeast Asia, and as a potential domino, it would lead to the fall of Thailand, Burma, Malaya, and Indonesia.[2] The threat of Vietnam falling, as both presidents Truman and Eisenhower pointed out, was a threat to U.S. global and regional policy. The U.S.

involvement in Southeast Asia was thus a result of the overarching strategic posture of its post-Second World War policies.

Containment policy played down the role of diplomacy because the Soviets were seen far more as an ideological threat than as a normal geopolitical power. In fact diplomacy had almost no place in containment policy that emerged after 1945 as the Soviets were considered fanatics.[3] Not only was diplomacy downplayed, but containment policy had an inherent tension within it, as it provided the need to intervene while limiting the means to prosecute policy.[4] The fear of nuclear war with the Soviets was extremely real, as was the perceived challenge to U.S. interests, so great care had to be taken in responding to the expanding communist threat and any conflict following a U.S. response needed to remain "limited."

What "limited war" meant in practice sparked much debate. For the John Kennedy administration (1961-63), the Cuban Missile Crisis had shown that limited "shows of force" allowed international crises to be managed.[5] The administration advocated a more politicized military policy of "flexible response" and, for example, set great store by counterinsurgency doctrine and training within the army to realize this. Kennedy's approach would be tested in Vietnam, as it was designed to meet just that kind of situation.[6] The policy faced opposition from the military, with the Joint Chiefs of Staff particularly opposed to a limited ground war in Asia.[7]

Successive administrations during the Cold War increased the executive role in national strategy.[8] The Vietnam War was also the product of the growing centralization of military policy-making by civilians looking to manage the national policy in pursuit of containment. President Kennedy had been disturbed during the Cuban Missile Crisis by his senior military advisers' inability to look beyond the military field.[9] The centralizing of military strategy was combined with the new administration's "belief that sheer intelligence and rationality could answer and solve anything."[10] The growth of political dominance over national military strategy was enhanced by the autocratic management style and focus on systems analysis of Robert McNamara, secretary of defense to presidents Kennedy and Johnson. McNamara had a scarcely concealed disdain for military advice, and the Vietnam War was seen as "McNamara's War."[11] Nonetheless, it was not the advocacy of new military options that led the military into Vietnam, but containment policy, especially as Kennedy gave new impetus to containment and energized the nation, proposing that the United States would "pay any price, bear any burden...in order to assure the survival and the success of liberty."

As it happened, the war the United States fought in Vietnam was not so much about Vietnam as about China and the Soviet Union. Conversely, for the Vietnamese it was not about the United States, but about the nature of the independent Vietnam that would emerge with the end of European colonization.[12] From the 1840s to 1890s the French had fought wars of colonization in Indochina, and they had ruled the region through to 1945, even despite Japanese occupation during the Second World War. Ho Chi Minh was the leader of the anti-Japanese resistance during the occupation, and with the end of the Second World War, his Viet Minh took control and declared the Democratic

Republic of Vietnam. In 1946 Ho set his sights on removing the French colonizers, and when war broke out, he looked to America for support against the French. In 1949 the French established a government under former emperor Bao Dai in Saigon to rival Ho Chi Minh's government.

By 1950 the Korean War had begun, China was under communist control, and China and the Soviet Union had recognized Ho's government. In response to communist recognition of the Democratic Republic of Vietnam, the United States recognized the Bao Dai government and provided political, economic, and military support to the French to prevent a Viet Minh victory. America's Mutual Defense Assistance Agreement with France, Vietnam, Cambodia, and Laos provided military supplies through a U.S. Military Advisory Group that comprised only four advisers when authorized in 1950; by 1954 the group had over three hundred advisers.[13] Supplies were channeled through the French.

Many U.S. policymakers, doubting French willingness to satisfy the nationalist aspirations of the Vietnamese, were skeptical about supporting the French in the Indochina War, but alternative courses of action were seen as far more perilous.[14] By 1953 Secretary of State John Foster Dulles felt that Indochina had the "top priority in foreign policy." The region was "more important than Korea because the consequences of loss there could not be localized, but would spread throughout Asia and Europe."[15] For example, Vietnam's fall would affect newly-independent Japan's trade as well as British and French interests in Southeast Asia, undermining the European Defense Community Treaty.

The fundamental difficulty was that the French forces were not winning against the Viet Minh forces, which were led by General Vo Nguyen Giap. French General Henri Navarre consolidated his forces in Vietnam, and Giap then invaded Laos, forcing Navarre to disperse his forces again. Deciding to lure Giap into a set-piece battle, Navarre stationed twelve battalions at Dien Bien Phu in the hills of northwestern Vietnam. Giap rose to the challenge. Outnumbering Navarre's forces and backed by Chinese matériel freed from the Korean peninsula, Giap encircled the French positions. The U.S. National Security Council spent much of January 1954 debating what its options were. Dulles agreed to the French proposal to add Indochina to the Geneva Conference scheduled to discuss the Korean Armistice. He did this to prevent France's Laniel government from falling and to protect the ratification of the European Defense Community.[16]

On the day of the French forces' final collapse at Dien Bien Phu in May 1954, Dulles kept open the option of sending U.S. military support to strengthen the Geneva negotiations, though the plan to intervene militarily (Operation Vulture) was not activated. Dulles thought it better to deal directly with the Indochinese rather than go through the French. This preference was reinforced by President Dwight Eisenhower and the army chief of staff, General Matthew Ridgway, who believed military force should be used only to defeat an opponent and nondecisive military interventions should be avoided, especially after the experience in Korea.[17] Dulles and Eisenhower gave up on French efforts but still looked to defend the broader Asian continent against communist incursion, a decision for which the administration was heavily criticized at the time.[18] The policy of shoring up the French allies collapsed with the defeat of their forces at Dien Bien Phu. The ceasefire became part of the negotiations in Geneva, and the French government soon fell.

The French requested help to withdraw from the region. The Anglo-American diplomatic effort was essential as Anthony Eden, the British foreign secretary, drove much of the negotiating. The transatlantic partners agreed to set up a regional defense pact, and the U.S. administration accepted Vietnam's partition. The Geneva Accords involved diplomats from the UN Security Council countries – the UK, United States, USSR, China, and France – and from Vietnam, Laos, and Cambodia. The end of the French influence in Indochina was marked in July 1954 with the signing of the accords with the Viet Minh, which gave Laos, Cambodia, and Vietnam independence. Vietnam was divided along the 17th parallel and was to be reunited by a free election in 1956. The accords also established an International Control Commission with India, Canada, and Poland to oversee the agreement's implementation. The United States pressured Bao Dai to appoint the nationalist and anticommunist Ngo Dinh Diem as prime minister of South Vietnam.

Neither the South Vietnam government nor the United States signed the Geneva Accords. In fact, "it was a document with participants but no contracting parties and thus no collective obligations."[19] Eisenhower had not mobilized a Western coalition in support of his plans, and so Dulles offered South Vietnam, Laos, and Cambodia unilateral guarantees. Such unilateralism weakened the position of the United States, which was to become increasingly isolated in its policy toward Vietnam. In its policy toward

Indochina, the United States dangerously conflated nationalism with the worldwide threat of communism, and this mindset, which was not shared by America's European allies, continued to plague U.S. perceptions of nationalist movements in Africa and South America throughout the Cold War. In addition to reading the ideology of the Vietnam War differently, the European allies such as Britain also did not agree on the scale of the threat to the West if Vietnam fell – the domino theory was primarily an American perception.[20] Also, Britain at this time faced its own problems with Malaya and Indonesia as it closed down its empire and withdrew by 1968 from "East of Suez," leaving the United States as the main security guarantor in the region. French President Charles de Gaulle was the main voice to express how foolish he thought U.S. policy was, and he advocated neutrality toward Indochina in accord with the 1954 settlement. Finally, even if the European allies had agreed with the later Lyndon Johnson administration in particular, the domestic opposition would have made any government action in favor of the United States extremely difficult. This is not to say that America's allies did not also see communism as a global threat – it was the place and nature of the U.S. response that was under question.

For his part, Eisenhower was determined not to lose Vietnam as Harry Truman had "lost" China. He aimed to stabilize Southeast Asia and prevent further losses to communism via expansion or overt aggression.[21] The difficulty was that the Geneva Accords primarily settled military rather than political issues, especially as the state of South Vietnam was present at Geneva but was excluded from discussions and did not sign the accords. Moreover, the Viet Minh anticipated that the

South would collapse quickly, and if it did not, then the rebels had sufficient arms hidden in the South to resume fighting – just as they had done earlier against the Japanese and the French. U.S. policy thus shifted to providing security through the establishment of a regional defense pact and support for an anticommunist government in South Vietnam that could stop Viet Minh expansion south of the 17th parallel.

In September 1954 the United States established the Southeast Asia Treaty Organization (SEATO) as a regional buffer with members (the UK, France, Australia, New Zealand, the Philippines, Thailand, and Pakistan) that could assist one another against armed attack. South Vietnam, Laos, and Cambodia joined the organization later. Through SEATO the United States justified its support for the South. As it developed SEATO, it had to ease the French out of Vietnam while keeping French support for collective security in Europe. Dulles and the French government argued frequently. Dulles ceded the initiative to Eden, and the British plan to restore German sovereignty through NATO was followed. The Nine Power conferences in 1954 led to the establishment of the Western European Union and the restoration of sovereignty to the Federal Republic of Germany, which then formally joined NATO. Atlantic unity was reinforced and Germany rearmed successfully.

In Southeast Asia, however, the establishment of a regional security organization was not sufficient to protect South Vietnam. The administration had to sponsor a politician to lead the state, and Eisenhower's choice fell on the autocratic Ngo Dinh Diem. Diem had lived in America since 1950, had many U.S. supporters, was anti-French, and was a Christian, a Catholic in a Buddhist country. American support of Diem, as with Syngman Rhee in South Korea and Chiang Kai-shek in Taiwan, was part of a broader pattern of backing Christian politicians against "godless communists," a policy reflective of the broader mood of 1950s America.[22] American policy, having avoided direct military intervention, became "sink or swim with Ngo Dinh Diem" – which led to incremental intervention and eventually full-scale military support.[23]

Diem deposed the head of state, Bao Dai, and gained control of South Vietnam in 1955. By 1956 his government, with huge amounts of U.S. aid, had brought about an economic miracle in agriculture policy. However, fearful of rigged elections in the North and the Viet Minh insurrection's effect on the Saigon government's viability and ability to unify the nation, Diem was expected to lose the 1956 elections.[24] He therefore refused to hold them, and the United States backed this decision. The following year Diem paid a state visit to the United States during which President Eisenhower hailed him as the "miracle man" of Asia. In return, and not inaccurately, Diem asserted that the Viet Minh had disintegrated in the South. As historian Stanley Karnow points out, Diem at this point might have sealed his control over the South had he not made a series of errors because of the nature of his regime and his misunderstanding of the task he faced. His regime, which supported wealthy landowners and alienated peasants with the creation of farm communities, was a narrow, corrupt oligarchy of relatives that saw the conflict as simply one of military security unrelated to social injustice.[25] This misconception was compounded by the nature of the U.S. military support.

The initial U.S. military advisory effort to support the South focused on creating a South Vietnamese military force that was conventional in tactics and equipment and whose organization was patterned after the U.S. Army.[26] It was geared to be capable of withstanding an invasion from the North. However, it was an army that was too centralized and its equipment was too heavy to cope with the internal insurgency that soon developed once the 1956 elections did not happen and Diem outlawed the opposition. Opposition in the South went underground. In 1959, Hanoi committed its military and political resources to the struggle for unification with the South. Thousands of trained leaders, or cadres, were sent south to build the military and political means to overthrow Diem.

Still, before Kennedy took office in 1961, the containment aim of averting an immediate communist takeover and improving domestic and economic stability had been achieved, though with huge levels of aid and the creation of a South Vietnamese government dependent on the United States. Therefore, when Eisenhower briefed Kennedy the day before his inauguration, he did not even mention Vietnam. Laos, a far more imperiled domino, was the focus. Once in office Kennedy faced a situation in Laos that deteriorated into a civil war, but the humbling experience of the failed invasion of Cuba at the Bay of Pigs kept him from using direct military force there.[27] Also Kennedy did not have a neutral option in Laos as the British co-chairman of the Geneva conference required Moscow's involvement and the Soviets (like the North Vietnamese) were backing the Pathet Lao. Vietnam was thus a more promising place to prevent the dominos from falling, a place where communists could be confronted rather than negotiated with as in Laos.

In November 1961 General Maxwell Taylor, a former army chief of staff and a favorite of the Kennedy administration, returned from a mission to Vietnam to report the need to raise morale and to show that the United States was serious about resisting a communist takeover.[28] Taylor recommended that military forces be introduced into South Vietnam.[29] By 1962 the U.S. Army had four thousand advisers there, under a Counterinsurgency Council chaired by Taylor.[30] However, as Andrew Krepinevich has shown in his book *The Army and Vietnam*, the complex political and physical nature of the developing war went against the conventional orientation and strengths of the U.S. military, which was at the time geared toward confronting the Soviets in northern Europe.[31] The war in Vietnam was frontless, with no defined battlefields or secure areas and with danger that was pervasive and chronic. Not only that, but the terrain in which the war was fought – including rain forest, flooding delta, and swampland – was far different from that of Europe. The United States was not prepared to fight an enemy it could hardly see and who was indistinguishable from the populace. The advisory role soon mutated. A key turning phase began on November 2, 1963, with President Diem's overthrow, which the United States had condoned. Diem had been losing control of the Buddhist population. But the resultant series of coups and ruling military commanders meant the United States faced a rising credibility issue and the eventual deterioration of the southern government's authority. At the time of President Kennedy's assassination later that same month, U.S. policy was on a cusp. Backing a failing Saigon government, the United States faced an enormous problem, especially as North Vietnam, already so successful with its guerrilla campaign, was gearing up for a full-scale war.

The situation continued to worsen for Saigon and Washington throughout 1964. In August, North Vietnamese forces allegedly attacked U.S. naval vessels in the Gulf of Tonkin. Congress quickly passed the Gulf of Tonkin Resolution, giving President Johnson a free hand to protect American forces in Vietnam – essentially the authority to fight a war without declaring one. This meant that Washington did not have to call for national mobilization, a key feature of the American military's nature. The failure to mobilize became the root of many domestic concerns about Vietnam and eventual opposition to the war. As H.R. McMaster explained in his book *Dereliction of Duty*, this policy led the United States to go to war "in a manner unique in American history...It slunk in on cat's feet."[32] However, the Johnson administration made more of an attempt to "manage" the North by coercion than to make war. Ironically, the U.S. policy of "limited war," in which limited amounts of force were used to coerce the opponent, left the North the most bombed country in the world at the time – and the South the second most.

The emphasis on the military option to augment diplomacy in Indochina containment policy greatly increased with President Johnson's tactic of using force in measured quantities to "coerce" the North to resume diplomatic negotiations. Johnson and his top advisers realized beginning in 1964 that the problems in Vietnam would have to be resolved through diplomatic negotiation.[33] His policy was thus to secure the South and increase the pressure on the North to withdraw. He had to deny Hanoi victory in the South while avoiding a regional war, especially as China had become a nuclear power in 1964 and there were fears that it would become directly involved as it had in the Korean War. In addition, in 1964 Nikita Khrushchev had fallen from power, and a change of policy in Moscow had led to an increase of military and economic aid to the North, as well as public assurances of full support in the event of a U.S. invasion. The United States was concerned about the impact of a communist takeover in the South on its SEATO allies, especially given the Indonesian communist situation – such an event would squeeze Malaysia and Thailand in particular. For Johnson, therefore, issues of U.S. credibility among the SEATO allies, China, and the Soviet Union were most significant.

Johnson also had to consider his domestic constituency and was reluctant to engage in a direct military confrontation with regional communist governments that supported the Viet Cong insurgency. He wished to avoid domestic public pressure for policy changes. His policy focused instead on generating pressure on the North by "escalation," a concept borrowed from nuclear strategy at the time, whereby gradually increased amounts of bombing would make the opponent consider the costs of his actions until he eventually capitulated to the aggressor's demands. For Johnson this policy was also matched by having a series of negative objectives that limited the campaign. However, by his use of damage-limiting expedients and measured actions, he was far closer to practicing crisis management than coercive pressure.[34]

The 1965-68 air campaign against the North is the clearest example of the escalation policy and its weaknesses. This campaign involved dropping graduated numbers of munitions on the North and taking periodic breaks from bombing to allow the North to consider the costs of its political position. In February 1965 the United States began to bomb industrial, logistical, and anti-aircraft sites in the North on a steady basis with Operation Rolling Thunder, which aimed not only to increase pressure but also to reduce the North's war-making capability, stiffen the South's morale, show U.S. resolve, and improve the U.S.-South's eventual negotiating position. However, a bombing pause in May and one in December produced no apparent reaction from the North. Hanoi did not abandon the insurgency in the South, as such warfare was much less dependent on industrial infrastructure than Washington had calculated. Ultimately, to be effective, the bombing had to eliminate the chance or hope of communist victory in the South, and this it could not do.[35] As Lawrence Freedman noted, there was a basic Catch 22 here: "The South could not be stabilized without pressure on the North; the North could not be pressurized without a more stable South."[36]

The difficulty for the United States was that for the North the war was aimed at national unification, and the break in the bombing did not make it reconsider its position and open negotiations. Instead, it shored up its position. In addition, Johnson limited the armaments used. The huge B-52s were used in support roles in the South but not sent to the North until 1966, and the targets were limited as well: the Chinese border, Hanoi, and Haiphong harbor were avoided. Johnson kept pausing the campaign too – eight times between March 1965 and March 1968 – sometimes as a propaganda effort and at times, notably in December 1965 and February 1967, in an attempt to prompt negotiation.[37] As befitted a coercive understanding of the war, the bombing was centrally managed at Tuesday lunchtime meetings in the White House.

The U.S. approach provoked the ire of Admiral Ulysses S. Grant Sharp, commander of Pacific Command and the war's overall senior commander. Admiral Sharp wrote that the most debilitating aspect of the war was "the political leadership's naïve hope that a major involvement could somehow be avoided by using a 'carrot and stick' sort of diplomacy as a means of initiating negotiations with the North Vietnamese." Sharp decried the "on again, off again" tinkering with coercive force.[38] Only with the arrival of Richard Nixon in the White House was the efficacy of airpower as a tool of diplomatic negotiation reestablished, but by then the war was different. The new administration had announced it was aiming to withdraw from the conflict "with honor."

However, while bargaining with airpower, the administration had to address the military problems on the ground in the South. As historian Larry Berman puts it, "The fundamental fact of international politics in July 1965 was South Vietnam's impending fall to Communist control, *unless* the United States provided enough ground support to deny Hanoi its goal of unifying Vietnam under communist leadership."[39] By July 1965 the options were leave the country, maintain the present force levels and lose, or increase troop numbers.[40] This was the crucial decision period. As Fredrik Logevall's 1999 study outlines, the forces at work in the decision to escalate were not quite as over-determined as has been traditionally held.[41] There was certainly a presumption of Chinese expansion, but historic Sino-Vietnamese and Sino-Soviet friction militated against that immediate possibility. The situation in the South was so poor that it was ripe for a communist takeover no matter what the United States did to the North, and Moscow wanted to improve relations with the United States despite the outcome in Vietnam. Logevall writes:

"The isolation of the United States on the war among its international allies at the end of 1964; the thin nature of domestic American popular support for the Vietnamese commitment; the downright opposition to a larger war among many elite American voices; the spreading war-weariness and anti-Americanism in urban and rural areas of South Vietnam; and the political chaos in Saigon – add all these elements together and you have a policy decision that is far less easily explained than many would suggest."[42]

Major escalation followed fifteen years of gradual escalation, and the exploration of military options was not matched, as some such as the British Foreign Office expected, by imaginative ways of getting the United States out of the disastrous situation. However, for all the long-term aspects, such as ideology and the bypassing of diplomacy and the containment mindset, short-term and personal factors prevailed within the inner war cabinet of Lyndon Johnson, Robert McNamara, McGeorge Bundy, and Dean Rusk.[43] The key factor was credibility.

The credibility problem was twofold, as it covered international American credibility and the need to preserve it by avoiding defeat in Vietnam, and personal credibility within the administration, especially following calls to stand firm since 1962, when the Cold War was much hotter and the commitment in Vietnam smaller. Johnson also had a personal credibility problem as he had committed himself after Kennedy's assassination to not being the president who lost Vietnam. Fundamentally, credibility was an issue of internal politics and self-perception, especially as international allies such as Britain advocated a negotiated settlement. Harold Wilson's government in Britain, despite needing U.S. support for its currency problems, was able to argue against sending British troops to support the United States because it had co-chaired the Geneva Conference and was in any case still disengaging from Malaya. Australia, New Zealand, and South Korea sent forces, but Johnson was enraged that the UK did not send even a token force, though a British Advisory Mission had been stationed in Saigon since 1961.[44] Other allies such as de Gaulle suggested neutralizing or removing the area from Cold War concerns, especially as the United States could not win there.

Ultimately the decision to introduce U.S. combat forces in 1965 saved the Republic of Vietnam from total military defeat at that time and thus the advisory phase was followed by an "Americanization" of the war and the commitment of half a million U.S. troops. The broader national policy had drawn them in, but the Saigon government had already become dependent on the U.S. military to survive. The United States thus ended up going to war – a very complex one. As Robert Komer, the president's special assistant for the civil pacification effort in Vietnam, writes, "It was a multi-dimensional politico-military conflict encompassing not only out-of-country bombing and a 'main force' war of more or less conventional forces, but a guerrilla struggle, a clandestine terror campaign, and the like. It was a 'war without fronts.'"[45]

The military effort to cope with the multifaceted war was fragmented. The U.S. Army and Marine Corps were primarily responsible for combating the North's regular forces and the Viet Cong guerrillas. During the war's peak from 1965 to 1968, these roles were under the overloaded command of General William Westmoreland at U.S. Military Assistance Command Vietnam (USMACV).[46] The air war was handled separately. Westmoreland explained that the U.S. military strategy employed in Vietnam was dictated by political – not military – decisions. This approach was shaped by the fact that a ground invasion of North Vietnam was not possible. Washington's aim in the war was not to conquer North Vietnam but rather to eliminate the insurgency in South Vietnam, which could be done "only by seeking, fighting, and destroying the enemy."[47] Additionally, if negotiations developed, avoidance of an invasion would provide some compensation for the leverage that the Viet Cong victories gave the other side. In Westmoreland's view this meant "We will have to grind him down. In effect, we are fighting a war of attrition, and the only alternative is a war of annihilation."[48] The land forces under Westmoreland, therefore, focused on bringing the North Vietnamese to battle, especially after the perceived success in the Battle of Ia Drang in 1965. Westmoreland's was a one-dimensional approach, and the military offered the president few alternatives in the war's prosecution.[49]

The North Vietnamese recognized the American military's propensity to fight conventionally. General

Giap developed a strategy that prevented the Americans from having a target on which they could mass and attack: by dispersing potential targets.[50] During the "big-unit" period of 1965-67 the U.S. Army found it difficult to bring the enemy to combat on its terms, so it developed the mass sweeps tactic, which became known under the blanket term "search and destroy." This approach's inadequacy led to the development in 1968-70 of the "constant pressure" tactic, an innovation that was still reliant on "excruciating direct military pressure."[51] More generally though, the U.S. response to Giap's strategy was to use its technology and firepower advantages: helicopter gunships, free-fire zones, defoliants, napalm, and bombing. The technological focus was applied to what was, as Michael Howard notes, a war in which the social dimension was the most important: "Of the four dimensions of strategy [operational, logistical, social, and technological] the social was incomparably the most significant."[52] The U.S. use of firepower devastated large portions of the South, the country it was trying to "save." It was a "technowar" approach.[53]

The U.S. military's view that the war's tactical and logistical aspects were successful, the disheartening nature of this approach, and the deficiencies in the technology on which it relied increased the American public's frustration as the United States continued to lose the war.[54] The scale of the effort in Vietnam was enormous, but the inability to achieve decisive victory on the battlefield increased the emphasis on American logistical superiority, which was expensive to run. The reliance on costly resources necessitated significant public support to fund and man the war effort, and this made the military vulnerable to congressional displeasure. Along with the selective draft, this automatically pushed the social aspect of strategy back home, where the war would also be fought in a country that had not been fully mobilized.

As disheartening as the war had become, the United States received a new shock with the Tet Offensive. During the Vietnamese New Year celebration in early 1968, the Viet Cong attacked all of the major cities and many towns in the South. Optimistic briefings from Westmoreland and the Pentagon were suddenly juxtaposed with shocking scenes of widespread Viet Cong assaults. Within a couple weeks all of the main cities (apart from Hue) were recaptured, but still the offensive was a seminal event in the war and the turning point for U.S. support and public perception. After Tet, one in five Americans shifted from being a "hawk" to a "dove."[55] For the U.S. military, the outcomes of the Tet Offensive were a success, as it recaptured all the lost ground and greatly diminished the Viet Cong as a fighting force. It took the North's General Giap until 1972 to rebuild his forces in the South sufficiently to attack in any strength again.

However, according to one of Giap's biographers, Peter MacDonald, "In Vietnam most soldiers realized for the first time that they would never win the war, while at home many people turned away from it with revulsion. During Tet, after the complete leveling of one town, Ben Tre, a weary American officer had told a reporter, 'We had to destroy it in order to save it.' For millions of Americans that phrase vividly summed up the futility of the war: nobody was winning, nobody could win."[56]

In a frustrating and perplexing war, the media's role became more important, although the military considered the media a weak link in the war's prosecution. According to General Westmoreland, the policy of escalating the war's costs was fatally flawed as it was garbled by the voices of dissent at home and the "sensational news reporting by the mass media."[57] Tet was the first time that the full horror of fighting came into people's living rooms, and the images of communist success overwhelmed the public. Before Tet, film footage had been edited and in the process most sharp images of injury and death were expunged.[58] Television coverage of the Tet Offensive provided the first live transmissions of war, as a satellite had been placed above the Pacific Ocean just weeks earlier. The coverage was combined with Walter Cronkite's practice of displaying the "body count" of American casualties on the wall behind him during his newscast.[59] Casualties were to become indicative of the failure of the political-military strategy in Vietnam. A greater national consensus to withdraw from Vietnam developed.

However, the U.S. media was not as universally critical as it is sometimes portrayed to have been.[60] What is beyond doubt is that there was a far closer examination of American actions than of its opponent's. As Guenter Lewy observes in his book *America in Vietnam*, "The VC were notoriously uncooperative in allowing Western cameramen to shoot pictures of the disemboweling of village chiefs or other acts of terror, while scenes of South Vietnamese brutality, such as the mistreatment of prisoners, were often seen on American TV screens."[61]

By 1968 the "war" had spread to U.S. streets with major anti-war demonstrations, especially among potential draftees. Vietnam was both a war abroad and a series of traumatic changes at home.[62]

For the military, the lack of mobilization (prior to the partial effort in April 1968) was a fundamental misuse of the country's military assets and a key problem concerning the nation at war. In Vietnam, unprepared officers and noncommissioned officers led to breakdowns in morale, discipline, and professional judgment, of which the My Lai massacre was one example. For the U.S. Army, this atrocity was an aberration, but for the public it exemplified the war, the nature of the U.S. military, and the regime the United States was supporting, a regime that utilized summary executions during Tet.[63] Tet brought the issue of public support to a head.

After Tet, President Johnson announced in a crucial speech to the nation on March 21, 1968, "Our objective in South Vietnam has never been the annihilation of the enemy. It has been to bring about a recognition in Hanoi that its objective – taking over the South by force – could not be achieved."[64] Johnson said he would devote himself to seeking "an honorable peace" and would not seek reelection. His announcement shocked the nation. The ensuing election saw the Republican challenger, Richard Nixon, running on a ticket promising an end to the war.[65]

After the Tet Offensive, negotiations between the United States and the North reopened in May 1968 in Paris. Hanoi had rejected Chinese Premier Zhou Enlai's suggestion of putting off the talks until the military situation improved for the North, because it wanted to discern Johnson's motives and garner public support. It had no intention of negotiating and sought only to frustrate Johnson as a peacemaker.[66] Both sides had firm positions: the North wanted the bombing stopped, and the United States wanted the North to recognize the South's government. With the U.S. election is imminent, Moscow wanted Hubert Humphrey rather than the hard-line cold warrior Richard Nixon to win, so it ordered the North to allow the Saigon delegates in. All sides agreed, so Johnson aimed to halt the bombings and let talks begin in November. The South was concerned about what would be talked about, and this situation was exploited by the Nixon camp, which encouraged South Vietnam's president Nguyen Van Thieu (who thought he would get a better deal under Nixon) to repudiate Johnson publicly by staying away from the talks.[67] The Nixon camp's deliberate sabotage of the talks undercut the Democrats, and Nixon won a close election. For such critics as Christopher Hitchens, 20,492 U.S. servicemembers and countless Vietnamese died unnecessarily between Nixon taking office and the eventual withdrawal because the settlement available in 1968 was accepted only in 1973.[68]

The new Nixon administration looked to move away from the distraction of Vietnam and back to its main focus on European aspects of the Cold War, on the Middle East, and on China. Europe was the core of the containment policy, and the U.S. focus on Vietnam raised serious questions about the nature of its commitments to NATO. The Soviet invasion of Czechoslovakia in 1968 did not ease this fear.

As Melvin Laird, Nixon's first secretary of defense, pointed out in 2005, Nixon did not have a plan of withdrawal from Vietnam when he took office.[69] Laird instead was tasked with coming up with a plan that focused on two key aspects of policy: the withdrawal of U.S. troops and the buildup of South Vietnamese capability through a policy of "Vietnamization" of the war. Air power was used to bridge the gap created by the drawdown of troops. The war's expansion under Nixon included the bombing of enemy bases and supply routes in neutral Cambodia. In 1970 a coup led to a more pro-American government there, but soon after a brief land invasion by U.S. and South Vietnamese forces, the country degenerated into a civil war won by the Communist Khmer Rouge in 1975. (The Hanoi government, interestingly, stopped the genocidal Khmer Rouge in 1979.) There was also an invasion of Laos in 1971, which only showed the incompetence of the South Vietnamese forces.

It is worth emphasizing that even though, beginning in 1968, the U.S. political will to continue the war had gone, the U.S. war in Vietnam continued for five more years – a point underrepresented by the major histories of the conflict.[70] More Americans were killed during this period than during the earlier phases.[71] In the post-Tet period, fundamental changes were made in the way the United States prosecuted the ground war as the army replaced Westmoreland with General Creighton Abrams, a man who had learned from the war and saw it as a single entity. Abrams immediately changed the tactics to population control, used different measures of success, and improved the South Vietnamese capability – all in a period of diminishing support and resources.[72]

As Ronald Spector points out in his book *After Tet*, "With the communists weakened militarily and organizationally by the losses in their repeated offensives, the U.S. and South Vietnam were able for the first time to gain a real measure of control in the countryside. Yet the continued weaknesses of the South Vietnamese regime, the communist powers of recuperation, and the U.S. decision to begin troop withdrawals in 1969 made this Allied ascendancy in the countryside only temporary."[73]

With U.S. credibility as the key issue, the military was being asked to provide sufficient options for the diplomatic negotiations. This policy was embodied in the controversial person of Henry Kissinger, the president's national security adviser.[74] Kissinger recognized that there was always a struggle to rescue choice from the pressures of circumstance.[75] He was concerned with reestablishing a balance of power with the Soviet Union and China, and he aimed to treat them as more normal states, rather than as centers of ideology as had been previous policy. Kissinger made a dramatic trip to China in 1971, and Nixon, the ardent anti-communist, made an official visit there and to Moscow in 1972. By this route, the Nixon administration played both communist superpowers off against each other, developing détente and looking for them to pressure North Vietnam. The policy, along with placing the burden of defending against communism on regional allies, was known as the "Nixon Doctrine."

Nixon centralized foreign policy making, which led to a greater disregard of democratic pressures such as the growing anti-war movement, whose widespread protest demonstrations included such incidents as the National Guard's killing of four students at Kent State University in 1970. Nixon and Kissinger distrusted the usual bureaucracy of foreign policy making, and their practices caused foreign policy under Nixon's administration to be identified far more with them personally than with the governmental agencies usually tasked with conducting it. Kissinger was both Nixon's personal adviser and his negotiator with North Vietnam.[76]

A devotee of back-channel meetings, Kissinger began secretly negotiating in August 1969 with North Vietnam's Xuan Thuy in Paris. Unlike Johnson, who wanted the North to withdraw from South Vietnam six months before the United States did, Nixon asked for mutual withdrawal of troops. However, the North did not see itself as an outside force, so it did not have any interest in mutual withdrawal. North Vietnam was then neither a traditional state nor a superpower and saw itself in a life-or-death struggle that did not involve issues of credibility concerning its broader policies. Thus, Kissinger faced fruitless negotiations. North Vietnam was a revolutionary state and not as susceptible to Moscow's influence as Kissinger had thought. And as Hanoi saw clearly, time was on its side. There was a shift in 1970 once the North sent a senior member of its Politburo, Le Duc Tho, to negotiate secretly with Kissinger, though talks again stalled on the question of mutual withdrawal.

Kissinger, however, helped the 1972 reelection campaign by saying in October that peace was at hand. It wasn't. In the previous March, the North had attempted to bypass negotiations with the United States by launching the Easter Offensive. With U.S. troop numbers run down, air power was used to blunt the offensive: B-52s were sent north for the first time since 1968. The offensive came at the onset of the American election campaigns, the opening of relations with China, and the Moscow summit. It demanded a coordinated political, military, and diplomatic response, and it was reliant on the U.S. military's ability to conduct its missions successfully.[77] U.S. policy seemed a shambles as Vietnamization was failing, weakening America's hand. As Kissinger noted, "We had seen enough of Le Duc

Tho to know that without a plausible military strategy we could have no effective diplomacy."[78] That was really the crux of the problem for the United States.

By October 1972, U.S. and North Vietnamese representatives were meeting in Paris to hammer out a peace agreement. Le conceded a crucial American requirement, namely that President Thieu's immediate removal was no longer a precondition for the ceasefire. The main points from the U.S. side were that once an agreement was signed, a ceasefire would come into place, U.S. and foreign troops would withdraw from the South within sixty days, American prisoners of war would be released, and a Council of National Reconciliation and Concord would be created to organize and oversee elections that would determine the South's political future. This agreement represented a victory for the North and gave the United States a way out of the war. Nixon approved its terms.

However, the cost of bilateral negotiations was soon apparent. Seeing the treaty as a sellout, South Vietnamese president Thieu stopped the process. The ceasefire would leave about 150,000 North Vietnamese soldiers positioned in the South, while the United States withdrew all of its troops. Since the South Vietnamese leader absolutely refused to consider such terms, the United States could not ratify it. The United States therefore reopened negotiations on the agreement's terms. In protest, the North reopened already settled aspects. By mid-December 1972 the talks had collapsed.

To address this diplomatic failure, Nixon, having won reelection, increased U.S. air power over Vietnam in an attempt to convince Hanoi that negotiating was preferable to continuing the war. He also wanted to reassure the South of America's commitment. The air campaign, dubbed "Linebacker II," focused on the enemy's capability and willingness to fight, rather than on the signaling emphasis of earlier campaigns. It involved bombing Hanoi and places above the 20th parallel and included 729 sorties by B-52s dropping 15,237 tons of bombs on thirty-four targets.[79] For some observers, by 1972 the North's air defense was comparable to NATO's highly sophisticated network in Europe,[80] but by the tenth day of bombing it was decimated. By the twenty-sixth, the North signaled that it would meet in January 1973. Nixon continued bombing for three more days to show the South both the effectiveness of U.S. air power and the necessity of supporting the agreement. In January 1973 all parties (including the South) signed the final agreement, which was identical to that reached in October 1972. South Vietnam simply had to accept the fate of U.S. withdrawal. It was a substitute for genuine peace.

For air-power advocates, the Christmas bombings showed how an air campaign could be a highly effective tool of coercive diplomacy. Unlike the earlier and fragmented Rolling Thunder campaigns, Linebacker II was tied to a clear strategy and brought the North back to the negotiating table. However, the context of Linebacker II was different. Fundamentally, not only were the political controls on bombing lighter than under Johnson, the war's nature had changed as well.[81] The Tet Offensive in 1968 had severely weakened the Viet Cong insurgency in the South, leaving the North Vietnamese army as Hanoi's only viable military tool. Thus the 1972 Easter Offensive was a conventional attack, and as such it was vulnerable to air power. Prior to 1968, victory from the air would have been unlikely because of the then-viable guerrilla war in the South. Also, the cessation of the North's support would not necessarily have led to the end of the Viet Cong insurgency. Nixon's political objectives were different because his clear goal was withdrawing U.S. troops without abandoning the South to imminent communist takeover. This was much easier than Johnson's goal: creating a South Vietnam capable of sustaining an independent existence while avoiding a third world war. In addition, Nixon and Kissinger's policy of détente with the Soviets had begun, leaving the North unable to receive increased assistance from its ally. Nixon had also opened the door to China to restore relations, and China recommended that the North let the Americans leave quickly.

On January 27, 1973, three days after his second inauguration (and coincidentally the day after Johnson died), President Nixon announced the halting of all hostile acts by U.S. forces in Vietnam after the signing of the Paris agreements by the North, South, and the United States. In March, the Military Assistance Command Vietnam (MACV) was deactivated and its last commander flew home. In December, Kissinger and Le Duc Tho were jointly awarded the Nobel Peace Prize, although Le refused to share it, blaming Kissinger for prolonging the war.

The 1973 "Agreement on Ending the War and Restoring Peace in Vietnam" actually achieved neither. Initially all the signatories gained something from the treaty, as the North saw U.S. forces depart from the country, the South had a written commitment from the United States, and the United States was able to leave Vietnam. However, the agreement only initiated a two-year pause in hostilities. In 1975 thirty North

Vietnamese divisions drove into the South, Saigon was overrun, and Vietnam was unified under Hanoi. Traditionally it is thought that the peace accords managed only to create a "decent interval" during which the United States could withdraw without an immediate collapse of the South. By 1975 Nixon was out of office and in disgrace, owing to the Watergate scandal, and Kissinger was the secretary of state. They liked to say that they won the war but that Congress lost the peace by not sending funds to the South in 1975, which President Gerald Ford had requested to help the Vietnamese repel the invasion. Battered by the war and Watergate, Congress indeed did not provide the funding to underwrite the pledges of the Paris Agreement. However, as Larry Berman argues, there was "no peace, no honor" because of the nature of the outcome and because Nixon had aimed to keep a stalemate going in Vietnam through airpower alone. Watergate undid his plans.[82]

For all the words, South Vietnam ceased to exist after April 1975. The conflict's last flutter was the U.S. raid to recapture the ship *Mayaguez* from the Cambodians and to rescue hostages in May, a U.S. show of "resolution" in which thirty-eight servicemembers died. The domino had fallen as North and South Vietnam became united under a communist government, the very outcome that the United States had borne and inflicted huge financial, military, social, and political costs to try to stop. The implementation of policy had failed.

As Fred Iklé noted in his book *Every War Must End*, "Wars transform the future...but it is the way a war is brought to an end that has the most decisive long-term impact."[83] The Vietnam War's later stages became a period of social fragmentation. The consensus over containment fell apart, and the American social identity split over criticism of the war. American political culture was also wracked by the Watergate scandal, and Congress challenged the power of the Executive Branch, especially with the reassertion of congressional power realized in the War Powers Resolution in 1973. The Vietnam War's legacy was to become a "syndrome," deforming U.S. strategic culture. Before the war, the United States had had an overly powerful potential,[84] but the conflict's result completely reversed this potential as it led to a reassessment of U.S. foreign policy. Nixon saw the war affecting American leaders so badly that it had turned the country "into a military giant and a diplomatic dwarf in a world in which the steadfast exercise of American power was needed more than ever."[85]

The war "left a deep national skepticism about the overall utility and legitimacy of American military power."[86] For example, the 1972 bombing escalation "hastened a transformation of the basic liberal argument against the war. Instead of stressing the hopelessness of the war, liberals now began to emphasize its immorality."[87] This shift reflects a growing influence of the "dovish" viewpoint in America during the war, coming as it did during the civil rights movement, and this led to the rise of human rights as a focus of the U.S. foreign policy agenda.[88] In the post-Vietnam period, both Jimmy Carter and Ronald Reagan emphasized the morality of their respective foreign policies.[89] For the Carter administration, for example, negotiating the second Strategic Arms Limitation Treaty, rather than using military intervention in areas of conflict, was seen as the primary way forward in diplomacy.

American military capability was therefore allowed to decline.[90]

The discrepancy between the dovish and hawkish mentalities within post-Vietnam America was particularly clear in the Carter administration, which illustrated the dilemmas of post-Vietnam intervention policy. Carter's secretary of state, Cyrus Vance, and national security adviser, Zbigniew Brzezinski, faced each other with divergent views as the administration focused on the détente process and on human rights issues.[91] A power-politics activist prepared to use force, Brzezinski saw a fundamental philosophical difference between himself and Vance, who embodied traditional diplomatic restraint.[92] Rather than resolving the problem of when use of military force is appropriate, Carter's presidency simply heightened it, especially once the U.S. embassy in Tehran was seized in November 1979 and Russia invaded Afghanistan in December. The final humiliation for Carter was his failed attempt to rescue the hostages in Iran. Vance resigned in protest at not having been consulted in the mission.

Carter's approach to foreign policy had failed, and Reagan arrived in office rejecting détente and referring to Vietnam as a "noble cause". A revision of the war's history had begun. The reluctance to use military force directly against a sizeable adversary (unlike Grenada and Panama), however, was not addressed until the 1991 victory in the Persian Gulf.[93] For Americans the Gulf War restored national pride after Vietnam. As President George H.W. Bush announced afterward, "It's a proud day for America. And, by God, we've kicked the Vietnam syndrome once and for all."[94] Though it is doubtful that U.S. foreign policy has fully recovered from the mistakes of the Vietnam War, especially after the events in Somalia in 1993, the Gulf War proved to have a cathartic effect on the crippling Vietnam legacy – sixteen years after the war ended. Military force could be used once more to support diplomatic policy.

What is clear is that in Vietnam the U.S. mix of policy and force, guided by a purposeful strategy developed by "America's overconfident military professionals, clever but arrogant civilian defense intellectuals, and overly ambitious politicians," failed.[95] The United States aimed to rebuff communism by supporting a flawed and corrupt embryonic state. It faced growing levels of isolation from allies and opposition from its own domestic constituency. It compensated for these shortcomings with the use of military force, and the poor military performance eventually led to U.S. withdrawal. Included in the North Vietnamese strategy of *dau tranh* was the concept that in the end victory goes to the side that is the best organized, stays the best organized, and can most successfully disorganize the other.[96] The United States was unable to match this coherence.

Still, it is worth discussing the broader diplomatic aspects of U.S. policy. The Vietnam War is a clear study of the difficulties of implementing broad national policies. The containment policy meant that the war was fought by a host government trying to unify its country against a foreign military, which was fighting because of its commitments elsewhere. Because of the containment policy, the U.S. conception of the war was narrowed, and successive administrations, ignoring the crucial aspects of North Vietnamese nationalism, misread the war as a Cold War fight. In doing so, the

United States isolated itself from its European allies, who had both experience and advice to offer.

Furthermore, the ideological focus of containment, which seriously downgraded diplomacy's role in foreign policy after the signing of the Geneva Accords, exacerbated U.S. isolation from its allies. The United States relied on military capability as a surrogate for diplomacy, using it to try to underpin diplomacy with the North and to generate enough costs in the North so that it would comply with American wishes. The use of the U.S. armed forces in this coercive manner went against the nature of the American military machine, as it was trained and configured for conventional warfare and for clear-cut victory. A state's diplomatic and military tools work in the context of their own traditions and approaches, and the Executive Branch has to use the tools of the state with an awareness of their strengths and limitations in this context.

The lack of success in Vietnam led to the war's escalation, and soon the military commitment became the policy. Once the United States committed active troops and victory in the South could not be assured, the issues of the country's and the administration's credibility became the interest defended by military forces, especially as the administration faced the ire of its domestic constituency.

The domestic critique of the war is noteworthy as it raised the issue of which constituencies are addressed in diplomatic negotiations and policymaking. Management of the war policy and diplomacy became gradually less democratic as more and more decision-making was pulled back to the White House up to the point when Kissinger and Nixon became involved in secret negotiations and invasions of countries. This centralized approach ultimately weakened the U.S. strategy in the region.

Isolated from their allies and their domestic constituency, the Johnson and Nixon administrations were shown that military might had limited political returns. Having repudiated diplomacy once it failed to achieve the desired outcome, Washington turned to the military option and then spent most of the war trying to revive diplomacy's role. Ultimately U.S. policy was unsuccessful because it had to compensate for the limits of its diplomacy.

THE FALKLANDS/ MALVINAS WAR

War in the South Atlantic came as a surprise to both Britain and Argentina in 1982. Argentina was preparing to use armed force if necessary against Britain later that year to force Britain to leave a collection of islands they had held since 1833. It rushed its plans forward because it erroneously believed that Britain was using a mini-crisis over the related dependency of South Georgia (a separate territory in the South Atlantic) to reinforce its military position in the region.

Britain, caught between Argentine demands for the return of contiguous territory and the determination of the local population to stay British, had been following a policy of procrastination for many years. A number of solutions had been explored, most recently a lease-back arrangement whereby sovereignty would be transferred to Argentina but then returned to Britain on a long lease to protect the islanders' way of life. It was understood that this policy was under strain. A new military junta in Buenos Aires wanted to regain the "Malvinas" Islands (*Islas Malvinas* in Spanish) – which the British call the "Falklands" Islands – by the 150th anniversary of their loss. It was, however, assumed that the first steps would be to isolate the islands by cutting off air and sea links. London was not expecting an invasion of sovereign territory by an otherwise friendly power.[1]

Although the islands had limited strategic and economic value, important issues of principle concerning sovereignty, territoriality, self-determination, and the use of force to resolve disputes were at stake. The conflict was relatively short. The crisis over South Georgia began in mid-March, the invasion took place at the start of April, a month later the British task force engaged with Argentine air and naval units, and by mid-June the Argentine army on the Falklands had surrendered. Though short, the conflict had a substantial political impact. It reinforced British Prime Minister Margaret Thatcher's reputation as a strong leader and helped her government to victory in the 1983 general election after a difficult first term. The conflict also brought down the military junta in Argentina and revived the fortunes of the Falkland Islands, which had up to this point been suffering from depopulation and poor economic prospects. Thatcher wrote in her memoirs, "The significance of the Falklands War was enormous, both for Britain's self-confidence and for our standing in the world. Since the Suez fiasco in 1956, British foreign policy had been one long retreat."[2]

Because of the conflict's surprising and intense nature, it provides a valuable example of how war and diplomacy are interlinked. In addition to the failures of diplomacy in preventing the conflict in the first place, once it had begun both sides tried to use their military position to influence the shape of a final settlement while limiting the amount of violence employed. They also had to demonstrate to allies and other supporters that they were sincere in seeking a peaceful resolution of the dispute. Institutions ranging from the

United Nations to NATO and the European Economic Community (EEC) were involved, as were countries as diverse as the Soviet Union, Jordan, New Zealand, and Japan.

This chapter, therefore, considers the diplomacy from the perspective of a variety of states that found themselves involved in the conflict. While it does not provide a day-by-day narrative, it provides an analysis of the conduct of diplomacy during the conflict and of its interplay with the international system.

The management of the conflict's diplomatic aspects was in its own way as difficult for the British Foreign Office as the military campaign was for the armed services. The timing was not good. The Argentine invasion had come at the exact moment when the head of the diplomatic service was changing, although the retiring Sir Michael Palliser was soon asked to continue to advise the government for the duration of the crisis. The two cabinet ministers from the Foreign and Commonwealth Office (FCO), Lord Carrington and Sir Humphrey Atkins, both resigned, as did Richard Luce, the minister who had been dealing with the Falklands. Some of the senior diplomats who had been handling the issue feared that they had been discredited, even though they were not sure what else they might have done, given the approach to the issue taken by the government as a whole. In Carrington's case, he believed that a senior resignation was needed to take the immediate heat off the government and that his position as a member of the House of Lords would prevent him from performing his role in the coming weeks.

The new foreign secretary, Francis Pym, was a figure respected in the Conservative Party and the House of Commons, but he was thrown in at the deep end of the Falklands conflict and was not notably close to the prime minister. In fact Pym had been considered a possible successor to Thatcher, who had given him the defense portfolio as a means of limiting his influence.[3] Pym's successor at the Ministry of Defence, Sir John Nott, had also offered his resignation, but Thatcher persuaded him to stay on in his post.

At the heart of the diplomatic problem facing the government was the fact that other countries, even among the most friendly, were not quite sure why Britain was putting in such an effort and accepting such high risks to retake an asset with so little real value, and they were less sure why they should put themselves out to help. Whatever Britain wanted – from access to facilities en route to the South Atlantic, to information on arms supplied to Argentina, to adherence to economic sanctions – the case had to be compelling and tenaciously argued. Ambassadors and British High Commissioners around the world had to become overnight experts on the dispute and its ramifications. At the same time as the FCO became bound up with the many practical demands of the crisis, it had to keep a close eye on the political implications of every military move being planned. It expected to be to the fore in the search for a negotiated outcome to the crisis, but here the prime minister was very much in charge, aware that any apparent concession to Argentina was political dynamite at home.

The critical advice on the diplomatic strategy to be adopted if compromises on the core issues of principle were to be avoided, while entreaties for moderation were respected, was provided largely from the two ambassadors at the most important posts in Washington and New York. The handling of the American government was going to be crucial in arranging any political settlement and a source of military support. Here the ambassador was Sir Nicholas Henderson, an unusually experienced and independent-minded diplomat, with a personality admirably suited to making a mark in Washington.[4] The most vital diplomatic battles would be fought in and around the United Nations, where Britain's ambassador was Sir Anthony Parsons, a shrewd and popular diplomat on the rebound from a difficult period as ambassador to Iran during the time of the Islamic revolution.[5] Parsons understood the culture of the UN and the conflicting pressures that would influence the collective response to the unfolding crisis. Henderson and Parsons together had a clear sense of the amount of flexibility it was appropriate and necessary to show as they faced the unusually demanding audiences of the Security Council and the American media.

Parsons helped redeem the FCO in the prime minister's eyes by securing a notable victory in the Security Council, pushing through a resolution that put the onus on Argentina to withdraw.[6] Institutionally Britain had an advantage as a permanent member of the Security Council, working from the commanding heights of the organization and with the capacity to veto any unfavorable resolution. Yet, while it had reason to expect solidarity from fellow members of the Western alliance and from Commonwealth countries, the UN had been a difficult arena for some time because of the strength of third-world opinion with its strong anti-colonial sentiment. The more the Falklands could be presented as a matter of colonialism, which is how it had previously been developed in the General

Assembly, the more awkward Britain's position could become. It did not help that the two European non-permanent members of the Security Council at this time – Spain and Ireland – had their own territorial disputes with Britain.

Moreover, the United States was represented in the UN by Jeane Kirkpatrick, who was closely associated with the Reagan administration's Latin America policy and led the pro-Argentina camp in Washington. Argentina's ambassador, Eduardo Roca, who had only arrived in late March to take up his position in New York, could take Latin American support for granted, hope for a helpful response from the Soviet bloc by opposing a leading member of NATO, and make the most of the UN's devotion to anti-colonialism, while at the same time relying on a sympathetic hearing from Kirkpatrick.

From the start of April, when few appreciated the affair's potential seriousness, to the end of May, when it was becoming a matter of real concern, international opinion developed in quite distinctive ways. National answers to these fundamental questions of principle varied considerably. Of Britain's traditional allies, only the old Commonwealth gave essentially unconditional backing. Canada, Australia, and New Zealand all stood firm; Prime Minister Robert Muldoon of New Zealand even offered a frigate to enable the Royal Navy to release another vessel for Falklands duties. By and large the new Commonwealth was also supportive. Many of the smaller African and Caribbean countries appreciated the need to put regional predators in their place. Although the Indian government adhered to its non-aligned position, Indian public opinion appeared to be with Britain, while publicity about possible South

African arms deliveries to Argentina helped reinforce black African support. Kenya and Guyana, both former colonies (and the latter with its own territorial dispute with Venezuela), were particularly helpful in the Security Council.

Elsewhere there was a clear preference for doing as little as possible. Japan, for example, was rarely disposed to disrupting trade on a point of principle. Japan voted for UN Security Council Resolution 502 (demanding an immediate cessation of hostilities and a complete withdrawal by Argentine forces), although there were reports of some hesitation. Thereafter, although the Japanese government claimed to have spoken firmly to Argentine representatives and to have warned of the possible economic consequences, it took no clear economic measures for several weeks.

France was in a pivotal position as both a leading member of the European Community and a permanent member of the UN Security Council. From the start it proved to be Britain's staunchest ally. President François Mitterrand ordered full support for Britain, which did not go down well in the French Foreign Ministry, where there were worries about the impact on relations with Latin America and an extension of Soviet influence. The immediate impact of this decision was an embargo on arms and trade with Argentina and support for Security Council Resolution 502. Crucially this meant that France would not provide any further Exocet anti-ship missiles to Argentina. France also provided valuable practical help to Britain's armed forces, particularly in its understanding of the capabilities and limitations of the equipment France had supplied to Argentina. It appears France came to Britain's aid during the crisis because of Mitterrand's genuine gratitude at the stance taken by Britain during the Second World War and because the French president wanted to demonstrate his Socialist government's reliability as a member of the Western camp.

Nevertheless, Mitterrand made clear that this support was for the duration of the crisis and no longer. He also took the opportunity to move against Britain over EEC issues on the budget and agricultural prices, assuming that the British government would make some concessions as a quid pro quo. Arguments over budgets and agricultural prices persisted. Britain refused to accept that concessions on these matters were a quid pro quo for European solidarity, arguing that the Falklands were a matter of international principle and not just a British national interest.

The German position was more equivocal. Chancellor Helmut Schmidt did not speak to Thatcher until April 7. The Germans joined enthusiastically in the NATO declaration of support, and despite their dislike of embargoes and their reluctance to set precedents that could later be used against them, they applied the arms embargo and agreed to the Community's economic sanctions on Argentina with uncharacteristic speed. So far this had been an instinctive gesture of support for an ally, a Community partner, and a close friend. At the same time they were cautious about endorsing British policies. They felt a genuine unease when observing the surge of patriotic enthusiasm in Britain, fully aware of how unhappy others would be if Germans betrayed the same tendencies. The aversion to armed conflict ran deep in Germany, with the supposition always that there must be a better way. For those of this view, it would be best if military action was delayed while the better way was found, even if this meant putting to one side the issues at stake. After the British sunk the Argentine cruiser *General Belgrano*, Germany's position on the issue became more difficult. The German interest in trade with Argentina was substantial as it took 28 percent of all the European Community's imports from Argentina in 1980. The Germans were also concerned that British forces would be diverted from their NATO tasks.

Spain illustrates the extent to which national problems influenced stances on the Falklands. The Spanish government found itself in a quandary. The Argentine junta represented exactly the sort of outmoded mentality that the fledgling Spanish democracy was dedicated to oppose. However, Spain also supported the Argentine claim to the Falklands, and the Spanish media (while almost unanimously opposing a similar use of force against Gibraltar) were jubilant at the Argentine invasion. It was in the midst of delicate negotiations with Britain over Gibraltar, and the unavoidable role Gibraltar played in support of the task force did not help. An announcement was due on April 20 concerning the opening of negotiations between the two foreign ministers "aimed at overcoming all the differences between them on Gibraltar" on the basis of the Lisbon Agreement of April 10, 1980. These were postponed, and as the conflict escalated Spain's concern led it to co-sponsor with Panama a proposed resolution calling for an immediate ceasefire and an immediate implementation of Resolutions 502 and 505, with voting scheduled for June 4. This was unacceptable for the British because it did not guarantee an Argentine withdrawal, and they vetoed the proposal.

Ireland, the other European state in a territorial dispute with the United Kingdom, was like Spain a temporary member of the Security Council. Irish attitudes were consistently exasperating to London and all too reminiscent of the assertion of neutrality during the Second World War, when London considered itself to be fighting for international principle while Dublin took the view that "England's difficulty is Ireland's opportunity." Initially Dublin had disapproved of Argentina's use of force and supported Resolution 502. It even went along with EEC sanctions, despite claims from the most Anglophobic sections of the community that this stance was inconsistent with Irish neutrality. The Irish were surprised, when claiming that they viewed the issue as a colonial one, by how many other ex-colonies, such as Kenya, Uganda, and Guyana, supported Britain. There was a 300,000-strong Irish community in Argentina, but perhaps more important was the difficulty in identifying with the Falkland Islanders: an intensely loyal but isolated British community facing a hostile neighbor was too redolent of the Unionist community in Northern Ireland.

Moreover, the crisis did not come at a good time in Anglo-Irish relations. After the traumas of the hunger strikes, there were serious divergences not only over Northern Ireland but also over a range of European Community issues. The announcement on April 18 that a British submarine had accidentally sunk the Irish trawler *Sharelga* caused further problems. The news of the *General Belgrano*'s sinking led the prime minister, Charles Haughey, to take control of policy toward the Falklands, and he drafted a statement that marked a decisive shift on May 4. This called for the Security Council to initiate an immediate ceasefire and to seek withdrawal of European Community sanctions. When the British asked for an explanation, the foreign minister explained that sanctions had been supported to maintain a balanced combination of economic, political, and military pressure, but that balance had now been lost with the increase in military activity. The posture adopted was not without costs for Ireland. In Britain, this maneuver encouraged views of the Irish as unreliable or hostile and even led to calls for the boycott of Irish goods. At this point the £9.4 million worth of exports to Argentina looked rather puny when compared to £1.5 billion to the UK.

In general, the U.S. was sympathetic to Britain's predicament. However, there were differences of view within the U.S. government, with the Defense Department largely on the British side and the State Department divided.[7] Much effort had recently gone into cultivating Argentina, and those in Washington most committed to this effort, notably Kirkpatrick and Thomas Enders, assistant secretary for inter-American affairs, argued vigorously for an "even-handed" approach. They pointed out that the United States had always been neutral on the substance of the Falklands issue. There seemed to be a strong argument for sustaining this neutrality, given the valuable role that Argentina was now playing in supporting Washington in its anti-communist campaigns in Central America and the need to correct the hemispheric suspicion that when it came to the crunch, the United States would always support Europeans rather than its closest neighbors.

The Europeanists, such as the assistant secretary for European affairs, Lawrence Eagleburger, were appalled by the very idea of failing to support a NATO ally in these circumstances, especially given the vigorous support that Thatcher had provided Reagan on a number of controversial matters. Anglo-American relations had taken time to recover from Suez in 1956, when the British had been in the wrong. It would be disastrous to desert the British now when they were clearly in the right. The promise to Henderson by White House chief of staff Alexander Haig that there "cannot be another Suez" was duly underlined.

The political weight was on Britain's side, as a democracy that had been wronged by a dictatorship and as a country that could call on close ties of affection and interest at all levels of the American political system. Britain received press coverage that remained favorable. Haig, however, thought the question for American policy to be more complex than a decision on whom to back. Obviously the United States could not support Argentina, but that did not mean that a more neutral stance should be ruled out, at least in the first instance. Haig was fearful that if the United States turned against Argentina, the main beneficiary would be Moscow. He tended to view most issues within the Cold War framework and was impressed by the opportunities the crisis presented "for Soviet mischief-making, either directly, or through their Cuban proxies, in Argentina." To this concern was added some sense of British responsibility for its poor management of this issue in the past, but most of all a belief that the United States was uniquely well placed to facilitate a negotiated settlement. The risk here, including for Haig personally, was that it would fail, and this was understood to be the most likely outcome given the past difficulties with this dispute and the added factor of military action by Argentina. Any hope here relied on the uncertainty both sides must face when contemplating further hostilities. Meanwhile, the mediator role would at least allow Washington off the hook when it came to taking sides immediately. All lines of communication would need to be kept open and no unnecessary offense proffered.[8]

Even before Haig's mediation effort ran its course at the end of April (although he did not give up even then), the material support provided by the Pentagon was remarkable. Even diplomatic support was provided when necessary, in keeping allies in line or defending Britain's position in forums as challenging as the Organization of American States. Yet for London the concern was with persistent appeals to Britain to offer concessions to Argentina to pave the way to some face-saving settlement. These had often been requested not so much to produce a better outcome for the Falklands but to help Argentine leader Leopoldo Galtieri hold onto power or to deflect Argentine irritation with Washington.

A post-landing assessment of May 23, 1982, in the *New York Times* was widely assumed to reflect the dominant view in U.S. political circles. The gravamen was that Britain could win the war but without necessarily bringing about the complete capitulation of the Argentines. Any new government in Buenos Aires would be revanchist, and attacks would continue indefinitely from the air, if necessary with borrowed aircraft and crews. This would impose an excessive long-term burden on Britain, provide opportunities for further Soviet and Cuban advances, and further damage U.S. interests. Accordingly, now that Britain had made its point, a settlement of some sort was needed. The administration could foresee the whole hemispheric system unraveling as a result of Latin American solidarity with a (probably) Peronist successor regime in Argentina, hell-bent on revenge. Previous reports that Galtieri would never deal with Moscow were now being discounted. There was now real fear that Argentina might turn to the Cubans and the Soviets as a last hope of averting total humiliation. Galtieri might be swept aside by elements even more opposed to Western interests. The expulsion of Argentine forces would not end the state of war, especially if Buenos Aires had been strengthened by communist support. The administration was further concerned that Britain wanted only a return to the status quo ante, without any consideration of the possibility of a long-term negotiated solution.

Against this, the British stressed how much sacrifice and intransigence had been endured. They could not come this far and suddenly pull out before the task was complete. The wear and tear on relations with the United States and Europe concerned ministers during the war but never became critical. What is also worth noting is the British skepticism with regard to the large geopolitical issues that were raised in these discussions with allies. Without exception all advice from friendly governments pointed in the same direction: compromise and magnanimity in relation to Argentina, to the point of sparing it from a humiliating defeat. While issues of proportionality and the readiness to "give peace a chance" animated this case, most governments' concerns were more pragmatic in nature. A British victory, it was widely assumed (including by many in Britain), would have three unfortunate consequences: it would (1) radicalize Argentina, (2) alienate Latin America, and (3) provide opportunities to the Soviet Union.

The validity of these concerns was rarely challenged directly, although there was good reason during the conflict to believe that they had been exaggerated and based on scanty evidence. The third danger was only true if the first two were real, because what was being postulated was a historic shift in alignments. The Argentines would be so frustrated at having their territory snatched away from them once again that they would never forgive the British or their North American and European accomplices. They would seek every available means of continuing the struggle, however foolish and futile these may be, and become even more extremist politically. The rest of Latin America would follow in sympathy, convinced of the rightness of the Argentine cause and the inadmissibility of Britain's military response.

Even as things stood in late May 1982, there were reasons to be skeptical of these assumptions. At one level they depended on ethnic stereotypes of passionate Latin Americans ready to give up everything on a point of honor. It supposed that the virulent anticommunism of recent years was extraordinarily superficial and could easily be thrown into reverse. If this adventure went awry and ended in humiliation, the right-wing Argentine junta would stagger into a communist embrace. It also supposed complete indifference to the conflict's economic aspects, for Western help would certainly be needed if Argentina was to sort out its shattered finances. As for the rest of Latin America, the gloomier analysis assumed a wholehearted identification with Argentina, when the tensions between Argentina and the other countries of the region were well known. It was quite apparent that support was largely rhetorical and that no Latin American country had been prepared to incur significant diplomatic, economic, or military costs on Argentina's behalf. Moscow and its local ally Cuba did try to exploit the conflict, but they were not successful. Buenos Aires used these contacts as a means of putting pressure on the West, but they were never going to lead to a move into the Soviet bloc.

Through May, Argentina stressed that it was a responsible member of the Western community rather than a potential convert to communism. Yet, it was feared, the military, including Galtieri himself, might hope to survive surrender and retain power if Argentine forces could hold on. Reports in early June that Argentina had signed a $100 million trade agreement with Cuba, expanding an already growing commercial and political relationship, could also, on one hand, confirm Washington's worst fears while, on the other, appear as a source of discomfort to a generally right-wing political and military elite. A photograph of Foreign Secretary Nicanor Costa Mendez (in Cuba to attend a meeting of the Non-Aligned Movement) embracing Fidel Castro had apparently irritated many officers. Even Costa Mendez was said to be unhappy about receiving assistance from communist countries. The more alarmist prognostications related more to the likely next government. It was assumed that the new leaders would be highly nationalistic, reluctant to negotiate with the British, and increasingly inclined to blame the United States for Argentina's defeat. Popular support for Argentina's claim would mean that even civilian leaders would have to sustain a nationalistic stance. In arguing against the need to "save" Galtieri, the British never accepted that the alternatives were likely to be more extreme or that post-hostilities Argentina would be easier to deal with if it had not been humiliated and allowed some return on its original aggression.

In retrospect we can see that not only would something have to be done about the economy and discontent with a repressive regime after the war, which was generally acknowledged, but defeat would also involve an enormous shock to the Argentine system, and this tended to be understated. Popular anger would be channeled internally, against the regime, rather than against foreign powers. The desire to get rid of military rule was underestimated, as was the need to work closely with Western powers if the economy was to recover. Any government would eventually have to cope with the sort of recurrent economic failures prompted by the surge of inflation resulting from the abandonment of fiscal austerity measures. As the conflict wore on, at issue was not whether Argentina was rejecting capitalism but whether capitalism was rejecting Argentina.

Equally, all of the economic and commercial arguments in Latin American countries were for strengthening rather than weakening relations with European countries, with whom there were close historical and cultural affinities, as well as an important market for commodities and sources of finance and technology. Britain had played a role in the Latin American independence struggle and in the region's economic development, while there were still sizeable British communities throughout Latin America. The responses to Argentine pressures had been slow and reluctant. Only Panama allowed its rhetoric to get out of hand, with chauvinistic comments about the prime minister that were deplored at home. British diplomats found little love for Argentina or for its military government in the region, and in private, if not in public, there was much condemnation of the Argentine aggression.

The basic interest in Latin America was to get the whole business over as soon as possible. The Latin American governments were aware of Western concerns about realignment, but in acknowledging these concerns, they took care not to suggest that realignment was inevitable. They remained the weaker parties in the relationship. Chile was officially neutral although in practice sympathetic to Britain. Brazil also had a recent history of quarrels with Argentina. The Mexicans accepted that Britain was the victim of aggression. When Argentina moved to reconvene the meeting of the Consultative Organ of the Rio Treaty states in late May to consider further action, a harsh resolution was adopted that condemned Britain, called on the United States to cease supporting Britain, and invited Rio Treaty signatories to assist Argentina individually or collectively. Four countries – the United States, Trinidad, Chile, and Colombia – voted against the resolution. It had no consequences.

The other issue in the Falklands/Malvinas War was Soviet support. Moscow, already a large importer of Argentine grain, used the crisis to ingratiate itself with Latin Americans, encouraging the media to denigrate British and American policies. Its diplomats advocated the exclusion of the United States and Canada from the Organization of American States (OAS) and promised to use the UN veto to help Argentina, although they had failed to do so with Resolution 502. The Americans saw Moscow seeking to capitalize on a major opportunity to improve its standing in Latin America. The British, however, always doubted that

Moscow would make much headway in improving its own position. There were no indications that Buenos Aires had requested Soviet military equipment, and in any case such material would probably have presented severe technical problems for the Argentines.

The Soviets made a strong protest to Britain over the disruption of the Soviet-Argentine grain trade caused by the British blockade. Grain shipments were piling up in Argentine ports and insurance rates for ships operating out of these ports had been pushed up. Britain – and by extension the United States – would be blamed by Moscow for domestic grain shortages. The Americans were worried that Argentina might seek to obtain new weapons from the USSR after the conflict, on the grounds that they would be offered at bargain prices, Western supplies had been restricted, and an arms deal would be a means of helping to pay for grain sales and would increase Soviet influence. However, even Moscow was wary of getting too close to Argentina. It had been caught on the hop by the invasion, avoided vetoing Resolution 502, and called for an Argentine withdrawal, even while condemning British colonial attitudes and describing the invasion as no more than an "occupation." Moscow was well aware of the junta's reputation among leftist groups in Latin America and had noted that third-world support for Argentina was hardly overwhelming, a critical criterion for Soviet foreign policy.

The problem therefore was not that Britain was seriously jeopardizing wider Western interests in Latin America by pushing its national interests so strongly, but that it was widely assumed by its friends and allies to be doing so. The government therefore had to work hard to prevent seepage.

Continuing military success helped. There were signs that Latin American countries were distancing themselves from Argentina as defeat seemed more likely. A more substantial help was the Versailles summit of the Group of Seven (G7) leading Western states of June 4 to 6. The summit was used to get the Americans and the other allies to understand this while they still appeared to be hankering after a compromise settlement of some sort. Solutions that might have been acceptable at an earlier stage of the crisis were no longer realistic in light of British military exertions and losses. This was coincident with the dramatic vote at the UN at which Britain at last had to use its veto, an event that was overshadowed by the American delegation's initial veto followed by the later observation that they wished they had abstained.

When Reagan, at the summit, made a public statement supporting Britain, the other countries fell in line. It was assumed that this was the green light for the battle for Stanley (the islands' capital city). After the summit Mitterrand stated, "We wanted to affirm our solidarity with Great Britain, who as it happens, had been the victim of aggression against both its national interests and its national pride, a solidarity which is natural. Great Britain must regain its right [*doit retrouver son droit*], it being understood that we shall do everything, once its right has been regained, so that peace triumphs over war."[9] At the same time it was already apparent that the other side of the coin was a conviction that, after the hostilities, Britain would be expected to be active in seeking the early lifting of economic sanctions. Slowly the diplomatic focus was shifting to the postwar situation. After the war, Britain would – and did – face arguments for magnanimity and pressure to find imaginative solutions to long-term problems and also to provide its allies with release from economic sanctions and arms embargoes.

As the final battle for Stanley began, allied governments had by and large been convinced that there was no longer any point in pressing London for some conciliatory gesture. The American media encouraged Britain to avoid a postwar strategy that could leave Argentina still determined to regain the island. The *New York Times* started to cast a skeptical eye on the "calamitous" harm that was being done to United States relations with Latin America.

Nearly thirty years on, it is apparent that the war helped Argentina back to democracy and not into further dictatorship and that it did the Soviet Union and Cuba no good at all. Western political relations with Latin America were soon in good repair, and in fact Argentine students were once again being trained at British staff colleges.

Critics are often dubious about "firm action." They assume that it produces an equal and opposite reaction from the opponent and antagonizes others. The evidence from this case suggests that governments make calculations out of their own sense of their interests (which may appear curious) and that the firm action of others can make them uncomfortable, but they rarely act out of pique or unbridled emotion.

It also shows that even wars about a relatively unimportant group of islands some 400 miles off the Argentine coast can end up involving countries from across the globe. Circumstance, such as the periodic rotation onto the UN Security Council, can suddenly thrust a nation into the midst of a situation for which it may have little or no interest. Moreover, when war begins, diplomacy does not end; in this case diplomacy continued even when the fighting had stopped. While it has been said that wars can be caused by the failure of diplomacy, in reality both diplomacy and war are means to achieve a desired end. They may run counter to one another, while in this case they acted in harmony.

THE KOSOVO WAR

The Kosovo War was important for a number of reasons. It was the first time that a "major use of destructive armed force had been undertaken with the stated purpose of implementing UN Security Council resolutions, but without Security Council authorization."[1] It also represented the first significant use of a "bombing campaign intended to bring a halt to crimes against humanity being committed by a state within its own borders."[2] It was a significant step in increasing the role of international military forces in humanitarian action and marked a change from earlier deployments within the Balkans region. It also highlighted the challenges of linking diplomacy with the threatened and actual use of the military arm.

The Balkans region has long been a potential conflict area, as it lies along what could be described as a fault line between civilizations – Western Christendom, Orthodox Christendom, and Islam.[3] Kosovo is frequently identified as the birthplace of the Serb nation: "Wipe away Kosovo from the Serb mind and soul, and we are no more."[4] For the Albanians, Kosovo is equally important: the Albanian national movement began in Kosovo in 1878. Centuries of conflict and dispute led to the Balkans providing the spark that caused the First World War.[5] The Paris Peace Conference that ended the war led to the creation of the state of Yugoslavia.

This brought together Serbs, Croats, Slovenes, and (against their will) half a million Albanians into a single state.[6] For the Albanians there was little obvious benefit, as they were generally dominated by an imported Serbian elite, which ran Kosovo. During the Second World War, a large part of Kosovo was temporarily united with Albania under Italian rule. After the Second World War, Yugoslavia was reunified and dominated by Marshal Josip Broz Tito. Nevertheless, Serb-Albanian relations continued to fluctuate until 1974, when a new Yugoslav constitution gave Kosovo considerable autonomy within Yugoslavia but not the independence many Kosovo Albanians sought. After Tito's death in 1980, Yugoslavia slowly began to disintegrate as the controlling grip associated with his regime steadily weakened.

The sources of the Kosovo tragedy can be seen in the rise to power of Serbian leader Slobodan Milošević. He sought to reassert Serbian dominance. In 1989 Kosovo's autonomous status was revoked, and it was brought under direct control of the Serbian government in Belgrade. Yugoslav Albanian parliamentary deputies responded by proclaiming Kosovo a republic within the Yugoslav Federation and seceding from Serbia. The secession was ignored by the Serbian government, which dissolved the Kosovo National Assembly and took full control of the province. In the years that followed, the majority Albanian population of Kosovo was progressively denied the right to govern its own affairs, to earn a living, to have access to the legal and judicial system, and to educate its children in their own language and culture.

As these repressive measures mounted, and against the background of conflict in Croatia and Bosnia-

Herzegovina (other "federal units" of the country), Yugoslavia disintegrated. The outgoing U.S. administration of President George H.W. Bush issued what became known as the "Christmas warning" in December 1992. U.S. diplomats informed President Milošević that the United States was prepared to respond militarily if the Serbs initiated an armed conflict in Kosovo.[7]

Initially the Kosovo Albanian response to repression was essentially peaceful; they effectively formed a shadow government and even held elections. But in 1995, the decision was made to leave Kosovo out of the Dayton Agreement (ending the war in Bosnia), and a number of Kosovo Albanians took up arms and formed the Kosovo Liberation Army (KLA or UCK).[8] The Serbian oppression intensified and a vicious spiral of violence grew as the KLA began guerrilla warfare and Milošević used Kosovo politically to retain his hold on power in Yugoslavia.

In December 1997, NATO foreign ministers confirmed that NATO's interest extended beyond Bosnia-Herzegovina to include the surrounding area. They expressed concern at the rising ethnic tension in Kosovo.[9] The following spring, NATO ministers called on all parties to seek a peaceful resolution to the crisis. The UN Security Council passed Resolution 1160, condemning the excessive use of force by the Former Republic of Yugoslavia's government and imposing a comprehensive embargo on the sale of arms and related material.[10] Many in NATO believed that Kosovo was in the same position Bosnia had been in 1991, and they did not want to see a repetition of that tragedy. In mid-May NATO sent a reconnaissance team to Albania to identify which facilities would be available if a military force needed to use Albania as a base for a monitoring force in Kosovo. NATO planners were then given authority to develop a range of military options involving 6,500, 10,000, and 13,000 troops. However, NATO's North Atlantic Council rejected all of these options.

As NATO's European members began to shift in favor of a potential military option to deter ethnic cleansing, the administration of President Bill Clinton remained unimpressed. Within the Defense Department and the Congress there was a desire to get out of the Balkans completely, rather than become further entangled, and a belief that the only way to deal with Milošević was by direct air strikes against Serbia. The risk of such a strategy was that NATO would effectively be encouraging the KLA. The issue of restraining KLA violence, while at the same time trying to coerce Milošević, remained a challenge throughout the conflict.

On May 28, 1998, NATO foreign ministers agreed on two main objectives for Kosovo: (1) to help achieve a peaceful resolution of the crisis by contributing to the response of the international community and (2) to promote stability and security in neighboring countries with particular emphasis on Albania and the Former Yugoslav Republic of Macedonia.[11] NATO's subsequent actions, including demonstration flights by NATO aircraft and enhanced "Partnership for Peace" activities with Albania and the Former Yugoslav Republic of Macedonia, seemed initially to have the desired inhibiting effect on Milošević.[12] However, the KLA leadership took advantage of this symbolic action against Milošević and changed its tactics.[13] The KLA sought to increase the area it controlled, and by July 1998 it claimed 40 percent of Kosovo. The Serbian response was brutal. They launched a counteroffensive, supplementing the Ministry of the Interior's Special Police Forces with the regular Yugoslav Army. The KLA's decision to stand and fight, matched by the indiscriminate use of violence by the Serb/Yugoslav forces, resulted in well over 200,000 people being displaced and 50,000 forced to camp in the open.[14] Moreover, the Serbian forces systematically destroyed homes and food stocks, slaughtered cattle, and prevented the harvest from being collected. This added an important complication to the international community's response. Within NATO, it was agreed that they wanted "to compel Milošević to halt his offensive and reduce the number of Serb security forces in Kosovo to the level that existed before the violence began. Milošević also had to agree to negotiate seriously with the Albanians to develop interim arrangements on autonomy."[15] However, there remained considerable disagreement about the best way to achieve this. The majority believed that Milošević was determined to move forward with a military solution. They also surmised that NATO would not take military action without a Security Council resolution, which the Russians would not allow to pass. A series of diplomatic initiatives tried to convince Milošević of NATO's seriousness.[16]

On September 4, 1998, the UN secretary-general reported to the Security Council that the number of displaced persons had increased tenfold since March.[17] This report had a galvanizing effect on the international community. As winter weather approached, a humanitarian disaster could occur whether the fighting had stopped or not. As a result, the Security Council passed Resolution 1199, expressing the international community's concern about the Serb military's excessive use of force, and called on all parties to comply with a ceasefire and negotiate.[18] To placate the Russians, it emphasized that both the KLA and the Yugoslav leadership needed to resolve the crisis and called for all parties to move toward a negotiated settlement, to stop human rights abuses, and to allow humanitarian efforts to take place.

The resolution also persuaded some other NATO members to back NATO action to tackle the threat posed by Milošević. General Wesley Clark, the supreme allied commander of Europe, was authorized to ask member states to provide the requisite military force to undertake a military intervention. On September 24, NATO defense ministers meeting at Vilamoura in Portugal agreed to prepare activation orders for two types of air operation.[19] The first was a five-phase operation designed to gradually increase the pressure on Milošević.[20] The second was a limited air response aimed at punishing him.[21] This marked a further political signal of NATO's commitment to dealing with Milošević. NATO began to increase its deployment of military aircraft within range of the Republic of Yugoslavia to increase the political pressure on him.

On October 3, the Security Council was told that Milošević had made no attempt to comply with Resolution 1199. Within NATO, attempts were made to agree on specific air strikes against Yugoslav targets. This failed in the absence of the required consensus. The next day Milošević claimed that he was withdrawing his forces from Kosovo. The Security Council met on October 6 to discuss the situation but could not reach agreement because both Russia and China were opposed to NATO air strikes.[22] Russian officials suggested that if the option were used, then Russia reserved the right to support the Federal Republic of Yugoslavia.[23] The Russian defense minister indicated that this would mark a return to the Cold War.[24] The Chinese foreign minister subsequently said on October 12, "The Chinese Government resolutely opposes the use of force or the threat to use force in international relations, and hopes that the Kosovo crisis will be resolved peacefully at an early date." For the UN, the proposal to use armed force against a nation-state on the basis of its government's improper actions broke new ground, and a number of countries were opposed to setting such a precedent. Within NATO, however, there was no dispute that NATO action would be legitimate under the UN Charter. The passing of Resolution 1199 had provided additional justification reinforcing this conclusion; the differences now were only over the timing of the decision to activate NATO's forces.

As a further step the Contact Group (including Russia, France, Germany, Italy, the United States, and the United Kingdom) demanded an end to Serb offensives in Kosovo, the withdrawal of Serb forces, freedom of access for the international community, full cooperation with the International War Crimes Tribunal, the safe return of refugees to their homes, and the start of a negotiated solution to the crisis on October 8. The U.S. administration took the lead in attempting to obtain Milošević's agreement that the Organization for Security and Cooperation in Europe (OSCE) rather than NATO would provide a monitoring force in Kosovo but that it would be accompanied by a NATO aerial surveillance operation. On October 12, Milošević appeared to make a number of important concessions to the American representative, Richard Holbrooke, by agreeing to comply with

UN demands. On October 13 NATO finally approved the activation orders, authorizing the use of force, but delayed implementing them until October 17 as a means of putting further pressure on Milošević. Two days later, Milošević gave permission for NATO reconnaissance flights, and shortly after he also agreed to allow the OSCE Kosovo Verification Mission (KVM) to enter Kosovo. The agreement to use the OSCE was a concession to Milošević that NATO would later regret. However, this temporary solution did allow the displaced persons to temporarily return to their homes for the winter, something that might not have proved possible if NATO had begun military action against targets in Serbia and Kosovo.

Reflecting on the agreement, Secretary of State Madeleine Albright acknowledged its problems: "The October agreement was more Band-Aid than cure. The commitments Milošević made could and would be reversed, but for the time being the agreement allowed hundreds of thousands of people to come down from the hills to spend winter in their homes. It reinforced the truth that Kosovo's fate was of international concern, and it established a set of formal obligations Milošević had accepted, and against which he could be held accountable."[25]

In the circumstances, it was the least bad option at that particular moment. NATO had simply run out of time. Beginning an air campaign as winter set in, and with so many displaced people in Kosovo living in the open, was not a practical military option. The compromise did at least bring about a temporary respite to the conflict and gave diplomacy further time to work.[26]

In terms of the detail, Milošević had ten days to reduce the number of Serb troops and police in

Kosovo. Refugees and displaced people would be allowed to return to their homes. Up to two thousand international observers would be deployed under the auspices of the OSCE. NATO was given authority to fly over Kosovo to verify Serb actions. Elections would be held within nine months, and a new multiethnic police force would be trained. Yugoslavia would have to cooperate with war-crimes tribunal investigations. Finally, Yugoslavia pledged to negotiate with leaders in Kosovo to achieve a settlement that would return autonomy to the province.[27]

President Milošević agreed to limit the number of security and military personnel in Kosovo to their pre-crisis level (12,000 Yugoslav Army and 10,000 Interior Ministry Police). The Security Council passed a further resolution on October 24, drafted by the United Kingdom, supporting the OSCE, KVM, and NATO aerial observation missions and demanding full compliance from all parties.[28] However, on Russian insistence, this resolution did not give NATO authority to use force if Milošević failed to comply with UN demands.

NATO also dispatched a task group to the Former Yugoslav Republic of Macedonia to assist in the event of an evacuation mission for the monitors becoming necessary. This idea was pushed through by the French government following its previous experience of hostage-taking in Bosnia, where French troops had been at the frontline.[29]

Winter's onset reduced the level of conflict, but it did not bring it to an end. The international community did accept that there was a sufficient level of compliance to prevent further action, not that it had any other option given the circumstances.[30] OSCE's monitoring mission (KVM) took time to deploy, and as a result, the smaller Kosovo Diplomatic Observer Mission (KDOM), which had been active in the region since June 1998, continued until January 1999. Part of the problem lay with the availability of qualified monitors. Although the mission had an authorized strength of up to two thousand, by the end of December the number actually deployed was only around six hundred. Attempts to move toward a negotiated settlement based on a peace plan drawn up by U.S. envoy Christopher Hill in September came to nothing, and the Albanians initially refused to meet the Serbs.

On the ground the KLA became more active, returning to certain areas vacated by withdrawing Serbian forces. In response Yugoslav/Serbian forces carried out an operation in the Podujevo area between Christmas and New Years, which killed at least nine Kosovo Albanians and forced over five thousand to flee.[31] In early 1999 the situation rapidly worsened.

On January 15, 1999, forty-five Kosovo Albanians, some of them children, were found murdered at Račak (a village in central Kosovo). Most had been shot in the head at close range.[32] This provided the catalyst for war. The incident convinced many within the international community that the prospect of a humanitarian catastrophe was once again real. NATO threatened military action against the Federal Republic of Yugoslavia if the ceasefire was not restored. The crisis escalated, and Yugoslav authorities ordered Ambassador William Walker, the head of the Kosovo Verification Mission, out of the country when he publicly accused the Serb authorities of being responsible for the atrocity. Walker refused to leave, but the Yugoslav authorities were able to deny Judge Louise Arbour, the chief prosecutor for the International Criminal Tribunal for Yugoslavia, access to Račak.[33]

In a final diplomatic effort to resolve the situation, the Contact Group called a conference on the future of Kosovo to be held at Rambouillet, a suburb of Paris, on February 6.[34] Meanwhile, NATO again raised its state of readiness. On January 28, NATO issued a further warning to Milošević and the Kosovo Albanian leadership.[35] NATO's North Atlantic Council also gave its secretary-general authority to authorize air strikes within the Federal Republic of Yugoslavia's territory when he believed it necessary, requesting that they be consulted in advance.

On February 23, an agreement was reached that granted Kosovo a high degree of autonomy and stipulated that Serb and Yugoslav security forces be withdrawn. The agreement was initially to last three years, and a follow-up meeting in Paris was supposed to sign it on March 15. It was made clear to the Serbian delegation that NATO's authority to use force remained in place.[36] After much delay, the Kosovo Albanian delegation eventually signed the Rambouillet Agreement on March 18, 1999, although some within the delegation were against continuing to be part of Yugoslavia. However, the Serbian delegation, led by Milan Milutinović, refused to sign. On March 19 the co-chairmen of the Contact Group sponsoring negotiations at Rambouillet – French Foreign Minister Hubert Védrine and British Foreign Secretary Robin Cook – announced the adjournment of the talks in the absence of an agreement from Yugoslavia. The talks' failure led the OSCE to withdraw the Kosovo Verification Mission on March 20. As OSCE monitors pulled out, they passed Yugoslav forces, which launched a major offensive in the Mitrovica region and along the Prizen-Djakovica-Pec axis, causing an estimated twenty thousand people to flee their homes. Serbian troops in Kosovo indicated that should NATO air strikes begin, it would punish the Kosovo Albanians even more.[37]

In yet another attempt to find a diplomatic solution, Holbrooke again traveled to Belgrade for talks with President Milošević. It quickly became clear that Milošević was not prepared to comply with NATO demands. Holbrooke briefed NATO ambassadors and announced that he was handing over the process to NATO Secretary-General Javier Solana. The last chance for a peaceful resolution had then passed; diplomacy could do no more. On March 22 the North Atlantic Council publicly delegated authority to Solana to decide when to begin air operations as a last and final attempt to get Milošević to back down.[38] The following day Solana directed General Clark to begin air strikes.

From the beginning the NATO members agreed to a set of five conditions for the conflict's termination: a verifiable end to all military action and the immediate ending of violence and repression; the withdrawal from Kosovo of Yugoslav military, police, and paramilitary forces; the stationing in Kosovo of an international military presence; the unconditional and safe return of all refugees and internally displaced persons and unhindered access to them by humanitarian organizations; and the establishment of a political framework for Kosovo, on the basis of the Rambouillet Accords, in conformity with international law and the UN Charter.[39]

Initially the use of ground forces was ruled out. Within NATO, ruling out this option was seen as a means of placating Russian hostility. There was a real fear that the Russian government might find itself forced by its own electorate to become involved on the Serb side. Moreover, for many NATO members, including Germany, Italy, and the United States, the involvement of ground troops was simply a political step too far at this stage.

The air campaign began in something of a rush, with the diplomatic position having jumped ahead of military preparations. Although air strikes commenced on March 24 under the code name Operation Allied Force, the force earmarked for the operation was relatively light. In the end the air campaign lasted seventy-eight days, far longer than most experts had predicted. The campaign plan retained the five phases outlined in October and was based on a gradual escalation of the air campaign, rather than starting with a full "shock and awe" strike designed to overwhelm the enemy. It was not intended to achieve a set level of physical destruction but rather involved a series of operations designed to lead to a change in behavior. In other words, it focused more on the psychological rather than the physical effect, which makes it far harder to gauge relative success until the behavior actually changes.

The air campaign highlighted the political and capability differences within NATO. Although all NATO members had eventually agreed to NATO action, they were not all prepared or even capable of actively participating.[40] On the first night, thirteen of the nineteen nations had military forces involved, of which only five (the United States, the United Kingdom, France, Canada, and Spain) dropped bombs, while aircraft from the Netherlands and the United States were engaged in air-to-air combat with the Yugoslav air force.[41] NATO started with a force of 366 aircraft and carried out 40 missions on the first night and finished the campaign with more than 900 aircraft, two-thirds of which were American, flying over 38,000 sorties of which more than 14,000 were strike sorties.[42]

The first targets were the Yugoslav air defense system and facilities linked to military units involved in Kosovo. These objectives proved problematic. The lack of engagement by the air defense system meant that it was difficult to target, while the majority of Serbian units had already dispersed from their barracks. As a result, Solana announced within a few days that he had directed General Clark to initiate a wider range of air operations against Yugoslavia.[43] The relatively light scale of early air strikes led to urgent calls for an increase in the size of the air forces committed to the operation.

The international reaction to NATO air strikes was disturbingly mixed. Both China and Russia referred to the "illegal" military action. President Boris Yeltsin issued a stark warning and ordered a temporary freeze on Russia's relations with NATO. On March 26 Russia put forward a draft resolution in the Security Council, co-sponsored by Belarus and India, which called for an immediate halt to NATO attacks and an urgent resumption of negotiations. Britain, the United States, and France all used their vetoes to defeat the proposal and were supported by nine other Security Council members, with only China, Russia, and Namibia voting in favor.

For an alliance dependent on consensus, disunity was its main vulnerability. Both Solana and Clark had to tread a careful line that did not undermine the consensus. Milošević sought to divide NATO by intensifying the ethnic cleansing in Kosovo while arguing that NATO's action was illegal. The problem for NATO was that in trying to prevent ethnic cleansing, it looked to some as though its actions were in fact having the reverse effect.

The bombing of Kosovo provoked a major humanitarian crisis in the region. Hundreds of thousands of ethnic Albanians were forced to flee their homes in an orchestrated policy of mass expulsion by Yugoslav forces known as Operation Horseshoe. This included an attempt to deny individuals their identities though the destruction of passports, birth certificates, and other documents. By March 30, the UN High Commission for Refugees (UNHCR) announced that some 94,000 ethnic Albanians had been forced out of Kosovo since the start of NATO military action less than a week earlier.

The NATO members agreed to reject the various calls for a halt to the bombing. The fear for the majority of them was that once the air war was suspended, it would be difficult to restart it, NATO would have failed, and Milošević would have got away with ethnic cleansing on an enormous scale. Yet Milošević continued to try to divide the alliance by making apparently reasonable offers. On March 30, for example, he offered elections based on Yugoslav citizenship, knowing that many of the refugees had had their documentation destroyed, effectively rendering them stateless.

From the second week onward, the air campaign was expanded to include the targeting of communication lines and transport routes, in an attempt to isolate Yugoslav forces in Kosovo and stop supplies flowing from Serbia to support the actions on the ground. The scale of air operations was also increased. On March 31 several thousand ethnic Albanian refugees arrived at the Macedonian border from Pristina (the largest city in Kosovo). They had been packed into trains and systematically transported to the Macedonian border by Serb forces in scenes reminiscent of the Holocaust. By April 2 an estimated 634,000 had been displaced from their homes, representing approximately one-third of the pre-war population. Not surprisingly, both Albania and the Former Yugoslav Republic of Macedonia appealed to the international community for help.

Most NATO members, including Italy, remained opposed to any ground option. The French government, led by President Jacques Chirac, remained in favor of a more gradualist approach without fully ruling out the use of ground troops. The Italian government wanted an end to the conflict and was prepared to compromise with Milošević far more than most. The Clinton administration was struggling with a sex scandal.

Nevertheless, the escalation in ethnic conflict and the lack of apparent success in the air campaign quickly persuaded the British government to try and shift both international and domestic opinion toward a possible ground option, recognizing that NATO needed to operate within a finite timeframe. As the experience of the previous year had shown, if the refugees were to be back in their homes before winter, then a ground campaign would ideally need to be over by the end of September.

The British government began to make the case for NATO deploying into a "semi-permissive" environment. Although the meaning of this was never fully defined, the British government suggested that NATO might deploy ground forces if it had achieved such a significant advantage in Kosovo that any opposition from the Yugoslav forces would be piecemeal and uncoordinated. The British change in language on the ground option and the announcement of further forces being committed to Macedonia led President Yeltsin to warn that, if NATO launched a ground offensive against the Federal Republic of Yugoslavia, then there would be a Russian military response. This further discouraged some NATO members from considering the ground option.

Without a change in policy, it was difficult for NATO air power to strike at the perpetrators of ethnic cleansing, who were frequently small bands of Serb men. The American and British governments therefore decided to support the KLA's military arm. The KLA could act as a counter to Serb forces on the ground. In response, the Serbs would have to concentrate their forces against the KLA, making them easier for NATO aircraft to target. Support for the KLA was therefore a mechanism to target Serbian forces, but the change in policy ran the risk of further encouraging the KLA's aspirations for independence.

As the air campaign intensified, strikes were made against Milošević's official residence and Serbian state television facilities. NATO argued that both were legitimate targets. At NATO's fiftieth anniversary summit in Washington (April 23-25), its leaders reassessed the campaign. They approved a further intensification of the air strikes to include the targeting of military-industrial infrastructure, the media responsible for promulgating propaganda, and other strategic targets, including the interests of those closest to Milošević. Further aircraft were deployed, again principally by the United States.

Both Solana and Clark believed that the summit gave them a green light to consider ground force options. However, the Quint Group of defense ministers (the United States, United Kingdom, France, Germany, and Italy) decided not to put the options before the North Atlantic Council in order to avoid a political debate too early within NATO, given the potential for division and a suspension of the development of options. Moreover, both President Clinton and his defense secretary had promised Congress that they would present any ground options to Congress for approval, and it was too early to do this successfully. The British government was content that it had begun the process toward a possible ground option without splitting NATO. Attention focused on an opposed assault into Kosovo, which in NATO jargon became known as "Option B(-)."

Meanwhile, bilateral discussions between Russia and the United States led to an agreement by the Group of Eight (G8) foreign ministers on a set of principles to resolve the crisis on May 6.[44] These principles subsequently formed the basis of what Milošević finally agreed to on June 3. They were significant because they were endorsed by Russia, marking a shift in Russian policy and Milošević's further isolation.

On the night of May 7-8, the Chinese embassy in Belgrade was bombed in error. Despite this tragedy, the air campaign finally began to expose cracks on the Yugoslav side. The police brutally put down protests in Kruševac, Serbia. Reports of soldiers deserting began to be received.[45] The international pressure on Milošević increased when an indictment was issued against him on three counts of crimes against humanity and one count of violations of the laws or customs of war on May 22, 1999, and made public five days later.[46] Despite this progress, there was real concern about the time available, given the need to return refugees to their homes before winter. NATO Secretary-General Solana pushed for Option B(-) to be decided on by the beginning of June, to allow sufficient time for it to be used before winter. Finally, on May 25, NATO's North Atlantic Council formally approved an increase in the force planned to enter Kosovo from 28,000 to 45,000.[47] The Quint ministers again met on May 26-27 but could not move ahead with Option B(-) because the French and Germans were against going beyond contingency planning.

Before this became necessary the European Union envoy, Finnish President Martti Ahtisaari, and Russian special envoy Viktor Chernomyrdin successfully negotiated a peace package with Milošević on the international community's behalf. Approved by the Serbian parliament on June 3, the plan's elements included a verifiable and rapid withdrawal from Kosovo of all Yugoslav Army, Paramilitary Forces, and Interior Special Police. It also called for the deployment under a UN mandate of an effective civil and security presence tasked with overseeing the return of refugees and internally displaced people. This international security presence was to include a substantial NATO participation with a unified command and control. An interim administration was to be established to effectively run the province under the aegis of the OSCE. This would lead to democratic self-governing institutions within Kosovo. Finally, the KLA was to be demilitarized.[48] No time limit was set for the NATO-led deployment, although the original Rambouillet Agreement had referred to a three-year period before a final settlement.

The revised deployment plan envisaged that the Kosovo Force (KFOR) would be a force of 48,000, almost double that planned under Rambouillet. Milošević's sudden agreement meant that putting together such a force was a real challenge. NATO's deployment plan divided Kosovo into five sectors, commanded respectively by the United States, France, Germany, Italy, and the United Kingdom. On June 5 the British commander of the NATO force in the Former Yugoslav Republic of Macedonia, Lieutenant-General Sir Mike Jackson, met his Yugoslav military counterparts to agree on a mechanism for the withdrawal of Yugoslav troops and paramilitaries. NATO did not see these meetings as negotiations but as a means for Yugoslav forces to comply with the international community's demands. The Serb generals sought to get around the previous agreement by retaining a Yugoslav/Serbian military and paramilitary presence in Kosovo. Jackson rejected these suggestions, and the discussions temporarily broke down. Given Milošević s track record, this was not entirely unexpected and was one of the main reasons for continuing the air campaign. In NATO the fear continued to be that any temporary suspension in the air campaign would be difficult to revoke, giving Milošević space to abrogate the June 3 agreement. Moreover, on the ground there was an upsurge in Serb/Yugoslav activity, and the violence continued.

The Serb/Yugoslav military returned to the negotiating table on June 8, and a "military technical agreement" was reached between Jackson and the Serb authorities the next day. This outlined a phased but complete withdrawal of Serbian military and security forces over eleven days.[49] This was a lesson learned from the previous fall, when it had been agreed to allow these forces to be reduced only to their pre-conflict levels in Kosovo. Milošević had continued to use these remaining forces, and it was never possible to properly establish whether he had fully complied with the overall numerical limitations.

On June 10, 1999, NATO agreed to suspend its air operations against the Federal Republic of Yugoslavia, following the start of the withdrawal by Yugoslav forces from Kosovo in accordance with a peace package agreed to by the G8 countries. The seventy-eight-day air campaign was over. The agreement was formalized by the Security Council with Resolution 1244, which was passed 14-0 (with China abstaining).[50] While not formally mentioning NATO, the agreement gave tacit retrospective approval for the air campaign, referring to relevant international organizations and approving the deployment of an international force to Kosovo with UN authority.

For Lieutenant-General Jackson, the challenge was to ensure the withdrawal of Serb forces and to secure the whole of Kosovo with a force that was still in the process of deploying to the region. Two days later, KFOR, consisting predominantly of NATO forces under NATO command, began to deploy. Jackson faced the prospect of sending a smaller force than the outgoing Serb forces into Kosovo.[51] He did not, therefore, want to provoke an incident while gaining control of Kosovo. He sought to advance quickly but not provocatively.

This led to a Russian response. On June 11, the day before NATO was scheduled to begin its movement into Kosovo, a small Russian force of fewer than two hundred unilaterally redeployed from Bosnia to Pristina Airport without consulting Western leaders. According to the Russian foreign minister, Igor Ivanov, this was a mistake, suggesting that the Russian Ministry of Defense had taken precipitous action.[52] The Russians were in breach of their NATO agreements, and General Clark was concerned that the Russians could effectively carve out their own sector and divide Kosovo. In response to a request from General Clark, Lieutenant-General Jackson put British and French forces on alert, with a plan prepared for an airborne assault on Pristina Airport. Jackson was not happy with this, however, and there was a significant disagreement with Clark. From Jackson's perspective, such an operation would have been contrary to the military technical agreement with the Serbs, which could have led to the shooting down of helicopters or a confrontation at the airport with a numerically larger Serb force. And such an action would have inevitably led to an armed confrontation with the Russians. Jackson believed that such a significant escalation of the crisis was unwise and unnecessary and that the Russian force could be dealt with through other means. With the support of Britain's political and military leadership, the airborne operation was cancelled and the originally planned deployment timetable was continued. By June 17, NATO had more than sixteen thousand troops deployed into Kosovo, with the British contingent amounting to over half the force (approximately nine thousand).[53]

To negate the Russian presence at the airport, British troops surrounded it, and the airspace around Yugoslavia was closed to Russian aircraft so that the Russians could neither reinforce nor resupply their force without NATO agreement. This effectively undermined the Russian position and ensured that a political resolution of the crisis was achieved.

From the beginning it was important for KFOR to be seen as impartial. As a result, one of its early goals was to protect the remaining Serbs in Kosovo from reprisals. With NATO in control of Kosovo, the KLA leadership agreed to disarm in accordance with the Security Council's Resolution 1244 and the Rambouillet Agreement on June 20.[54] This required complete disarmament within 120 days, with a series of defined interim decommissioning steps.

Almost as soon as NATO forces began entering Kosovo, more significant population movements began as ethnic Albanians started to return while ethnic Serbs fled to Serbia. On June 17, 1999, the UNHCR had estimated that 234,000 Kosovo Albanians were in Macedonia, 424,600 in Albania, 69,700 in Montenegro, and 21,700 in Bosnia. In addition, a total of 87,156 were reported to have been evacuated to other countries, including 4,056 to the United Kingdom.[55] Offsetting this were the 100,000-plus Serbs and Roma who were estimated to have fled Kosovo to Serbia, Montenegro, or the Former Yugoslav Republic of Macedonia.

Operation Allied Force was ultimately successful: Slobodan Milošević's ethnic cleansing of Kosovo was reversed, and over one million refugees were able to return home. NATO came through its first war victoriously. For better or worse, the conflict set a precedent for international coalitions to intervene in the domestic affairs of another state for humanitarian reasons.

The Kosovo crisis also illustrated that often there can be no ideal outcome. The international community had no interest in either the Serbs or the KLA achieving ascendancy. The best that could be hoped for was some form of constitutional compromise between the ethnic groups.

The main protagonist in the conflict, Slobodan Milošević, died in 2006 at the UN War Crimes Tribunal's detention center. Still the future of Kosovo is not guaranteed. The Assembly of Kosovo approved a declaration of independence on February 17, 2008, and as of late 2010, sixty-nine UN states recognize the independence of Kosovo. But the UN Security Council remains divided on the question. Of the five members with veto power, the United States, United Kingdom, and France have recognized the declaration of independence. China has expressed concern, while Russia considers it illegal. Kosovo has not made a formal application for UN membership, in view of a possible veto from Russia and China. On October 8, 2008, upon request of Serbia, the UN General Assembly adopted a resolution asking the International Court of Justice for an advisory opinion on the issue of Kosovo's declaration of independence. The advisory opinion, which is legally non-binding but had been expected to carry "moral" weight, was rendered on July 22, 2010, holding that Kosovo's declaration of independence was not in violation of international law

The Kosovo campaign demonstrated that traditional military conflict, with a direct clash between opposing militaries of different states, is becoming less common. In this conflict, asymmetrical warfare came to the fore with NATO seeking to press home its advantage in the air and the Yugoslav forces using a variety of means to offset NATO's advantages. Ethnic cleansing was a disturbing aspect of this.

U.S. Secretary of Defense William Cohen also argued, "As a nation, as an alliance we face something of a superpower paradox. Our supremacy in the conventional arena is prompting adversaries to pursue increasingly unconventional and asymmetrical methods of warfare. There is a tendency to view this paradox largely in terms of stateless or state-sponsored actors who seek to wield terror with nuclear, biological, or chemical weapons. But we have learned in Kosovo to stretch this sensibility of asymmetric warfare to include not merely tools but also tactics. In Slobodan Milošević, NATO faced a foe who saw rape, pillage, and slaughter as appropriate and even preferred military tactics; who created a humanitarian crisis as a combat strategy; and who viewed mass executions and expulsions as in his national interest."[56]

The operation was a successful example of coalition warfare, but it also demonstrated the challenges this brings. It showed the problems of working with international partners and the limitations that this imposes. In her autobiography, Madeleine Albright identified working with partners as one of the key problems confronting policymakers,[57] and this partly explains the George W. Bush administration adopting "coalitions of the willing" rather than formal alliances in Afghanistan and Iraq. The conflict also showed that managing the peace that follows the war can be as complex and at times more difficult than the war itself. NATO's commitment to Kosovo looks set to continue for some time to come.

ORIGINS OF THE IRAQ WAR

The Iraq War remains the subject of profound disagreement and controversy around the globe. Despite elections within Iraq, increasing Iraqi self-rule, and improved security, the country's future remains in doubt. Until 2010 the post-war U.S. troop presence, in the midst of a "surge" to try and combat the insurgency, remained far higher than that which conducted the conventional war in March and April 2003.[1]

The war has also had a far wider impact. Not only did it come to dominate the George W. Bush and Barack Obama presidencies in the United States and the Tony Blair and Gordon Brown premierships in the United Kingdom.[2] It has also contributed to further terrorist attacks in Europe, which have had profound effects there. The Madrid railway bombings of March 2004 changed the course of the Spanish elections,[3] while the London bombings of July 7, 2005, have had a significant impact on British community relations.[4]

Transatlantic relations are still unsettled despite the replacement of a number of Europe's long-serving leaders: Angela Merkel became Germany's first female chancellor in 2005, and Nicolas Sarkozy became France's president in 2007. The title of a 2007 paper from the International Institute for Strategic Studies, "Repairing the Damage: Possibilities and Limits of Transatlantic Consensus," hinted at the need to rebuild the transatlantic consensus.[5] Moreover, the UN-authorized operations in Afghanistan have become enmeshed in the minds of many with the "illegality" of the war in Iraq, with profound consequences.

In the Middle East the ramifications are no less significant. The traditional balance of power has been upset, and the United States is being confronted by a resurgent and hostile Iran at a time when support for the Western governments is at an all-time low.[6] For many within the region there are fears of a Shia-dominated Iraq working in conjunction with Iran against the other Sunni states, which could result in a full-scale regional war.

In many ways the war's origins can be traced to the failure to fully resolve the situation following the Iraqi invasion of Kuwait in August 1990.[7] In response to the seizure of Kuwait, an international coalition was rapidly put together to liberate the country. Iraqi forces were successfully expelled from Kuwait in March 1991, and there followed uprisings in Iraq's north (Kurds) and south (Shias) against Saddam Hussein's brutal regime. These conflicts were brutally suppressed, and thousands were killed.

As part of the ceasefire conditions associated with Kuwait's liberation, Iraq was required to admit United Nations weapons inspectors (UNSCOM) tasked with supervising the elimination of Iraq's ballistic missile capability and weapons of mass destruction programs.[8] The Iraqi government did not at any stage offer unreserved cooperation to the UN inspectors as required by the UN Security Council. In 1998 Richard Butler, the UN chief weapons inspector, added a number of presidential palaces to a list of sites to be inspected. This led Saddam Hussein to ban the inspectors. In response, the British and U.S. governments launched a short air campaign in December 1998 known as Operation Desert Fox.[9] This failed to secure Iraqi cooperation, and in their final report to the Security Council in January 1999, the UNSCOM inspectors raised significant continuing concerns.[10] Their final report concluded that a number of questions had been left unanswered, and real doubts remained about Iraqi capabilities. This resulted in a standoff between the Iraqi government and the UN. Iraqi noncooperation was seen by almost everyone at the time as further evidence that they were concealing a continuing program.

To encourage Iraqi compliance with UNSCOM, the Security Council imposed sanctions on Iraq that prevented it from trading with the rest of the international community, except through the UN-sponsored oil-for-food program established in 1995.[11] Many viewed the sanctions policy as unfair because it allowed the Iraqi leadership to exert an even greater control over the country. It encouraged anti-Western feelings in the region as pictures of the Iraqi people's suffering were broadcast around the world.

In the meantime, the United Kingdom and the United States continued to enforce two no-fly zones in Iraq's north and south. These had been established in 1991 and 1992, respectively, and were designed to help protect the Kurds in the north and the Shias and Marsh Arabs in the south from attacks by Saddam Hussein after their unsuccessful uprisings immediately following the end of the 1991 Gulf War. While the no-fly zones did not necessarily prevent brutal repression on the ground, they did prevent the Iraqi government from using its full arsenal of weaponry. However, American and British forces charged with enforcing the zones were subjected to repeated attacks from Iraqi surface-to-air missiles.[12] Although no aircraft were shot down, there was a feeling within military circles that such a loss was only a matter of time.[13] Moreover, the requirement to maintain these forces represented a continuing drain on American and British air forces. It also involved basing Western forces in Saudi Arabia, which galvanized Arabic opinion against the United States in favor of Saddam Hussein, who was seen by some as the only Arab leader prepared to stand up to America. Rather than being seen as the protectors of the Iraqi people, the American and British forces were identified by propagandists with the oppression of the Arabs and as occupiers of holy Muslim land.

Although the inauguration of a new American president in January 2001 brought into the White House a group of neoconservatives who felt that the existing U.S. policy toward Iraq was harming U.S. interests,[14] it was the tragic events of September 11, 2001, that galvanized the American and British governments into looking harder at the threat posed by Iraq.[15] The attacks appeared to bring together the challenge of global terrorism and the danger of weapons of mass destruction. Many in the United States were shocked to realize that they were no longer safe from international terrorism at home.[16] The U.S. government subsequently identified Iraq as one of a number of near-term threats that needed to be tackled.[17] The events of September 11 did not change the problem of Iraq's noncompliance with the UN. Rather they increased the problem's importance, as the United States and the world began to look much more searchingly at potential threats. The issue of the proliferation of weapons of mass destruction had risen to the top of the political agenda, and Iraq appeared to be one example in which something could be done militarily to prevent further developments.

The challenge for both the U.S. and British governments was to explain and justify, both domestically and internationally, why the previous policy needed to change and why Iraq's failure to comply with the Security Council's calls for it to relinquish its weapons of mass destruction was now so important. Some in the United States wanted rapid action.[18] However, the British government did not and was fearful that the United States would undertake unilateral military action. Tony Blair therefore saw his task as ensuring the action's legitimacy.[19] Over the summer of 2002, he successfully encouraged the Bush administration to make a further effort to persuade the UN to deal with the Iraqi weapons of mass destruction issue. In a speech to the UN General Assembly on September 12, 2002, a year and a day after the tragic events of 9/11, President Bush challenged the United Nations to act, stating that it should confront the "grave and gathering danger" presented by Iraq or stand aside and let the United States do so.[20] Four days later, Iraq apparently agreed to the unconditional return of the UN weapons inspectors. The U.S. and British governments insisted that there could be no more second chances and that a final UN resolution should set out the obligations placed on Iraq.

The next month the U.S. Senate was briefed in a closed session that Saddam Hussein could deliver chemical and biological weapons to America's East Coast[21] and, within a few days, passed a resolution authorizing the use of force against Iraq. A few weeks later, after a considerable amount of diplomatic activity, especially by the United Kingdom, the Security Council unanimously adopted Resolution 1441.[22] At the time all of the Security Council members, including France, Russia, and Syria, accepted that Iraq had weapons of mass destruction. They gave the Iraqi government one last chance and authorized the deployment of a new inspection commission, UNMOVIC, to send inspectors into Iraq.

On the insistence of the U.S. defense secretary, Donald Rumsfeld, the military campaign would be different from that of the 1991 Gulf War. As commander of the U.S. Central Command, General Tommy Franks had inherited a fairly traditional plan based on the previous war.[23] Under Rumsfeld's direction, Franks looked at various alternatives until the secretary was finally satisfied. The new approach was to focus on the desired strategic effect – the downfall of the Iraqi regime and the elimination of its weapons of mass destruction.

Franks therefore shifted the operation's focus away from the destruction of the opponent's military and economic infrastructure to the regime's removal by taking control of Baghdad. The reasoning behind this was straightforward. As occupying powers, the American-led coalition would be legally responsible for rebuilding Iraq. It was therefore in the U.S. interest to minimize the damage to Iraq's infrastructure and protect its means of generating future wealth. The seizure and protection of the Iraqi oil fields and their key distribution elements was therefore a major component of the plan, not least because in the 1991 Gulf War Iraqi forces had caused significant environmental damage by setting light to Kuwaiti oil wells and pumping oil into the northern Persian Gulf. Franks wanted to avoid a repetition of this.

The plan that emerged emphasized speed, maneuver, and accuracy of firepower. It reflected much of the new thinking embraced by Rumsfeld,[24] which involved fighting wars with much smaller forces that used speed and surprise to offset numerical inferiority. The problem would be that the smaller U.S. forces were ill-equipped to deal with the situation they confronted after the end of the conventional battle.

The real challenge for General Franks lay with the ground forces. At the start of the war, Iraq still had a substantial amount of armor and artillery. Iraq's troop numbers were significantly larger than the coalition's, although once all of the conventional measures of capability were included, such as air power, the opposing forces seemed more evenly matched. The original plan went through a number of iterations. Initially it entailed forces moving from the south into Iraq only, as this was part of Central Command's area of operation. However, the British pointed out that there was a northern option available: coalition forces could attack southward from Turkey. This came under U.S. European Command but was eventually accepted. The revised plan envisaged this southern movement matched with an advance from Kuwait, with the seizure of Baghdad as the primary objective. However, despite an intense diplomatic effort, the Turkish government refused access initially for the British and then subsequently for the Americans (see below for the reasoning behind this).

The plan had to be changed yet again. This time it called for an initial deployment of American, British, and Australian Special Forces into Iraq's north and west. Their aim was to cause as much confusion in the minds of the Iraqi leadership as possible and to prevent the use of weapons of mass destruction against Israel and the Gulf states. Once these units were inserted and ready to operate, an initial two-day air campaign – the "shock and awe" – that many had predicted would commence. On the ground British and U.S. Marine forces would take the al-Faw Peninsula through a combined helicopter and land assault. Their goals were to secure the key oil nodes in the south, open up the port of Umm Qasr to support the land offensive, allow humanitarian aid to be brought in, and prevent any ecological attack. After the two-day air campaign, the U.S. Third Infantry Division and the First Marine Expeditionary Force would advance on Baghdad from the south, bypassing potential pockets of resistance such as major towns and cities. Baghdad was seen as the absolute key; once the city was taken, the regime would effectively have lost control. The British division's role was to secure the southern oil fields, isolate Basra, watch the border with Iran, and act as a reserve if the U.S. forces ran into difficulty.

As in the Suez campaign, the diplomatic and military elements of the Iraq War were intertwined, which caused considerable problems on both the diplomatic and military fronts. With the passing of the Security Council's Resolution 1441, the first elements of what would become the invasion force began to deploy to the region. The pace of deployment and the diplomatic tempo began to quicken after Christmas 2002. British Secretary of State for Defence Geoff Hoon visited Turkey, where it was made clear that although U.S. forces would be able to use Turkish bases for the invasion of Iraq from the north, the British would be denied access. As a result, the British looked to provide a full division to support the invasion from the south and left the United States to run the northern option on its own.

As the military buildup continued, disagreements within the international community about how to proceed emerged into full public glare. French Foreign Minister Dominique de Villepin publicly criticized America's position. U.S. Secretary of State Colin Powell made a presentation to the Security Council in February 2003 which purported to illustrate Iraq's weapons program.[25] Most people found the presentation, unlike the satellite photographs that the United States was able to reveal during the Cuban Missile Crisis, unconvincing. Moreover, Hans Blix, head of the new UN mission in Iraq, was equally ambiguous about whether Iraq indeed had weapons of mass destruction. Both Washington and London announced further force deployments, which would bring their forces up to the strength envisaged by the Franks plan.

As tensions rose, Turkey invoked Article IV of the Washington Treaty (which formed NATO and acts as its constitution), formally seeking consultations within the alliance. Turkey requested that Patriot air defense missiles be deployed for protection against a feared Iraqi surface-to-surface missile attack.[26] France, Germany, and Belgium plunged NATO into crisis by blocking any alliance deployments to Turkey, arguing that to do otherwise was for NATO to accept the "logic of war."[27] In other words, they argued that the inspections were irrelevant and merely a pretext for a U.S.-led invasion, whereas the Security Council had set out a prescribed route involving weapon inspections. In reality, both French President Jacques Chirac and German Chancellor Gerhard Schröder were working to other agendas. Chirac wanted to isolate the United Kingdom from Europe and reinstall the Franco-German axis as the dominant power bloc within the European Union. Schröder wanted simply to be reelected. The two therefore issued a joint statement with the Russian government, calling for the UN inspectors' reinforcement.

In his February 14 report to the Security Council, Blix highlighted continuing problem areas but signaled that he was encouraged by the progress he had made with the Iraqi regime, arguing in favor of continuing an expanded inspection program.[28] In contrast, the British and American governments argued that either UNMOVIC receive cooperation in full, or the Iraqi regime would be in breach of the Security Council's resolution. A new draft resolution was tabled on February 24. The French, German, and Russian governments responded with the statement, "We will not let a proposed resolution pass that would authorize the use of force."[29] For the British government, the statement seemed wholly irresponsible since it undermined the key element encouraging Iraqi cooperation within UNMOVIC. The three governments were effectively saying that a failure to comply with Resolution 1441 would not have any further consequences. Other motives appeared more plausible.

After Hans Blix delivered his next report on Iraq's compliance on March 7, 2003,[30] the British government tried to secure agreement by arguing in favor of a series of five or six targets against which Iraqi compliance could be measured. In effect this was an argument for one final chance. The French government, however, made it clear that it would veto any resolution allowing the use of force. The British government decided to withdraw its proposals, given the inevitability of a French veto.[31] A coalition was then formed to use military force to remove the Iraqi regime and oversee its disarmament consistent with UN resolutions.

From the beginning the plan had to be changed. When information was received about the likely location of Saddam Hussein and his two sons on March 19, the coalition seemed suddenly to have the opportunity to bring the conflict to a rapid and successful conclusion. Two F-117 aircraft were tasked to strike a house where Saddam and his sons were thought to be. All three survived, and the initial order of the campaign had been thrown into confusion.

The assault on the al-Faw Peninsula took place under the leadership of the Royal Marines' 3 Commando Brigade. A nighttime helicopter assault from land and sea bases landed 40 Commandos on top of their targets, the manifold metering station and pipeline heads, which were successfully seized after a brief firefight.[32] At the same time, America's 15th Marine Expeditionary Unit moved across land from Kuwait toward the port of Umm Qasr. The port was identified as a key objective to help bring in the humanitarian relief supplies that the people of southern Iraq needed. On hearing that some of the southern oil wells had been set alight, General Franks brought the remainder of the ground offensive forward.

The attempted attack on Saddam and his sons completely altered the air campaign. Rather than preceding the invasion with the planned two-day air campaign, the ground war kicked off early and the initial air campaign supported the ground war. After a couple days, this dramatically changed. On the night of March 21, the bombing campaign against Baghdad began with munitions targeting key installations associated with the regime. The significance of these strikes lay both in their intensity and in the nature of their targets. Traditional strategic targets such as electricity and the Umm Qasr-Basra railway line were left alone because they would be needed after the war to help Iraq's rebuilding. Instead, the strikes were precisely focused on the organs of state that supported Saddam's regime, including the Republican and Special Republican Guard.

Over the first five days, U.S. forces advanced at unprecedented speed toward Baghdad, while the Rumaila oil fields in the south were secured virtually intact. The few oil wells that were set alight were rapidly dealt with by accompanying British-American-Kuwait oil crews. As the U.S. V Corps moved on to Baghdad from the southwest, it sought to avoid becoming entangled in the major urban areas. Nevertheless, it needed to seize a number of bridges in urban areas to support its supply routes. Its supply convoys came under attack by the Iraqi irregular forces called *fedayeen*, and a number of U.S. military personnel were killed or captured. After some five days, the advance appeared to stall as intense sandstorms hit Iraq. Media commentators began to talk about it being bogged down and complained about the coalition's failure to deploy sufficient troops for the task at hand.[33] In reality most advances inevitably tend to slow for the simple reason that in twenty-four-hour warfare, people eventually need to sleep. Moreover, as supply lines become longer, the ability to sustain the frontline becomes more difficult. And the slowing down was inevitable so that U.S. forces could build up their supplies before pushing through the Karbala Gap, where they expected to face the strongest resistance from the Republican Guard (including the use of weapons of mass destruction). At no point did the invasion grind to a halt, as a number of TV experts alleged, but the storms reduced visibility to zero and slowed progress.

From a coalition point of view, the delay had its plus side. As the storms hit, *fedayeen* and other irregular forces emerged from the bypassed cities to attack U.S. troops, believing that the sandstorms would allow them to achieve surprise. However, the American troops, equipped with night-vision goggles, were able to see their enemy charging, often in pickups with mounted weapons reminiscent of the vehicles used in Somalia. As a result, the *fedayeen* suffered heavy casualties, caused the Americans only minor problems, and survivors were tracked back to their bases in the cities, which precision air strikes hit. The Iraqi Republican and Special Republican Guard forces also hoped to use the weather as cover to deploy south of Baghdad to close the Karbala Gap. Again they were detected and coalition air power inflicted significant damage. Some of these units were so comprehensively hit that, with the desertions, they virtually ceased to exist as military units by the time U.S. forces met them on the ground. The Iraqis had failed to take account of the new generation of precision munitions, which could be accurately guided even through sandstorms. Nevertheless, a brigade of the 82nd Airborne Division and one of the 101st Air Assault Division were deployed to protect the vulnerable supply lines.[34] These units also provided humanitarian support to the many communities that welcomed the coalition into Iraq.

In the south, once the oil fields were secured and Basra was isolated, opening the port of Umm Qasr to bring humanitarian aid to the Iraqis became the priority. 3 Commando Brigade cleared the whole of the al-Faw Peninsula, while naval units cleared the waterway mines so the first humanitarian supplies could be delivered quickly into Umm Qasr. In addition, aid convoys were escorted to Umm Qasr, Az Zubair, and Safwan. As areas were cleared of elements of the former regime, British troops rapidly shifted away from a warfighting mode of operation to peacekeeping. British forces also secured Basra following a carefully orchestrated campaign. Rather than launch a headlong assault into the city, British forces carefully targeted the remaining elements of Saddam loyalists until the city was ready to fall. A more direct approach would have resulted in higher casualties among British personnel and Iraqi civilians. Moreover, 7 Armoured Brigade was the main heavy reserve force for the coalition until America's 4th Infantry Division arrived in Kuwait. This division had formed part of the U.S. northern force, to which Turkey subsequently decided to deny access. As a result, the advance from the north did not occur and the forces involved were rerouted via the Suez Canal to Kuwait, much to the annoyance of the Bush administration.

Instead, Kurdish forces were used to pin down Iraqi troops in northern Iraq, and the American 173rd Airborne Brigade was flown directly into the area from Italy. The brigade began a series of operations in conjunction with U.S. Special Forces and Kurdish Peshmerga guerrillas, leading to the securing of the northern oil fields and the key cities of Mosul and Kirkuk. Throughout these operations in the north, coalition partners performed a delicate balancing act between supporting the Kurds and not upsetting the Turks, who had threatened to invade if Kurdish forces alone took control of both Kirkuk and Mosul.

By April 5, American forces had reached Baghdad's outskirts. V Corps, approaching from the southwest, seized Baghdad International Airport as a supply base. (Prior to the Americans' arrival, it was named Saddam International Airport.) Aircraft were soon bringing in supplies while A-10 attack aircraft began operating from the airfield. To test the level of opposition in Baghdad, U.S. armor forces then began a series of raids into the city called "thunder runs."[35] At the same time, U.S. Marines approached the city from the southeast. During the second of the thunder runs, the U.S. forces decided that the opposition was sufficiently light and they could risk staying overnight in the city.[36] The following day the regime was effectively toppled as the relative lack of opposition became apparent and U.S. forces pushed still further into the city. The war was basically over as pockets of resistance in Baghdad were dealt with and U.S. forces moved northward to take control of Tikrit, Saddam's hometown.

At the beginning of May 2003, President Bush confirmed in a speech made aboard a U.S. aircraft carrier returning from Iraq that the war-fighting was officially over.[37] The assumption for many was that the hard work had been done. This did not prove to be the case, although Saddam Hussein's subsequent capture seemed for a time to lead to a reduction in the overall level of opposition to the coalition. In the immediate aftermath of the regime's fall, there was widespread looting in Baghdad and Basra, partly in response to years of repression. Many of the symbols of the old regime were destroyed. The looting also spread to hospitals and museums, although not always on the large scale reported in the media.

Insufficient preparations had been undertaken for this next phase of the conflict, and the speed of victory and the collapse of the Iraqi civil administration posed far greater problems than had been predicted. Moreover, the sheer scale of the rebuilding task in Iraq was not anticipated. Although the coalition had specifically sought to preserve Iraq's infrastructure, it faced the legacy of the Iran-Iraq War, the Gulf War, and UN sanctions, which meant that most public facilities had not been properly maintained for over two decades. Moreover, in the south, Saddam Hussein had deliberately starved the Shia of resources as a punishment for their uprisings after the Gulf War. The initial U.S.-led coalition authority also made a series of errors. The de-Ba'athification of the military, the police, and the civil service led to their virtual elimination and the need to recreate a complete government infrastructure. And a sizeable element of the Sunni community had lost a great deal with the prospect of a Shia-dominated state before them.

For much of Iraq the situation has significantly improved, but the seemingly slow pace of improvement has frustrated many Iraqis. The development of new political structures for Iraq has been particularly challenging.[38] The dilemma is how to encourage a democracy in which the majority's will is recognized but not at the expense of the minority's rights. A majority viewpoint would mean the domination of Iraq by the Shia to the frustration of the Sunni minority, historically used to being in control. In January 2005 the first democratic elections in decades were held to elect an interim authority tasked with drafting a new constitution. Since then, elections have been conducted largely peacefully, although participation within the Sunni community has sometimes been disappointing.

However, opposition to the interim government, subsequent governments, and the coalition forces has remained, requiring the retention of a large foreign-military presence in Iraq with an urgent requirement to rebuild the Iraqi army, border, and civilian police forces. As the violence increased, the coalition unsuccessfully looked for international support to help reduce the overall burden. The results were mixed: a significant number of countries supplied forces, but few were willing to take overall responsibility for the country's major sectors. Moreover, as casualties among coalition forces grew, a series of partners withdrew their forces. As a result, the coalition has now focused on the training of indigenous security forces to provide for long-term security. While the existing coalition has shouldered much of the burden, the security situation has generally deteriorated and resulted in Bush's 2007 move toward a troop surge in Iraq to try and halt the spiraling level of violence. There is now, during Barack Obama's presidency, concern among coalition leaders that the coalition is confronted with the prospect of strategic failure in Iraq and a destabilized Middle East. This was underlined by the withdrawal of British troops from Iraq in 2009 and the American plan to withdraw in 2011 or 2012.

The 2003 war in Iraq showed the interaction of diplomacy with the threatened and actual use of force. From the moment the British successfully shifted the Bush administration's thinking toward obtaining UN support in September 2002, the diplomatic effort had the countdown to war in the background. In particular, much of the British buildup was directly linked to the diplomatic campaign with successive deployment announcements linked to Iraqi noncompliance with the UN weapon inspectors. Even more stark was the situation in March 2003. As the British pushed for a second resolution, they were faced with calls from various nations demanding that more time be given to the weapon inspectors. At the same time, they were aware of the military preference for fighting before the fast-approaching Iraqi summer. In the end the diplomacy was halted and the military was given the go-ahead to conduct operations, primarily because the size of the military force deployed was unsustainable for very long and the troops sitting in bases in Kuwait had to be either used in war or withdrawn. In other words, this campaign showed not only how diplomacy can shape the use of armed forces, but also how the military's needs can shape diplomacy.

The Iraq War has also shown the importance once again of not only winning the military war but also winning the peace. The emphasis on the humanitarian and media elements reflect this. The Iraq War has shown that parallel rather than sequential warfare, with forces having to engage in a variety of different operational activities simultaneously, is here to stay. This requires not only joint forces, but also different elements of government to be brought together to operate within the conflict. It means that military commanders in the field need to be even more aware of the political dynamic of their actions and to take this into account. The failures in nation-building were largely the result of bureaucratic infighting, particularly in Washington and also London.

CONCLUSION

This volume has shown that there is no neat division between war and diplomacy: they are interconnected and their relationship is not always symbiotic. When the military theorist Carl von Clausewitz referred to war as "the continuation of politics by other means," he was emphasizing that war, like diplomacy, is an instrument that a government will use to try and achieve its own political goals. War – and more generally the use of force – should therefore be used, in theory, to complement and sometimes replace diplomacy as a means of achieving the desired goal. For example, the Argentine junta's decision to use military force to take control of the Falklands/Malvinas was, in part, the result of a failure to achieve their transition to Argentina via diplomatic means.

The various case studies have shown that war is an exceptionally blunt instrument. Yet it is an instrument that is frequently grasped when diplomacy fails to deliver what one or more of the protagonists want and they have effectively run out of ideas. In other words, rather than being used to reinforce diplomacy, war is frequently used when diplomacy is perceived to have failed, with the implicit assumption that diplomacy then ends until the war resolves itself. However, war will, at best, leave one state victorious and one defeated. It is unlikely to resolve the war's basic causes. Diplomacy, as part of conflict resolution, will still be needed to avoid further conflict in the future. For example, while the British may have been victorious in the 1982 Falklands conflict, the basic dispute over ownership remains, tensions between Argentina and the United Kingdom continue to periodically resurface, and the British now feel obliged to maintain a substantial military presence on the islands.

This volume has also shown that war remains a far less predictable instrument than diplomacy. Few imagined before the Falklands conflict that a British government that had continuously sought to offload the islands would fight to regain them. More generally war as an instrument has its own dynamic and own requirements. Both Iraq and Kosovo show how a crisis can at times become a side issue within the wider international system. In Kosovo that issue became NATO's credibility and whether it would survive as an international organization. In Iraq the use of the military buildup as a mechanism of trying to coerce Saddam ultimately failed and also limited the diplomacy. By March 2003 the U.S.-led coalition had deployed significant forces to the region, which could not be left indefinitely at their desert staging posts. For the United Kingdom, in particular, it was a case of using the military instrument or withdrawing the troops. The challenge for many politicians is how war and the threat of war can be harnessed as part of a diplomatic process without placing too many limitations on that process.

There is also the question of where diplomacy fits within a war. The stop-start element to the U.S. air campaign in Vietnam is a good example of how the diplomatic effort can at times undermine the military effort. It is also clear that diplomacy must continue throughout a conflict if some sort of political solution is ultimately to be achieved. As Iraq now shows, rarely does one side so defeat another that a war cannot be continued if the other party so wishes. Moreover, as the dynamic of the war itself develops, so too do the goals of the protagonists and also those outside. It is, therefore, necessary for future commanders to be fully aware of the political consequences of their proposed actions and to understand the context in which they operate and the political ends they want to achieve.

Diplomats as well must be vigilant to ensure that their continued role within the war-fighting environment is not seen as irrelevant until the shooting stops. When the military and political aspects of the attempts to restrict the use of force diverge, each working in its own solitude, the tendency for failure in both the military and the diplomatic realms is enhanced immeasurably. To wage war of any size or scale without a clear political objective that is achieved by a combination of diplomacy and military power, as well as the application of other types of power, all still tied to the diplomacy and negotiation required to achieve a peace, is the height of folly. These case studies have outlined some of the successes and failures in that relationship and may serve as a useful guide for practitioners of all sorts involved in the task of creating and maintaining peace.

NOTES

The Origins of the First World War

[1] E.L. Woodward, *Short Journey* (Oxford: Oxford University Press, 1942), 72-73.

[2] Joachim Remak, *Sarajevo: The Story of a Political Murder* (London: Weidenfeld & Nicolson, 1959); Vladimir Dedijer, *The Road to Sarajevo* (New York: MacGibbon & Kee, 1966).

[3] David MacKenzie, *Apis: The Congenial Conspirator: The Life of Colonel Dragutin T. Dimitrijević* (Boulder, Colorado: East European Monographs, 1989).

[4] Nicolson to de Bunsen (private), July 20, 1914, De Bunsen Mss, Bodleian Library, Oxford, De Bunsen 15; D.C. Watt, "British Press Reactions to the Assassination at Sarajevo," *European Studies Quarterly* 1, no. 3 (1971), 22-40.

[5] H. Kohn, *Nationalism: Its Meaning and History* (Princeton, New Jersey: Van Nostrand, 1965), 9.

[6] Matthew S. Anderson, *The Eastern Question, 1774-1923: A Study in International Relations* (London: St. Martin's Press, 1966); Barbara Jelavich, *History of the Balkans* (Cambridge: Cambridge University Press, 1983), 1:171-376; Nadine Lange-Akhund, *The Macedonian Question, 1893-1908* (Boulder, Colorado: East European Monographs, 1998), 146-155; F.R. Bridge, "Izvolsky, Aehrenthal, and the End of the Austro-Russian Entente, 1906-08," *Mitteilungen des Österreichischen Staatsarchivs* 29 (1976), 315-362.

[7] Owen Chadwick, *The Secularization of the European Mind in the 19th Century* (Cambridge: Cambridge University Press, 1995); Nicholas Mansergh, *The Unresolved Question: The Anglo-Irish Settlement and Its Undoing, 1912-72* (New Haven, Connecticut: Yale University Press, 1991), 43-78; Eric Cahm, *The Dreyfus Affair in French Society and Politics* (London: Longman, 1996); James N. Retallack, *Notables of the Right: The Conservative Party and Political Mobilization in Germany, 1876-1918* (Boston: Unwin Hyman, 1988); Edward C. Thaden, *Russification in the Baltic Provinces and Finland, 1885-1914* (Princeton, New Jersey: Princeton University Press, 1981), 54-87; Arthur J. May, *The Hapsburg Monarchy, 1867-1914* (Cambridge, Massachusetts: Harvard University Press, 1951), 362-385.

[8] David Gates, *Warfare in the Nineteenth Century* (Basingstoke, United Kingdom: Palgrave Macmillan, 2001); Hew Strachan, *European Armies and the Conduct of War* (London: Allen & Unwin, 1983), 108-129.

[9] Figures compiled from B.R. Mitchell with Phyllis Deane, *Abstract of British Historical Statistics* (Cambridge: Cambridge University Press, 1962), 8-11; Hans-Ulrich Wehler, *Deutsche Gesellschaftsgeschichte* (Munich: C.H. Beck, 1987-2003), 3:494-503; Andre Armengaud, *La Population française au XIXe siècle* (Paris: Presses Universitaires de France, 1971), 115. The figures for Russia exclude the Grand Duchy of Finland and the Central Asian protectorates. The data for Austria-Hungary, France, and Russia were taken from the contemporary statistics in the *Encyclopaedia Britannica*, 11th ed. (1911).

[10] T.G. Otte and Keith Neilson, eds., *Railways and International Politics: Paths of Empire, 1848-1945* (London: Routledge, 2006);

Allan Mitchell, *The Great Train Race: Railways and the Franco-German Rivalry, 1815-1914* (New York: Berghahn, 2000); Denis E. Showalter, *Railroads and Rifles: Soldiers, Technology and the Unification of Germany* (Hamden, Connecticut: Archon, 1975).

[11] Andrew Porter, *European Imperialism, 1860-1914* (Basingstoke, United Kingdom: Macmillan, 1994); Ronald Robinson and John Gallagher, *Africa and the Victorians: The Official Mind of Imperialism*, 2nd ed. (London: Macmillan, 1981); John Darwin, "Imperialism and the Victorians: The Dynamics of Territorial Expansion," *English Historical Review* 112, no. 3 (1997), 614-642.

[12] Michael R. Gordon, "Domestic Conflict and the Origins of the First World War: The British and German Cases," *Journal of Modern History* 46, no. 3 (1974), 191-226; Volker R. Berghahn, *Germany and the Approach of War in 1914*, 2nd ed. (London: Palgrave Macmillan, 1993); Dietrich Geyer, *Russian Imperialism: The Interaction of Domestic and Foreign Policy, 1860-1914* (Leamington Spa, United Kingdom: Berg, 1987); Arno J. Mayer, *The Persistence of the Old Regime: Europe to the Great War* (London: Pantheon, 1981).

[13] David Stevenson, *Armaments and the Coming of War: Europe, 1904-14* (Oxford: Oxford University Press, 1996); David G. Herrmann, *The Arming of Europe and the Making of the First World War* (Princeton, New Jersey: Princeton University Press, 1996); Peter Gatrell, *Government, Industry and Rearmament in Russia, 1900-14: The Last Argument of Tsarism* (Cambridge: Cambridge University Press, 1994); Gerd Krumeich, *Armaments and Politics in France on the Eve of the First World War: The Introduction of Three-Year Conscription* (Leamington Spa, United Kingdom: Berg, 1984).

[14] Lauren Sondhaus, *Naval Warfare, 1815-1914* (London: Taylor & Francis, 2001).

[15] Paul M. Kennedy, *The Rise of the Anglo-German Antagonism, 1860-1914* (London: Allen & Unwin, 1980); E.L. Woodward, *Great Britain and the German Navy, 1898-1912* (London: Faber & Faber, 1964); John H. Maurer, "Churchill's Naval Holiday: Arms Control and the Anglo-German Naval Race, 1912-14," *Journal of Strategic Studies* 15, no. 2 (1992), 102-127.

[16] George Frost Kennan, *The Fateful Alliance: France, Russia, and the Coming of the First World War* (Manchester, United Kingdom: Manchester University Press, 1984); Holger Afflerbach, *Der Dreibund. Europäische Großmacht–und Allianzpolitik vor dem Ersten Weltkrieg* (Vienna: Böhlau Verlag, 2002).

[17] Ian Nash, *The Origins of the Russo-Japanese War*, 2nd ed. (London: Longman, 1987); Keith Neilson, "'A Dangerous Game of American Poker': Britain and the Russo-Japanese War," *Journal of Strategic Studies* 12, no. 1 (1989), 63-87; T.G. Otte, "The Fragmenting of the Old World Order: Britain, the Great Powers and the War," in Rotem Kowner, ed., *The Impact of the Russo-Japanese War* (London: Routledge, 2006), 91-108.

[18] Christopher Andrew, *Théophile Delcassé and the Making of the Entente Cordiale* (London: Macmillan, 1996); T.G. Otte, "The Elusive Balance: British Foreign Policy and the Entente before the First World War," in Alan Sharp and Glyn Stone, eds., *Anglo-French Relations in the Twentieth Century: Rivalry and Cooperation* (London: Taylor & Francis, 2001), 471-504; idem., "From 'War-in-Sight' to Nearly War: Anglo-French Relations in the Age of High Imperialism, 1875-98," *Diplomacy & Statecraft* 17, no. 4 (2006), 693-714.

[19] Heiner Raulff, *Zwischen Machtpolitik und Imperialismus: Die deutsche Frankreich-Politik, 1904-06* (Düsseldorf: Droste, 1976).

[20] S.L. Mayers, "Anglo-German Rivalry at the Algeciras Conference," in Posser Gifford and William Roger Louis, eds., *Britain and Germany in Africa: Imperial Rivalry and Colonial Rule* (New Haven, Connecticut: Yale University Press, 1967), 215-244; Samuel R. Williamson, *The Politics of Grand Strategy: Britain and France Prepare for War, 1904-14* (London: Ashfield, 1990), 59-88; T.G. Otte, "'Almost a Law of Nature?' Sir Edward Grey, the Foreign Office, and the Balance of Power in Europe, 1905-12," in Brian J.C. McKercher and Eric Goldstein, eds., *Power and Stability: British Foreign Policy, 1865-1965* (London: Frank Cass, 2003), 85-89.

[21] W.N. Medlicott, *The Congress of Berlin and After: A Diplomatic History of the Near Eastern Settlement, 1878-80*, 2nd ed. (London: Longman, 1963); F.A.K. Yasamee, *Ottoman Diplomacy: Abdülhamid II and the Great Powers, 1878-88* (Istanbul: Isis, 1996); F.R. Bridge, "Austria-Hungary and the Ottoman Empire in the Twentieth Century," *Mitteilungen des Österreichischen Staatsarchivs* 34 (1981), 234-240.

[22] Bernadotte E. Schmitt, *The Annexation of Bosnia* (Cambridge: Cambridge University Press, 1937); Norman Stone, "Moltke-Conrad: Relations between the Austro-Hungarian and German Staffs, 1909-14," *Historical Journal* 9, no. 3 (1996), 201-228; F.R. Bridge, Die jungtürkische Revolution aus öster-reichischen-ungarischer Sicht," *Österreichischen Osthefte* 38, no. 1 (1996), 23-52.

[23] M.L. Dockrill, „British Policy during the Agadir Crisis of 1911," in Francis H. Hinsley, ed., *British Foreign Policy under Sir Edward Grey* (Cambridge: Cambridge University Press, 1977),

271-287; Richard C. Hall, *The Balkan Wars, 1912-13: Prelude to the First World War* (London: Frank Cass, 2000); J.C.G. Röhl, "Admiral von Müller and the Approach of War, 1911-14" *Historical Journal* 12, no. 4 (1969), 651-673.

[24] Gerhard Ritter, *The Schlieffen Plan* (London: Oswald Wolff, 1958); Annika Mombauer, *Helmuth von Moltke and the Origins of the First World War* (Cambridge: Cambridge University Press, 2001); Terence Zuber, *Inventing the Schlieffen Plan: German War Planning, 1870-1914* (Oxford: Oxford University Press, 2002). For critiques of Zuber, see Hans Ehlert, Michael Epkenhans, and Gerhard P. Gross, eds., *Der Schlieffenplan: Analysen und Dokumente* (Paderborn, Germany: Ferdinand Schöningh, 2006).

[25] Fritz Fischer, *Germany's Aims in the First World War* (London: Norton, 1975); F.R. Bridge, *The Hapsburg Monarchy among the Great Powers, 1815-18* (New York: Oxford University Press, 1990); Norman Stone, "Hungary and the July Crisis 1914," *Journal of Contemporary History* 1, no. 2 (1966), 153-170; Samuel R. Williamson Jr., "Vienna and July 1914: The Origins of the Great War Once More," in idem. And Peter Pastor, ed., *Essays on World War I: Origins and Prisoners of War* (New York: St. Martin's Press, 1983), 8-36.

[26] Jack Snyder, *The Ideology of the Offensive: Military Decision-Making and the Disasters of 1914* (Ithaca, New York: Cornell University Press, 1984); L.C.F. Turner, "The Role of the General Staffs in July 1914," *Australian Journal of History and Politics* 11, no. 3 (1965), 305-323; Jack S. Levy, Thomas S. Christensen, and Marc Trachtenberg, "Mobilization and Inadvertence in the July Crisis," *International Security* 16, no. 2 (1991), 189-203; Steven E. Miller et al., eds., *Military Strategy and the Origins of*

the First World War, rev. ed. (Princeton, New Jersey: Princeton University Press, 1991).

[27] David Stevenson, "War by Timetable? The Railway Race Before 1914," *Past & Present* 162 (1999); D.C.B. Lieven, *Russia and the Origins of the First World War*, rev. ed. (London: Palgrave Macmillan, 1987), 139-151; Zara S. Steiner and Keith Neilson, *Britain and the Origins of the First World War*, 2nd ed. (Basingstoke, United Kingdom: Palgrave Macmillan, 2003), 229-257.

The Origins of the Second World War

[1] See, for example, the two contributions in the Longmans Origins of Modern Wars series: Akira Iriye, *The Origins of the Second World War in Asia and the Pacific* (London: Longman, 1987); and P.M.H. Bell, *The Origins of the Second World War in Europe*, 2nd ed. (London: Longman, 1997).

[2] The approach taken in the valuable work edited by Robert Boyce and Joseph A. Maiolo, *The Origins of World War Two: The Debate Continues* (Basingstoke, United Kingdom: Palgrave, 2003).

[3] Francis Harris Hinsley, *Power and the Pursuit of Peace: Theory and Practice in the History of Relations between States* (Cambridge: Cambridge University Press, 1963), 289-308.

[4] For two accounts that introduce the literature, see Manfred F. Boemeke, Gerald D. Feldman, and Elisabeth Glaser, *The Treaty of Versailles: A Reassessment after 75 Years* (Cambridge: Cambridge University Press, 1998); and Michael Dockrill and John Fischer, eds., *The Paris Peace Conference, 1919. Peace without Victory?* (Basingstoke, United Kingdom: Palgrave, 2001).

[5] A.J.P. Taylor, *The Origins of the Second World War* (London: Hamish Hamilton, 1961).

[6] Geoffrey Roberts, "Military Disaster as a Function of Rational Political Calculation: Stalin and 22 June 1941," *Diplomacy and Statecraft* 4, no. 2 (1993), 313-330; Evan Mawdsley, "Crossing the Rubicon: Soviet Plans for Offensive War in 1940-41," *International History Review* 25, no. 4 (2003), 817-865; and Brian Villa and Timothy Wilford, "Signals Intelligence and Pearl Harbor: The State of the Question," *Intelligence and National Security*, 21, no. 4 (2006), 520-556.

[7] The approach used in Keith Neilson, *Britain, Soviet Russia and the Collapse of the Versailles Order, 1919-39* (Cambridge: Cambridge University Press, 2006). See also E.H. Carr, *The Twenty Years' Crisis, 1919-39: An Introduction to the Study of International Relations* (London: Macmillan, 1939).

[8] The key work here is Alan Cassels, *Ideology and International Relations in the Modern World* (London: Routledge, 1996).

[9] This is the approach taken by Zara Steiner in her magisterial *The Lights That Failed: European International History, 1919-33* (Oxford: Oxford University Press, 2005). Steiner is essential reading for anyone interested in the period. A second volume, *The Triumph of the Dark*, covering the period from 1933 to 1939, is being published in late 2010.

[10] Erik Goldstein and John Mauer, eds., *The Washington Conference, 1921-22* (London: Frank Cass, 1992); Dick Richardson, *The Evolution of British Disarmament Policy in the 1920s* (London: Pinter, 1989); Carolyn J. Kitching, *Britain and the Geneva Disarmament Conference* (Basingstoke, United Kingdom: Palgrave, 2003);

Emily O. Goldman, *Sunken Treaties: Naval Arms Control between the Wars* (Philadelphia: Pennsylvania State University Press, 1994).

[11] The classic work is Jon Jacobson, *Locarno Diplomacy: Germany and the West, 1925-29* (Princeton, New Jersey: Princeton University Press, 1972). The subsequent literature is best pursued via Gaynor Johnson, ed., *Locarno Revisited: European Diplomacy, 1920-29* (London: Routledge, 2004).

[12] Robert Self, *Britain, America and the War Debt Controversy: The Economic Diplomacy of an Unspecial Relationship, 1917-41* (London: Routledge, 2006), replaces the older literature.

[13] Ian Nish, *Japan's Struggle with Internationalism: Japan, China and the League of Nations, 1931-33* (London: Kegan Paul International, 1993).

[14] Patricia Clavin, *The Failure of Economic Diplomacy: Britain, Germany, France and the United States, 1931-36* (Basingstoke, United Kingdom: St. Martin's Press, 1996).

[15] Keith Neilson, "The Defence Requirements Sub-Committee, British Strategic Foreign Policy, Neville Chamberlain and the Path to Appeasement," *English Historical Review* 118, no. 477 (2003), 651-684; David G. Anderson, "British Rearmament and the 'Merchants of Death': The 1935-36 Royal Commission on the Manufacture of and Trade in Armaments," *Journal of Contemporary History* 29 (1994), 5-37.

[16] Joseph A. Maiolo, *The Royal Navy and Nazi Germany, 1933-39: A Study in Appeasement and the Origins of the Second World War* (London: Macmillan, 1998), 11-37; Greg Kennedy, "Becoming Dependent on the Kindness of Strangers: Britain's Strategic

Foreign Policy, Naval Arms Limitation and the Soviet Factor: 1935-37," *War in History* 1, 1 (2004), 34-60.

[17] Robert Mallett, *Mussolini and the Origins of the Second World War, 1933-40* (Basingstoke, United Kingdom: Palgrave Macmillan, 2003), 18-19, 63-64.

[18] Jill Edwards, *The British Government and the Spanish Civil War, 1936-39* (London: Macmillan, 1979); Christian Leitz and David J. Dunthorn, eds., *Spain in an International Context, 1936-59* (New York: Berghahn, 1999).

[19] Antony Best, *Britain, Japan and Pearl Harbour: Avoiding War in East Asia, 1936-41* (London: Routledge, 1995), 27-28.

[20] G. Bruce Strang, *On the Fiery March: Mussolini Prepares for War* (Westport, Connecticut: Praeger, 2003), 60, 73.

[21] Chamberlain's career and policy are best followed in Robert Self, *Neville Chamberlain: A Biography* (Aldershot, United Kingdom: Ashgate, 2006).

[22] Greg Kennedy, "'Rat in Power': Neville Chamberlain and the Creation of British Policy, 1931-39," in T.G. Otte, ed., *The Makers of British Foreign Policy: From Pitt to Thatcher* (Basingstoke, United Kingdom: Palgrave, 2002), 173-189.

[23] The useful study of Anglo-American relations in the 1930s is Greg Kennedy, *Anglo-American Strategic Relations and the Far East, 1933-39: Imperial Crossroads* (London: Frank Cass, 2002); for Eden, see 229-241.

[24] Andrew J. Crozier, *Appeasement and Germany's Last Bid for Colonies* (Basingstoke, United Kingdom: Macmillan, 1998).

[25] Reynolds M. Salerno, *Vital Crossroads: Mediterranean Origins of the Second World War, 1935-40* (Ithaca, New York: Cornell University Press, 2002), 49-59.

[26] For Munich, see Watt, *How War Came*, passim; Neilson, *Collapse of the Versailles Order*, 241-253; and Peter Jackson, *France and the Nazi Menace: Intelligence and Policy Making, 1933-39* (Oxford: Oxford University Press, 2000), 278-289.

[27] Compare R.A.C. Parker, *Chamberlain and Appeasement: British Policy and the Coming of the Second World War* (Basingstoke, United Kingdom: Macmillan, 1993), and George C. Peden, *British Rearmament and the Treasury* (Edinburgh: Scottish Academic Press, 1979). For a discussion, see Crozier, *Causes of the Second World War*, 226-259.

[28] Talbot C. Imlay, *Facing the Second World War: Strategy, Politics, and Economics in Britain and France, 1938-40* (Oxford: Oxford University Press, 2003), 135-185; Jackson, *France and the Nazi Menace*, 337-378.

[29] Neilson, *Collapse of the Versailles Order*, 280-317.

[30] Best, *Britain, Japan*, 71-86.

[31] Neville Wylie, ed., *European Neutrals and Non-Belligerents during the Second World War* (Cambridge: Cambridge University Press, 2002).

[32] Alvin D. Coox, *Nomonhan: Japan Against Russia, 1939* (Stanford, California: Stanford University Press, 1985).

[33] Patrick R. Osborn, *Operation Pike: Britain Versus the Soviet Union, 1939-41* (Westport, Connecticut: Greenwood Press,

2000); Gabriel Gorodetsky, *Grand Delusion: Stalin and the German Invasion of Russia* (New Haven, Connecticut: Yale University Press, 1999).

[34] Nicholas Tarling, *Britain, Southeast Asia and the Onset of the Pacific War* (Cambridge: Cambridge University Press, 1996), 123-192.

[35] Antony Best, *British Intelligence and the Japanese Challenge in Asia, 1914-41* (Basingstoke, United Kingdom: Palgrave, 2002), 160-187.

Anglo-American Diplomacy, 1939-45

[1] Greg Kennedy, *Anglo-American Strategic Relations and the Far East, 1933-39: Imperial Crossroads* (London: Frank Cass, 2002); Greg Kennedy and Keith Neilson, eds., *Incidents and International Relations: Personalities, Perceptions and Power* (New York: Praeger-Greenwood Press, 2002); Keith Neilson, *Britain, Soviet Russia and the Collapse of the Versailles Order, 1919-39* (Cambridge: Cambridge University Press, 2006).

[2] Kevin Smith, *Conflict Over Convoys: Anglo-American Logistics Diplomacy in the Second World War* (Cambridge: Cambridge University Press, 1996).

[3] W.N. Medlicott, *The Economic Blockade*, 2 vols. (London: Her Majesty's Stationery Office, 1952-59); George C. Peden, *Arms, Economics and British Strategy: From Dreadnoughts to Hydrogen Bombs* (Cambridge: Cambridge University Press, 2007); Arnold Hague, *The Allied Convoy System, 1939-45: Its Organization, Defense and Operation* (Annapolis, Maryland: Naval Institute Press, 2000).

4   Warren F. Kimball, *The Most Unsordid Act: Lend-Lease, 1939-41* (Baltimore: Johns Hopkins University Press, 1969); J.R.M. Butler, *Grand Strategy*, vol. 2, *September 1939-June 1941* (London: Her Majesty's Stationery Office, 1957).

5   Basil Collier, *The Lion and the Eagle: British and Anglo-American Strategy, 1900-50* (London: MacDonald Publishing, 1972); William Roger Louis, *British Strategy in the Far East, 1919-39* (London: Clarendon, 1971); idem, *Imperialism at Bay, 1941-45: The United States and the Decolonization of the British Empire* (Oxford: Oxford University Press, 1977); Paul Haggie, *Britannia at Bay: The Defence of Britain's Far Eastern Empire, 1919-41* (Oxford: Oxford University Press, 1981); Christopher Thorne, *Allies of a Kind: The United States, Britain and the War against Japan, 1941-45* (Hamish Hamilton, 1978); Robert Dallek, *Franklin D. Roosevelt and American Foreign Policy, 1932-45* (Oxford: Oxford University Press, 1979).

6   Halifax Papers, Borthewick Research Institute, York, United Kingdom, A7.8.19 "Most secret" wartime dieraies, 1941-45. Dec. 27, 1941.

7   There is material throughout Robert E. Sherwood, *The White House Papers of Harry L. Hopkins: An Intimate History*, vols. 1 and 2, *September 1939-July 1945* (London: Eyre & Spottiswoode, 1948, 1949), that speaks to this issue. See also, Warren F. Kimball, ed., *Churchill & Roosevelt: The Complete Correspondence*, 3 vols. (London: Collins, 1984-88).

8   George C. Marshall, "Selected Speeches and Statements of General of the Army George C. Marshall: Chief of Staff, United States Army," *Infantry Journal*, 1945; Forrest C. Pogue, *George C. Marshall*, 3 vols. (London: MacGibbon & Kee, 1964,

1967, 1987); Thomas B. Buell, *Master of Sea Power: A Biography of Fleet Admiral Ernest J. King* (Annapolis, Maryland: Naval Institute Press, 1995); Henry Adams, *Witness to Power: The Life of Fleet Admiral William D. Leahy* (Annapolis: Maryland: Naval Institute Press, 1985); William D. Leahy, *I Was There: The Personal Story of the Chief of Staff to Presidents Roosevelt and Truman, Based on His Notes and Diaries Made at the Time* (London: Gollancz, 1950).

[9] David Reynolds, Warren Kimball, A.O. Chubarian, *Allies at War: The Soviet, American, and British Experience, 1939-45* (New York: St. Martin's Press, 1994); Alex Danchev, *Very Special Relationship: Field-Marshal Sir John Dill and the Anglo-American Alliance, 1941-44* (London: Brassey's Ltd., 1986); Alex Danchev and Daniel Todman, eds., *War Diaries, 1939-45: Field Marshal Lord Alanbrooke* (Berkely: University of California Press, 2001); Alex Danchev, *On Specialness: Essays in Anglo-American Relations* (New York: St. Martin's Press, 1998).

[10] Dwight D. Eisenhower, *The Papers of Dwight David Eisenhower: The War Years, 1941-45*, 5 vols., Alfred D. Chandler Jr., ed. (Baltimore: Johns Hopkins University Press, 1970); Patrick G. E. Murray, *Eisenhower versus Montgomery: The Continuing Debate* (Westport, Connecticut: Praeger, 1996); Nigel Hamilton, *Master of the Battlefield: Monty's War Years, 1942-44* (New York: McGraw-Hill, 1983); Martin Blumenson, *The Patton Papers*, vol. 2, *1940-45* (New York: Da Capo Press, 1996); Omar N. Bradley and Clay Blair, *A General's Life* (London: Sidgwick & Jackson, 1983).

[11] Raymond E. Lee, *The London Observer: The London Journal of General Raymond E. Lee, 1940-41* (Boston: Little, Brown, 1971); Ted Schwarz, *Joseph P. Kennedy: The Mogul, the Mob, the Statesman, and the Making of an American Myth* (Hoboken, New Jersey: Wiley, 2003).

[12] John G. Winant, *A Letter from Grosvenor Square* (London: Hodder & Stoughton, 1947); George Bilainkin, *Diary of a Diplomatic Correspondent* (London: Allen & Unwin, 1942); idem, *Second Diary of a Diplomatic Correspondent* (London: Sampson, Low, Marston, 1946).

[13] Ian Cowman, *Dominion or Decline: Anglo-American Naval Relations on the Pacific, 1937-41* (Oxford: Berg, 1996); Roy F. Harrod, *The Life of John Maynard Keynes* (London: Macmillan, 1951); Steven B. Shepard, *American, British, Dutch, and Australian Coalition: Unsuccessful Band of Brothers* (Fort Leavenworth, Kansas: Army Command and General Staff College, 2003); Robert Skidelsky, *John Maynard Keynes: Fighting for Freedom, 1937-46* (New York: Penguin, 2000).

[14] Edward Frederick Lindley Wood, *Fullness of Days* (London: Collins, 1957); David Reynolds, *Lord Lothian and Anglo-American Relations, 1939-40* (Philadelphia: American Philosophical Society, 1983); Royal Institute of International Affairs, *The American Speeches of Lord Lothian, July 1939 to December 1940* (London: Oxford University Press, 1941).

[15] Winston Churchill, *The Second World War*, vol. 4, *The Hinge of Fate* (Boston: Houghton Mifflin, 1950), 569; H.P. Willmott, *Empires in the Balance: Japanese and Allied Pacific Strategies to April 1942* (Annapolis, Maryland: Naval Institute Press, 1982).

[16] James Leutze, *Bargaining for Supremacy: Anglo-American Naval Collaboration, 1937-41* (Chapel Hill: North Carolina Press, 1977); David Reynolds, *The Creation of the Anglo-American Alliance, 1937-41: A Study in Competitive Cooperation* (Chapel Hill: University of North Carolina Press, 1982).

[17] John Wheeler-Bennett, *Special Relationships: America in Peace and War* (London, Macmillan, 1975); Frederick Leith-Ross, *Money Talks* (London: Hutchinson, 1968); Alan P. Dobson, *The Politics of the Anglo-American Economic Special Relationship, 1940-87* (New York: St. Martin's Press, 1987); idem, *U.S. Wartime Aid to Britain, 1940-46* (New York: St. Martin's Press, 1986).

[18] Nicholas Cull, *Selling War: The British Propaganda Campaign against American "Neutrality" in World War II* (Oxford: Oxford University Press, 1995); William H. McNeill, *America, Britain and Russia: their Cooperation and Conflict 1941-46* (Oxford: Oxford University Press, 1953), 129-150.

[19] Theodore A. Wilson, *The First Summit: Roosevelt and Churchill at Placentia Bay, 1941* (Lawrence: University of Kansas Press, 1991).

[20] Kimball, *Churchill & Roosevelt*, vol. 1, *Alliance Emerging, October 1933-November 1942*; David J. Bercuson and Hoger Herwig, *One Christmas in Washington: Churchill and Roosevelt Forge the Grand Alliance* (London: Weidenfeld & Nicolson, 2005).

[21] H.G. Nicholas, ed., *Washington Despatches, 1941-45: Weekly Political Reports from the British Embassy* (London: Weidenfeld & Nicolson, 1981), entry for Jan. 5, 1942, 10.

[22] Mark A. Stoler, *Allies and Adversaries: The Joint Chiefs of Staff, the Grand Alliance, and U.S. Strategy in World War II* (Chapel Hill: University of North Carolina Press, 2000); Andrew B. Cunningham, *A Sailor's Odyssey: The Autobiography of Admiral of the Fleet Viscount Cunningham of Hyndhope* (New York: Dutton, 1951); Michael Simpson, ed., *The Cunningham Papers, 1942-46*, vol. 2 (Aldershot, United Kingdom: Navy Records Society /

Ashgate, 2006); idem., *The Somerville Papers* (Aldershot, United Kingdom: Navy Records Society / Ashgate, 1995).

[23] Marc Milner, *Battle of the Atlantic* (Stroud, United Kingdom: Tempus, 2005); W.J.R. Gardner, *Decoding History: the Battle of the Atlantic and Ultra* (Annapolis, Maryland: Naval Institute Press, 1999); Samuel E. Morison, *History of United States Naval Operations in World War II*, vol. 10, *The Atlantic Battle Won, May 1943-May 1945* (Oxford: Oxford University Press, 1956).

[24] Richard Overy, *Why the Allies Won* (New York: Norton, 1995); Evan Mawdsley, *Thunder in the East: The Nazi-Soviet War, 1941-46* (London: Arnold, 2005).

[25] Mark A. Stoler, *The Politics of the Second Front: American Military Planning and Diplomacy in Coalition Warfare, 1941-43* (Westport, Connecticut: Praeger, 1977); Keith Sainsbury, *The Turning Point: Roosevelt, Stalin, Churchill, and Chiang Kai-Shek, 1943: The Moscow, Cairo and Teheran Conferences* (New York: Oxford University Press, 1986); Danchev and Todman, *War Diaries, 1939-45*.

[26] Gill Bennett, *Churchill's Man of Mystery: Desmond Morton and the World of Intelligence* (London: Routledge, 2007); John DeNovo, "The Culbertson Economic Mission and Anglo-American Tensions in the Middle East, 1944-45," *Journal of American History* 63 (March 1977), 913-936.

[27] Frances Perkins, *The Roosevelt I Knew* (New York: Viking, 1946), 81-85; David Dilks, ed., *the Diaries of Sir Alexander Cadogan, 1938-45* (New York: Cassell, 1972), 580-585; John Charmley, *Chruchill's Grand Alliance: The Anglo-American Special Relationship, 1940-57* (New York: Harcourt Brace, 1995).

[28] Williamson Murray and Allan R. Millett, *A War to Be Won: Fighting the Second World War* (Cambridge, Massachusetts: Belknap Press, 2000); Randall B. Woods, *A Changing of the Guard: Anglo-American Relations, 1941-46* (Chapel Hill: University of North Carolina Press, 1990).

[29] Terry H. Anderson, *The United States, Great Britain and the Cold War, 1944-47* (Columbia: University of Missouri Press, 1981); David B. Woolner, ed., *The Second Quebec Conference Revisited: Waging War, Formulating Peace: Canada, Great Britain and the United States, 1944-45* (New York, St. Martin's Press, 1988); D.C. Watt, "Britain and the Historiography of the Yalta Conference and the Cold War," *Diplomatic History* 13 (1989), 67-98; Andrew Whitfield, *Hong Kong, Empire and the Anglo-American Alliance at War, 1941-45* (Basingstoke, United Kingdom: Palgrave, 2001).

The Algerian War

[1] An important contribution to the field is the mammoth edited collection *La guerre d'Algérie, 1954-2004: La fin de l'amnésie*, Mohammed Harbi and Benjamin Stora, eds. (Paris: Hachette, 2004).

[2] The best account of the talks, written from the perspective of a key Algerian participant, is Redha Malek, *L'Algérie à Evian: Histoire des négociations secrètes 1956-1962* (Paris: Éditions du Seuil, 1995).

[3] Regarding the war's internationalization, see Matthew Connelly, *A Diplomatic Revolution: Algeria's Quest for Independence* (Oxford: Oxford University Press, 2002); Martin Thomas, *The French North African Crisis: Colonial Breakdown and Anglo-French Relations, 1945-62* (London:

Macmillan, 2000); Irwin M. Wall, *France, the United States, and the Algerian War* (Los Angeles: University of California Press, 2001). See also Irwin M. Wall, "The United States, Algeria, and the Fall of the French Fourth Republic," *Diplomatic History* 18, no.4 (1994), 489-511; Martin Thomas, "Defending a Lost Cause? France and the United States Vision of Imperial Rule in French North Africa, 1945-56," *Diplomatic History* 26, no. 2 (2002), 215-247; Matthew Connelly, "Rethinking the Cold War and Decolonisation: The Grand Strategy of the Algerian War of Independence," *International Journal of Middle East Studies* 33 (2001), 221-244; Jacob Abadi, "Great Britain and the Maghreb in the Epoch of Pan Arabism and Cold War," *Cold War History* 2, no. 2 (2002), 125-160.

[4] Connelly, *A Diplomatic Revolution*; Yahia H. Zoubir, "The United States, the Soviet Union and Decolonisation of the Maghreb, 1945-62," *Middle Eastern Studies* 31 (1995), 58-84; and Zoubir, "U.S. and Soviet Policies toward France's Struggle with Anti-Colonial Nationalism in North Africa," *Canadian Journal of History* 30 (1995), 439-466.

[5] Cited in Pierre Dabezies, "Subversion, anti-subversion, auto-subversion," in Olivier Forcade, Eric Duhamel, and Philippe Vial, eds., *Militaires en République 1870-1962: Les Officiers, le Pouvoir et la Vie Publique en France* (Paris: Publications de la Sorbonne, 1999), 554.

[6] Omar Carlier, "Mouvements de jeunesse, passage des générations et créativité sociale: La radicalité inventive algérienne des années 1940-50," in Nicolas Bancel, Daniel Denis, and Youssef Fates, eds., *De l'Indochine à l'Algérie: La jeunesse en mouvement des côtés du miroir colonial 1940-62* (Paris: Découverte, 2003), 169-170.

[7] The most detailed analysis of the FLN is Gilbert Meynier, *Histoire Intérieure du FLN, 1954-62* (Paris: Fayard, 2002).

[8] Charles-Robert Ageron, "L'Opinion française à travers les sondages," in Jean-Pierre Rioux, ed., *La guerre d'Algérie et les Française* (Paris: Fayard, 1992), 26-27.

[9] Charles-Robert Ageron, "L'insurrection du 20 août 1955 dans le nord Constantinois: De la résistance armée à la guerre au people," in *La guerre d'Algérie et les Algériens, 1954-62* (Paris: Armand Colin, 1997), 27-50; Anthony Clayton, *The Wars of French Decolonization* (London, Longman, 1994), 118-119.

[10] Regarding these earlier measures, see *DDF* I, doc. 300 (1955), Antoine Pinay to Couve de Murville, May 26, 1955; TNA, FO 371/113788, Algiers consular note to FO African Dept., July 8, 1955.

[11] Philippe Bourdrel, *La dernière chance de l'Algérie française: Du gouvernement socialiste au retour de De Gaulle, 1956-58* (Paris: Albin Michel, 1996). See also Gérard Bossuat, "Guy Mollet: La puissance française autrement," *Relations Internationales* 57 (1989), 25-48.

[12] Paul Clay Sorum, *Intellectuals and Decolonization in France* (Chapel Hill: University of North Carolina Press, 1977), 107.

[13] Service Historique de l'Armée, Vincennes, 1H1374/D3, "Situation des effectifs des trios armées en Algérie, 1956."

[14] On the SAS, see Grégor Mathias, *Les Sections administrative spécialisées en Algérie: Entre ideal et réalité, 1955-62* (Paris: L'Harmattan, 1998); Sylvian Bartet, "Aspect de la pacification en Grande Kabylie, 1955-62: Les relations entre les sections

administrative spécialisées et les populations," *Revue Française d'Histoire d'Outre-Mer* 85, no. 319 (1998), 3-32.

[15] The consequences of army action are explored in Raphaëlle Branche, *La torture et l'armée pendant la Guerre d'Algérie: 1954-1962* (Paris: Gallimard, 2002); for the judicial system's involvement, see Sylvie Thénault, *Une drôle de justice: Les magistrats dans la guerre d'Algérie* (Paris: La Découverte, 2001), especially part 2.

[16] Michel Cornaton, *Les Camps de regroupement de la guerre d'Algérie* (Paris: L'Harmattan, 1998); Keith Sutton, "Army Administration Tensions over Algeria's *Centres de regroupement*, 1954-62," *British Journal of Middle Eastern Studies* 26, no. 2 (1999), 243-270.

[17] George Armstrong Kelly, *Lost Soldiers: The French Army and Empire in Crisis, 1947-62* (Cambridge, Massachusetts: MIT Press, 1965); Maurice Vaïsse *La Grandeur. Politique étrangère du général de Gaulle, 1958–1969* (Paris: Fayard, 1998), 60-103.

[18] William Stivers, "Eisenhower and the Middle East," in Richard A. Melanson and David Mayers, eds., *Reevaluating Eisenhower: American Foreign Policy in the Fifties* (Urbana, Illinois: University of Chicago Press, 1987), 193, 204.

[19] Matthew Connelly, "Taking Off the Cold War Lens: Visions of North-South Conflict during the Algerian War for Independence," *American Historical Review* 105 (2000), 753-769.

[20] Martin Thomas, "The British Government and the End of French Algeria, 1958-62," *Journal of Strategic Studies* 25, no. 2 (2000), 172-173, 185-189.

[21] Connelly, *A Diplomatic Revolution*, 130-141; Martin Thomas, "France Accused: French North Africa before the United Nations, 1952-62," *Contemporary European History* 10, no. 1 (2001), 91-121.

[22] For details, see Wall, "The United States, Algeria, and the Fall of the French Fourth Republic," 489-511.

[23] The FLN's approach is explained in Connelly, *A Diplomatic Revolution*.

[24] Raymond Betts, *France and Decolonization, 1900-60* (Basingstoke, United Kingdom: Macmillan, 1991), 107-108.

[25] Martin S. Alexander, "Seeking France's 'Lost Soldiers': Reflections on the Military Crisis in Algeria," in Kenneth Mouré and Martin S. Alexander, eds., *Crisis and Renewal in France, 1918-62* (Oxford: Berghahn, 2002), 246-250, 260 n. 13.

[26] *DDF*II, doc. 7 (1960), "Conclusions sur les entretiens de Melun," July 5, 1960; Malek, *L'Algérie à Evian*, 62-66; Agulhon, *The French Republic*, 395-396.

[27] For insights into OAS attitudes, see Alexander Harrison, *Challenging De Gaulle: The O.A.S. and the Counterrevolution in Algeria, 1954-62* (New York: Praeger, 1989).

[28] Jim House and Neil MacMaster, *Paris 1961: Algerians, State Terror, and Memory* (Oxford: Oxford University Press, 2006), 88-89.

[29] The subtlest analysis of the war's impact on French society is Todd Shepard, *The Invention of Decolonization: The Algerian War and the Remaking of France* (Ithaca, New York: Cornell University Press, 2006).

[30] House and MacMaster, *Paris 1961*, 95-111, 162-179. Through research of police and hospital records, the authors estimate "well over" 120 police killings of Algerians in the Paris region during September and October 1961.

[31] Jim House and Neil MacMaster, "'Une journé portée disparue': The Paris Massacre of 1961 and Memory," in Mouré and Alexander, *Crisis and Renewal*, 267-90.

[32] Jean-Paul Brunet, *Police contre F.L.N.: Le drame d'octobre 1961* (Paris: Flammarion, 1999), 12.

[33] Martin Evans, *The Memory of Resistance: French Opposition to the Algerian War, 1954-62* (Oxford: Berg, 1997), 36-37, 122-125, 205.

[34] SHA, 1H2036/D1, no. 30/ART, Final artillery report, March 30, 1962.

[35] Malek, *L'Algérie à Evian*, annex IV.

[36] Colette Zytnicki, "L'administration face à l'arrivée des repartriés d'Algérie: L'exemple de la region Midi-Pyrénées, 1962-64," *Annales du Midi* 110, no. 224 (1998), 501-521.

The Suez Crisis

[1] See, for instance, Martin Woollacott, *After Suez: Adrift in the American Century* (London: IB Tauris, 2006).

[2] Peter Lyon, "The Commonwealth and the Suez Crisis," in William Roger Louis and Roger Owen, eds., *Suez 1956: The Crisis and Its Consequences* (London: Clarendon Press, 1991), 257-273.

[3] J.C. Hurewitz, "The Historical Context," in Louis and Owen, *Suez 1956*, 19-29.

[4] Derek Varble, *The Suez Crisis 1956* (Oxford: Osprey, 2003).

[5] Eden had twice previously served as foreign secretary, successively in Stanley Baldwin's and Neville Chamberlain's Conservative governments, before resigning over the policy of appeasement, and again for the majority of the Second World War in Churchill's coalition government.

[6] Nasser espoused these ideas in numerous speeches, synthesizing many in his record of the Egyptian revolution, Gamal Abdel Nasser, *Egypt's Liberation: The Philosophy of the Revolution* (Washington, D.C.: Public Affairs Press, 1955). For a succinct summary of Nasser's thoughts, see A. Hillal Dessouki, "Nasser and the Struggle for Independence," in Louis and Owen, *Suez 1956*, 31-42.

[7] Keith Kyle, *Suez* (London: Weidenfeld & Nicolson, 1991), 72-73.

[8] BBC Summary of World Broadcasts, Part 4, September 30, 1955, 17-18, quoted in Scott Lucas, ed., *Britain and Suez: The Lion's Last Roar* (Manchester, United Kingdom: Manchester University Press, 1996), 16.

[9] Scott Lucas, *Divided We Stand: Britain, the U.S. and the Suez Crisis* (London: Hodder & Stoughton, 1991), 104-108.

[10] Anthony Nutting, *No End of a Lesson: The Story of Suez* (London: Constable, 1967), 17. Also quoted in Lucas, *Divided We Stand*, 95.

[11] Evelyn Shuckburgh, *Descent to Suez* (London: Navy Records Society, 1986), 345. Quoted in Kyle, *Suez*, 95.

NOTES

[12] Nutting, *End of a Lesson*.

[13] Memorandum from Secretary of State Dulles to President Eisenhower, March 28, 1956, Ann Whitman Series, DDE Diaries, box 13, Eisenhower Papers, Eisenhower Library, Abilene, Kansas.

[14] U.S. Department of State, *Foreign Relations of the United States (FR US), 1955-57*, vol. 15, *Arab-Israeli Dispute, January 1-July 26, 1956* (Washington, D.C.: Government Printing Office, 1989); Lucas, *Britain and Suez*, 22-38.

[15] Shuckburgh, *Descent to Suez*, 345.

[16] It is worth noting that the Omega Memorandum caveats cooperation by stating that U.S. Middle (or "Near") East strategy "would in the main be coordinated with the United Kingdom."

[17] See for instance Wilbur C. Eveland, *Ropes of Sand: America's Failure in the Middle East* (London: Norton, 1980).

[18] *FR US, 1955-57*, vol. 15, doc. 197, Eden to Eisenhower, May 15, 1956.

[19] The details of MI6's three-phased plan are contained in a cable from the CIA's London Station to the director of the CIA. For a summary see Lucas, *Britain and Suez*, 38-39.

[20] M. Johnson, Treasury to J. Phillips (FO), June 6, 1956, FO 371/119055. Quoted in Kyle, *Suez*, 126.

[21] For a good insight into Nasser's mindset, see Mohamed H. Heikal, *Cutting the Lion's Tail* (London: Andre Deutsch, 1986).

[22] Message from Eden to Eisenhower, July 27, 1956, *FR US, 1955-57*, vol. 16, *Suez Canal Crisis, July 27-December 31, 1956*, 9-11.

[23] Message from Eisenhower to Eden, July 31, 1956, *FR US 1955-57*, vol. 16, 69-71.

[24] See for instance Ian Speller, *The Role of Amphibious Warfare in British Defence Policy, 1945-56* (Basingstoke, United Kingdom: Palgrave, 2001), 173-200.

[25] André Beaufre, *The Suez Expedition 1956* (London: Faber & Faber, 1969).

[26] Selwyn Lloyd, *Suez 1956: A Personal Account* (New York: Cape, 1978).

[27] This basis was Lloyd's so-called Six Principles: free and open transit of the canal without discrimination, respect of Egyptian sovereignty, insulation of canal operations from the politics of any one country, canal dues to be decided between Egypt and the canal users collectively, a "fair" proportion of the revenue to be earmarked for Egyptian development, and all outstanding issues between the Suez Canal Company and the Egyptian government to be settled by independent arbitration.

[28] Presidential Press Conference, October 12, 1956.

[29] See Mahmoud Fawzi, *Suez 1956: An Egyptian Perspective* (London: Shorouk, 1987).

[30] Kyle, *Suez*, 272-278.

[31] See letter from Secretary of State Dulles to Foreign Secretary Lloyd, October 15, 1956, *FR US, 1955-57*, vol. 16, doc. 347, and letter from Foreign Secretary Lloyd to Secretary of State Dulles, October 15, 1956, *FR US, 1955-57*, vol. 16, doc. 348.

[32] Telegram from the Department of State to the Embassy in the United Kingdom, October 17, 1956, *FR US, 1955-57*, vol. 16, doc. 351.

[33] Letter from Lloyd to Dulles, October 15, 1956, *FR US, 1955-57*, vol. 16.

[34] National Archives (NA Kew), PREM 11/1102 Eden to Lloyd, T 445/56, August 10, 1956.

[35] See, for instance, the telegram from the Department of State to the Embassy in the United Kingdom, October 26, 1956, *FR US, 1955-57*, vol. 16, doc. 384.

[36] See for instance Keith Kyle, "Britain and the Crisis, 1955-56," in Louis and Owen, *Suez 1956*, 107-109.

[37] See for instance Mordechai Bar-On, "David Ben Gurion and the Sèvres Collusion," in Louis and Owen, *Suez 1956*, 145-160; Michael Bar-Zohar, *The Armed Prophet: A Biography of David Ben-Gurion* (London: Arthur Baker, 1995); David Ben-Gurion, *Recollections* (London: MacDonald, 1970).

[38] See Bar-On, "David Ben Gurion and the Sèvres Collusion," 149.

[39] Ibid., 157.

[40] Message from President Eisenhower to Prime Minister Ben Gurion, October 28, 1956, *FR US*, 1955-57, vol. 16, docs. 394 and 395.

[41] See, for example, the telegram from the U.S. Embassy in the UK to Department of State, October 29, 1956, *FR US, 1955-57*, vol. 16, doc. 405.

[42] Memorandum of a telephone conversation between the president and the secretary of state, Washington, October 28, 1956, *FR US, 1955-57*, vol. 16, doc. 398.

[43] Lucas, *Britain and Suez*, 100.

[44] Letter from Prime Minister Bulganin to President Eisenhower, May 11, 1956, *FR US, 1955-57*, vol. 16, doc. 505.

[45] Memorandum of Discussion at the 302nd Meeting of the National Security Council, January 11, 1956, *FR US, 1955-57*, vol. 16, doc. 455.

[46] Hugh Thomas, *The Suez Affair* (London: Weidenfeld & Nicolson, 1966), 146.

[47] Message from Eden to Eisenhower, May 11, 1956, *FR US, 1955-57*, vol. 16, doc. 499.

[48] Draft message from Eisenhower to Eden, May 11, 1956, *FR US, 1955-57*, vol. 16, doc. 502.

[49] See Ian Speller, "The Suez Crisis: Op MUSKETEER, Nov 1956," in Tristan Lovering, ed., *Amphibious Assault: Manoeuvre from the Sea* (Suffolk, United Kingdom: Seafarer Books, 2007), 421-436.

The Vietnam War

[1] John Lewis Gaddis, *Strategies of Containment*, rev. ed. (Oxford: Oxford University Press, 2005), 24-52.

[2] Larry Berman, *Planning a Tragedy: The Americanization of the War in Vietnam* (New York: Norton, 1982), 9.

[3] Fredrik Logevall, *Choosing War: The Lost Chance for Peace and the Escalation of War in Vietnam* (Berkeley: University of California Press, 1999), 385.

[4] Henry Kissinger, *Diplomacy* (London: Simon & Schuster, 1994), 480.

[5] For example, Lawrence Freedman, "Escalation/Limited War: The U.S. View," in Carl G. Jacobsen, ed., *Strategic Power: USA/USSR* (London: Macmillan, 1990), 159.

[6] Gaddis, *Strategies of Containment*, 235-271.

[7] Roger Hilsman, *To Move a Nation: The Politics of Foreign Policy in the Administration of John F. Kennedy* (New York: Doubleday, 1967), 128-129; Lawrence Freedman, *Kennedy's Wars: Berlin, Cuba, Laos, and Vietnam* (New York: Oxford University Press, 2000), 290-291.

[8] Presidents Kennedy, Nixon, and Johnson's powers were in excess of their predecessors' and perhaps in excess of the Constitution. See Leslie H. Gelb, *The Irony of Vietnam: The System Worked* (Washington, D.C.: Brookings Institute, 1979), 362.

---

[50] The Israelis would not withdraw until March of the following year.

[9] Robert Kennedy, *Thirteen Days: A Memoir of the Cuban Missile Crisis* (New York: Norton, 1969), 36.

[10] David Halberstam, *The Best and the Brightest* (New York: Random House, 1969), 44.

[11] Dave R. Palmer, *Summons of the Trumpet: U.S.-Vietnam in Perspective* (Novato, California: Presidio Press, 1978), 204.

[12] Robert D. Schulzinger, *A Time for War: The United States and Vietnam, 1941-75* (Oxford: Oxford University Press, 1997), 328.

[13] Andrew F. Krepinevich Jr., *The Army and Vietnam* (Baltimore, Maryland: Johns Hopkins University Press, 1986), 18.

[14] Schulzinger, *A Time for War*, 23-43.

[15] U.S. Department of State, *Foreign Relations of the United States (FR US), 1952-54*, vol. 13, *Indochina* (Washington, D.C.: Government Printing Office), 419.

[16] Richard H. Immerman, *John Foster Dulles: Piety, Pragmatism and Power in U.S. Foreign Policy* (Wilmington, Delaware: Scholarly Resources, 1999), 89-90.

[17] Christopher M. Gacek, *The Logic of Force: The Dilemma of Limited War in American Foreign Policy* (New York: Columbia University Press, 1994), 94-123.

[18] Townsend Hoopes, *The Devil and John Foster Dulles* (London: Andre Deutsch, 1973), 226-228.

[19] Ibid., 239.

[20] For a brief summary see Serge Ricard, "Europe and the Vietnam War: A Thirty Year Perspective," review in *Diplomatic History* 29, no. 5 (2005), 879-883.

[21] Berman, *Planning a Tragedy*, 12.

[22] Seth Jacobs, *America's Miracle Man in Vietnam: Ngo Dinh Diem, Religion, Race and U.S. Intervention in Southeast Asia* (Durham, North Carolina: Duke University Press, 2004).

[23] Jacobs, *America's Miracle Man in Vietnam*, 2.

[24] *FR US, 1955-57*, vol. 1, *Vietnam*, 411.

[25] Stanley Karnow, *Vietnam: A History*, rev. ed. (London: Penguin, 1991) 245-249.

[26] James Lawton Collins Jr., *The Development and Training of the South Vietnamese Army, 1950-72* (Washington, D.C.: Government Printing Office, 1975).

[27] Freedman, *Kennedy's Wars*, 293-304.

[28] For the papers of the Taylor mission, see *FR US, 1961-63*, vol. 1, *Vietnam, 1960*, 380-614.

[29] "Maxwell Taylor Proposes U.S. Combat Troops for Vietnam," in George C. Herring, ed., *The Pentagon Papers*, abr. ed. (New York: McGraw-Hill, 1993), 55-57.

[30] Michael Maclear, *Vietnam: The Ten Thousand Day War* (London: Methuen, 1981), 57.

[31] Krepinevich, *The Army and Vietnam*.

[32] H.R. McMaster, *Dereliction of Duty: Lyndon Johnson, Robert McNamara, the Joint Chiefs of Staff, and the Lies That Led to Vietnam* (New York: HarperCollins, 1997), 323, 334.

[33] William E. Simons, "U.S. Coercive Pressure on North Vietnam, Early 1965," in Alexander L. George and William E. Simons, eds., *The Limits of Coercive Diplomacy*, 2nd ed. (Oxford: Westview Press, 1994), 155.

[34] Simons, "U.S. Coercive Pressure on North Vietnam, Early 1965," 133-173.

[35] Mark Clodfelter, *The Limits of Airpower: The American Bombing of North Vietnam* (New York: Free Press, 1989), 140.

[36] Lawrence Freedman, "Vietnam and the Disillusioned Strategist," *International Affairs* 72, no. 1 (1996), 136.

[37] Clodfelter, *The Limits of Airpower*, 20.

[38] U.S.G. Sharp, *Strategy for Defeat: Vietnam in Retrospect* (Novato, California: Presidio, 1978), 2, 4, 268.

[39] Berman, *Planning a Tragedy*, xi-xii.

[40] *FR US, 1964-68*, vol. 3, *Vietnam, July-December 1965*, 209-217.

[41] Fredrick Logevall, *Choosing War*.

[42] Ibid., 383.

[43] Ibid., 385.

44 Ibid., 279, 372-373; Peter Busch, *All the Way with JFK? Britain, the U.S., and the Vietnam War* (Oxford: Oxford University Press, 2003).

45 Robert W. Komer, foreword in Thomas C. Thayer, *War without Fronts: The American Experience in Vietnam* (Boulder, Colorado: Westview, 1985), xxi. Komer wrote an excellent book on the Vietnam War, *Bureaucracy at War: U.S. Performance in the Vietnam Conflict* (Boulder, Colorado: Westview Press, 1986).

46 George S. Eckhardt, *Command and Control 1950-69* (Washington, D.C.: Government Printing Office, 1974).

47 William C. Westmoreland, *A Soldier Reports* (New York: Dell, 1976), 198-199.

48 Ibid., 296.

49 Eliot A. Cohen, *Supreme Command: Soldiers, Statesmen, and Leadership in Wartime* (New York: Free Press, 2002), especially 17-88.

50 Peter MacDonald, *Giap: The Victor in Vietnam* (London: Norton, 1993). This book is based on interviews by the author with Giap.

51 Julian J. Ewell and Ira A. Hunt Jr., *Sharpening the Combat Edge: The Use of Analysis to Reinforce Military Judgment* (Washington, D.C.: Government Printing Office, 1974), 83.

52 Michael Howard, "The Forgotten Dimensions of Strategy," in *The Causes of War* (London: Unwin, 1984), 101, 115.

[53] James William Gibson, *The Perfect War: Technowar in Vietnam* (Boston: Atlantic Monthly Press, 1986).

[54] Harry G. Summers Jr., *On Strategy: A Critical Analysis of the Vietnam War* (Novato, California: Presidio Press, 1982), 1.

[55] Guenter Lewy, *America in Vietnam* (New York: Oxford University Press, 1978), 434.

[56] MacDonald, *Giap*, 266, 269.

[57] William C. Westmoreland, "A Military War of Attrition," in W. Scott Thompson and Donaldson D. Frizzell, eds., *The Lessons of Vietnam* (New York: Crane, Russack and Co., 1977), 57-71.

[58] Adam Garfinkle, *Telltale Hearts: The Origins and Impact of the Vietnam Antiwar Movement* (London: Macmillan, 1995), 100.

[59] Ibid., 100.

[60] William M. Hammond, *Public Affairs, the Military and the Media, 1968-73: The U.S. Army in Vietnam* (Washington, D.C.: Government Printing Office, 1996).

[61] Lewy, *America in Vietnam*, 433.

[62] For example, see Robert Buzzanco, *Vietnam and the Transformation of American Life* (Oxford: Blackwell, 1999).

[63] See Seymour Hersh, *My Lai 4: A Report on the Massacre and Its Aftermath* (New York: Vintage Books, 1970). General Nguyen Ngoc Loan's summary execution of a Viet Cong prisoner came to be symbolic as it was captured on film; see Schulzinger, *A Time for War*, 261.

[64] Lyndon B. Johnson, "The President's Address to the Nation Announcing Steps to Limit the War in Vietnam and Reporting His Decision Not to Seek Reelection," March 21, 1968, *Public Papers of the Presidents, Lyndon B. Johnson 1968-69*, vol. 1 (Washington, D.C.: Government Printing Office, 1970), 469-476.

[65] H.G. Nicholas, "The 1968 Presidential Elections," *Journal of American Studies* 3, no. 1 (1969), 4-5.

[66] Larry Berman, *No Peace, No Honor: Nixon, Kissinger, and Betrayal in Vietnam* (New York: Simon & Schuster, 2001), 21ff.

[67] Ibid., 33.

[68] Christopher Hitchens, *The Trial of Henry Kissinger* (London: Verso, 2001), 6-18, 21.

[69] Melvin Laird, "Iraq: Learning the Lessons of Vietnam," *Foreign Affairs* 84, no. 6 (November/December 2005), 22-43.

[70] Lewis Sorley, *A Better War: The Unexamined Victories and Final Tragedy of America's Last Years in Vietnam* (New York: Harcourt Brace, 1999), xiv. For example, Karnow's *Vietnam* has 103 pages out of 670 on this period, and there are 60 out of a possible 281 pages in George C. Herring, *America's Longest War: The United States and Vietnam 1950-75*, 4th ed. (New York: Knopf, 2001).

[71] Ronald H. Spector, *After Tet: The Bloodiest Year in Vietnam* (New York: Free Press, 1993), xv.

[72] See Sorley, *A Better War*. The standard account is William Shawcross, *Sideshow: Nixon, Kissinger and the Destruction of Cambodia* (New York: Simon & Schuster, 1979). For a more

current example of the controversy and its associated issues, see Hitchens, *The Trial of Henry Kissinger*.

[73] Spector, *After Tet*, xvi.

The criticisms of Kissinger have been recently revived by Christopher Hitchens, *The Trial of Henry Kissinger*, particularly 6-43.

[75] John Lewis Gaddis, "Rescuing Choice from Circumstance: The Statecraft of Henry Kissinger," in Gordon A. Craig and Francis L. Loewenheim, eds., *The Diplomats 1939-79* (Princeton, New Jersey: Princeton University Press, 1994), 564-592.

[76] Walter Isaacson, *Kissinger: A Biography* (London: Faber & Faber, 1992), 242; T.G. Otte, "Kissinger," in G.R. Berridge, Maurice Keens-Soper, and T.G. Otte, *Diplomatic Theory from Machiavelli to Kissinger* (Basingstoke, United Kingdom: Palgrave, 2001), 188-190.

[77] Stephen P. Randolph, *Powerful and Brutal Weapons: Nixon, Kissinger, and the Easter Offensive* (Cambridge, Massachusetts: Harvard University Press, 2007).

[78] Isaacson, *Kissinger*, 260.

[79] Clodfelter, *The Limits of Airpower*, 194.

[80] MacDonald, *Giap*, 316.

[81] Clodfelter, *The Limits of Airpower*.

[82] Berman, *No Peace, No Honor*.

[83] Fred Charles Iklé, *Every War Must End*, rev. ed. (New York: Columbia University Press, 1991), vii.

[84] Edward N. Luttwak, "The Impact of Vietnam on Strategic Thinking in the United States," in Patrick J. Hearden, ed., *Vietnam: Four Perspectives* (West Lafayette, Indiana: Purdue University Press, 1990), 71.

[85] Richard Nixon, *No More Vietnams* (London: W.H. Allen, 1985), 13.

[86] Richard A. Melanson, *Reconstructing Consensus: American Foreign Policy since the Vietnam War* (New York: St. Martin's Press, 1991), 189.

[87] Gelb, *The Irony of Vietnam*, 357.

[88] Garfinkle, *Telltale Hearts*, 214.

[89] Gaddis Smith, *Morality, Reason and Power: American Diplomacy in the Carter Years* (New York: Hill & Wang, 1986), especially 12-33; and John Lewis Gaddis, *The United States and the End of the Cold War: Implications, Reconsiderations, Provocations* (Oxford: Oxford University Press, 1992), 47-64.

[90] Mackubin T. Owens, "Strategy and Resources: Trends in the U.S. Defense Budget," in Williamson Murray, ed., *Brassey's Mershon American Defense Annual 1995-96* (Washington, D.C.: Brassey's, 1995), 171.

[91] Smith, *Morality, Reason and Power*, 35-45; Jay Winik, *On the Brink* (New York: Simon & Schuster, 1996), 83.

[92] Zbigniew Brzezinski, *Power and Principle: Memoirs of the National Security Adviser 1977-81*, rev. ed. (New York: Farrar, Strauss, Giroux, 1985), 42-44.

[93] Richard Lock-Pullan, *U.S. Intervention Policy and U.S. Army Innovation: From Vietnam to Iraq* (London: Routledge, 2006).

[94] "Remarks to the American Legislative Exchange Council, March 1, 1991," http://bushlibrary.tamu.edu/papers/1991/91030101.html.

[95] Colin S. Gray, *Weapons Don't Make War: Policy, Strategy, and Military Technology* (Lawrence: University of Kansas Press, 1993), 174.

[96] Douglas Pike, *PAVN: People's Army of Vietnam* (Novato, California: Presidio Press, 1986), 217.

The Falklands/Malvinas War

[1] The best account of Thatcher's diplomatic activity during this timeframe is Paul Sharp, *Thatcher's Diplomacy: The Revival of British Foreign Policy* (New York: St. Martin's Press, 1997). Overviews of the conflict include Lawrence Freedman, *The Official History of the Falklands Campaign*, vols. 1 and 2 (London: Routledge, 2005); Max Hastings and Simon Jenkins, *The Battle for the Falklands* (London: Pan Books, 1983); and the essays in Stephen Badsey et al., eds., *The Falklands Conflict Twenty Years On: Lessons for the Future* (London: Frank Cass, 2005).

[2] Margaret Thatcher, *The Downing Street Years* (London: Harper-Collins, 1993), 173. In addition to Thatcher's memoirs, for the political background, see Peter Carrington, *Reflect on Things Past* (London: Collins, 1988); John Nott, *Here Today, Gone Tomorrow: Reflections of an Errant Politician* (London: Politico's,

2002); and William Whitelaw, *The Whitelaw Memoirs* (London: Headline Book, 1990). A critical intervention came from First Sea Lord Henry Leach. See Henry Leach, *Endure No Makeshifts: Some Naval Recollections* (London: Leo Cooper, 1993).

[3] Andrew Dorman, *Defence under Thatcher* (London: Palgrave, 2002).

[4] See Nicholas Henderson, *Mandarin: The Diaries of an Ambassador, 1969-82* (London: Weidenfeld & Nicolson, 1994).

[5] Anthony Parsons, "The Falklands Crisis in the United Nations, 31 March-14 June 1982," *International Affairs* 59, no. 2 (Spring 1983), 169-178.

[6] UN Security Council Resolution 502 (1982) was passed April 3, 1982, http://daccessdds.un.org/doc/RESOLUTION/GEN/NR0/435/26/IMG/NR043526.pdf?OpenElement, accessed June 23, 2010.

[7] Caspar Weinberger, *Fighting for Peace: Seven Critical Years at the Pentagon* (London: Michael Joseph, 1990), 144-145; Henderson, *Mandarin*, 442.

[8] Alexander Haig, *Caveat* (London: Weidenfeld & Nicolson, 1984).

[9] Freedman, *The Official History of the Falklands Campaign*, vol. 2, 531.

The Kosovo War

[1] Adam Roberts, "NATO's 'Humanitarian War' over Kosovo," *Survival* 41, no. 3 (Autumn 1999), 102-133. See also Larry

Minear, Ted van Baarda, and Marc Sommers, "NATO and Humanitarian Action in the Kosovo Crisis," occasional paper no. 36, Thomas J. Watson Jr. Institute for International Studies (2000), v, www.unhcr.ch.

[2] Roberts, "NATO's 'Humanitarian War' over Kosovo." See also Minear, van Baarda, and Sommers, "NATO and Humanitarian Action in the Kosovo Crisis."

[3] Samuel P. Huntington, *The Clash of Civilizations and the Remaking of World Order* (New York: Simon & Schuster, 1997).

[4] Cited in M.A. Smith, "Kosovo: Background and Chronology" (Camberley, United Kingdom: Conflict Studies Research Centre Paper G72, April 1999), 1.

[5] Barbara W. Tuchman, *August 1914* (London: Macmillan, 1980); A.J.P. Taylor, *War by Time-Table: How the First World War Began* (London: Macdonald & Co., 1969); Zara Steiner, *Britain and the Origins of the First World War* (Basingstoke, United Kingdom: Macmillan, 1977).

[6] See Margaret MacMillan, *Peacemakers: The Paris Peace Conference of 1919 and Its Attempt to End the War* (London: John Murray, 2001).

[7] Madeleine Albright, *Madam Secretary: A Memoir* (New York: Macmillan, 2003), 379-380.

[8] The Dayton Agreement had identified Kosovo as an issue that could potentially have prevented the signing of the agreement, and it was therefore agreed that it should be identified as an issue for subsequent resolution; United Nations Security Council Resolution 1031 (1995), December 15, 1995,

http://ods-dds-ny.un.org/UNDOC/GEN/N95/405/26/PDF/N9540526.pdf?OpenElement.

9 "Final Communiqué: Ministerial Meeting of the North Atlantic Council Held at NATO Headquarters, Brussels, on December 16, 1997," *Press Release M-NAC-2 (97), 155*, December 16, 1997, www.nato.int/docu/pr/1997/p97-155e.htm.

10 United Nations Security Council Resolution 1160 (1998), March 31, 1998, http://ods-dds-ny.un.org/UNDOC/GEN/N98/090/23/PDF/N9809023.pdf?OpenElement.

11 "Background to the Conflict," Official Kosovo Force website, www.nato.int/kfor/kfor/intro.htm; "Final Communiqué: Ministerial Meeting of the North Atlantic Council in Luxembourg on May 28, 1998," *NATO Press Release M-NAC-D 1 (98) 77*, June 11, 1998, www.nato.int/docu/pr/p98-059e.htm.

12 "Statement on Kosovo," issued at the meeting of the North Atlantic Council in Defence Ministers Session, *NATO Press Release M-NAC-D 1 (98) 77*, June 11, 1998, www.nato.int/docu/pr/1998/p98-077e.htm.

13 Albright, *Madam Secretary*, 360.

14 "Report of the Secretary-General prepared pursuant to Resolution 1160 (1998) of the Security Council," *s/1998/834*, September 4, 1998, www.un.org/Docs/sg/reports/1998.htm.

15 Albright, *Madam Secretary*, 388.

16 See Wesley K. Clark, *Waging Modern War* (New York: Public Affairs Press, 2001).

[17] "Report of the Secretary-General prepared pursuant to Resolution 1160 (1998) of the Security Council," *S/1998/834*, September 4, 1998, http://ods-dds-ny.un.org/doc/UNDOC/GEN/N98/279/96/PDF/N9827996.pdf?OpenElement.

[18] United Nations Security Council Resolution 1199 (1998), *S/RES/11 99 (1998)*, September 23, 1998, http://ods-dds-ny.un.org/doc/UNDOC/GEN/N98/279/96/PDF/N9827996.pdf?OpenElement.

[19] "Statement by the Secretary General following the ACTWARN decision," Press Statement, September 24, 1998, www.nato.int/docu/pr/1998/p980924e.htm; "Kosovo/Operation Allied Force After-Action Report," (Department of Defense, January 31, 2000), 21, www.defenselink.mil/pubs/kaar02072000.pdf.

[20] Phase 0: Deploy to region, begin a series of air exercises to signal intent, and begin information operations. Phase 1: Following on from North Atlantic Council (NAC), the extension of the No-Fly Zone to include the Federal Republic of Yugoslavia, attacks against the Yugoslav Integrated Air Defense System, command and control system, and aircraft. Phase 2: Further NAC decision – strike military and special police targets in Kosovo. Phase 3: Further NAC decision – extension of strikes to cover Yugoslavia with targets geared towards destroying/neutralizing the capability to undertake military operations and compel the Yugoslav authorities to end the conflict.

[21] The problem of this alternative was that it could only be undertaken by the United States and thus might not be seen to be a NATO action.

[22] "Report of the Secretary-General prepared pursuant to Resolutions 1160 (1998) and 1199 (1998) of the Security

Council," *S/1998/912*, October 3, 1998, http://ods-dds-ny.un.org/UNDOC/GEN/N98/289/78/PDF/N9828978.pdf?OpenElement.

[23] "Statement by the Russian government on NATO plans to attack targets in Yugoslavia," press release by the Russian Embassy, London, October 6, 1998.

[24] *The Scotsman*, October 12, 1998.

[25] Albright, *Madam Secretary*, 390.

[26] "Press Release by Foreign Secretary, Mr. Robin Cook," NATO HQ, Brussels, October 13, 1999.

[27] Albright, *Madam Secretary*, 390.

[28] United Nations Security Council Resolution 1203, October 24, 1998, http://daccessdds. Un.org/doc/UNDOC/GEN/N98/321/21/PDF/N9832121.pdf?OpenElement.

[29] Paddy Ashdown, *The Ashdown Diaries*, vol. 2, *1997-99* (London: Penguin Press, 2001), 361.

[30] Youngs, "Kosovo."

[31] "Kosovo: Lessons from the Crisis" (London: Ministry of Defence, 2000), www.mod.uk/publications/kosovo_lessons/contents.htm.

[32] *An Analysis of the Human Rights Findings of the OSCE Kosovo Verification Mission October 1998-June 1999*, www.osce.org/documents/mik/1999/11/1620_en.pdf.

[33] www.un.org/icty.

[34] The six-nation Contact Group was set up in 1992 by the London Conference on the Former Yugoslavia and consisted of France, Germany, Italy, Russia, the United Kingdom, and the United States.

[35] "Statement to the Press by NATO Secretary General, Dr. Javier Solana," *NATO Press Release (99) 11*, January 28, 1999, www.nato.int/docu/pr/1999/p99-011e.htm; "Interview given by the Foreign Secretary, Robin Cook Friday," *Today* radio program, January 29, 1999.

[36] See "Prepared Statement for Walter B. Slocombe, Undersecretary of Defense Policy, Before the Senate Armed Services Committee Hearing on Kosovo," February 25, 1999, 4, http://armed-services.senate.gov/hearings/1999/c990225.htm.

[37] "Chris Roberts, Sky News, at Briefing by Mr. George Robertson, Secretary of State for Defence, and General Sir Charles Guthrie, Chief of the Defence Staff," March 25, 1999, www.kosovo.mod.uk/brief250399.htm.

[38] "Statement by the North Atlantic Council on the Situation in Kosovo," *NATO Press Release (1999) 038*, March 22, 1999, www.nato.int/docu/pr/1999/p99-038e.htm.

[39] "Press Statement by Dr. Javier Solana, Secretary-General," *NATO Press Release (1999) 040*, March 23, 1999, www.nato.int/docu/pr/1999/p99-040e.htm.

[40] See "Combined Prepared Statement of General Wesley Clark, Admiral James Ellis Jr., and Lieutenant-General Michael

Short of the United States European Command before the Senate Armed Services Committee Hearing on Kosovo," October 21, 1999, http://armed-services.senate.gov/hearings/1999/c991021.htm.

[41] Andrew Dorman, "The Irrelevance of Air Power: The Potential Impact of Capability Divergence in NATO Post-Kosovo," *Airman Scholar* (Spring 2000), 53-58, www.usafa.af.mil/wing/34edg/air-man/A-Spring00.pdf.

[42] "Briefing by Mr. George Robertson, Secretary of State for Defence, and General Sir Charles Guthrie, Chief of the Defence Staff," March 25, 1999, www.kosovo.mod.uk/brief250399.htm.

[43] See "Combined Prepared Statement of General Wesley Clark, Admiral James Ellis Jr., and Lieutenant-General Michael Short of the United States European Command before the Senate Armed Services Committee Hearing on Kosovo," October 21, 1999, http://armed-services.senate.gov/hearings/1999/c991021.htm.

[44] "G8 Foreign Ministers' Principles, May 6, 1999," www.kosovo.mod.uk/account/principles.htm.

[45] George Robertson, "Briefing by the Secretary of State for Defence, Mr. George Robertson, and the Deputy Chief of the Defence Staff (Commitments), Air Marshal Sir John Day," May 20, 1999, www.kosovo.mod.uk/briefing200599.htm.

[46] For full details of the case, initial and subsequent indictments, see Milosevic (IT-02-54), "Kosovo, Croatia and Bosnia," www.un.org/icty/cases/indictindex-e.htm.

[47] George Robertson, "Briefing by the Defence Secretary, Mr. George Robertson, and the Deputy Chief of the Defence Staff (Commitments), Air Marshal Sir John Day," May 26, 1999, www.kosovo.mod.uk/brief260599.htm.

[48] Tim Youngs and Paul Bowers, "Kosovo: KFOR and Reconstruction," House of Commons Library Research paper 99/66, June 18, 1999, 8, www.parliament.uk/commons/libresearch/rp99/rp99-066.pdf.

[49] "Military Technical Agreement between the International Security Force (KFOR) and the Governments of the Federal Republic of Yugoslavia and the Republic of Serbia," June 9, 1999, www.nato.int/kosovo/docu/a990609a.htm.

[50] United Nations Security Council Resolution 1244, *S/RES/1244 (1999)*, http://ods-dds-ny.un.org/doc/UNDOC/GEN/N99/172/89/PDF/N9917289.pdf?OpenElement.

[51] Mike Jackson, "Kosovo: The Inside Story," *The RUSI Journal* 145, no. 1 (February 2000), 13-19.

[52] Doug Henderson, "Briefing by the Armed Forces Minister, Mr. Doug Henderson, and the Chief of Joint Operations, Admiral Sir John Garnett," June 12, 1999, www.kosovo.mod.uk/brief120699.htm.

[53] Geoffrey Hoon, "Briefing by the Foreign Office Minister, Mr. Geoffrey Hoon, and the Chief of Joint Operations, Admiral Sir Ian Garnett," June 17, 1999, www.kosovo.mod.uk/brief170699.htm.

[54] "Undertaking of demilitarization and transformation by the UCK," signed June 20, 1999, www.nato.int/kfor/kfor/docu/a990620a.htm.

[55] "UNHCR Kosovo Crisis Update," June 17, 1999, www.unhcr.ch/news/media/kosovo.htm.

[56] "Text: Defense Secretary Cohen on Lessons Learned in Kosovo," October 9, 1999, www.usembassy.it/file9909/alia/99091010.htm.

[57] Albright, *Madam Secretary*, 378.

Origins of the Iraq War

[1] David H. Petraeus, "Report to Congress on the Situation in Iraq," September 11, 2007, http://foreign.senate.gov/testimony/2007/PetraeusTestimony070911a.pdf.

[2] James Dobbins, "Who Lost Iraq? Lessons from the Debacle," *Foreign Affairs* 86, no. 5 (September-October 2007), 61-74; Anthony Seldon, *Blair Unbound* (London: St. Martin's Press, 2007), 557.

[3] "The Legacy of the Madrid Bombings," *BBC News Online*, February 15, 2007, http://news.bbc.co.uk/1/hi/world/europe/6357599.stm.

[4] "Police Chief Urges Muslim Inquiry," August 7, 2006, http://news.bbc.co.uk/1/hi/uk/5251346.stm.

[5] Dana H. Allin, Gilles Andréani, Philipe Errera, and Gary Samore, "Repairing the Damage: Possibilities and Limits of Transatlantic Consensus," *Adelphi Paper 389* (London: Taylor & Francis for the IISS, 2007).

[6] Barbara Slavin, *Bitter Friends, Bosom Enemies: Iran, the U.S., and the Twisted Path to Confrontation* (New York: St. Martin's Press, 2007).

[7] See Lawrence Freedman and Efraim Karsh, *The Gulf Conflict 1990-91: Diplomacy and War in the New World Order* (London: Faber & Faber, 1993).

[8] See http://www.un.org/av/photo/subjects/unscom.htm.

[9] See http://www.defenselink.mil/specials/desert_fox/.

[10] "Letter dated 25 January 1999 from the Executive Chairman of the Special Commission established by the Secretary-General pursuant to paragraph 9 (b) (i) of Security Council Resolution 687 (1991) addressed to the President of the Security Council," www.un.org/Depts/unscom/s99-94.htm.

[11] See http://www.un.org/Depts/oip/background/inbrief.html.

[12] Geoff Hoon, *House of Commons Parliamentary Debates*, November 25, 2002, col. 124, www.publications.parliament.uk/pa/cm200203/cmhansrd/vo021125/debtext/21125-34.htm#21225-34_spmin0.

[13] Geoff Hoon, *House of Commons Parliamentary Debates*, Statement to the House, February 6, 2003, vol. 299, session 2002-03, col. 455, www.publications.parliament.uk/pa/cm200203/cmhansrd/vo200206/debtext/30206-11.htm#30206-11_spmin0.

[14] Jacob Heilbrunn, *They Knew They Were Right: The Rise of the Neocons* (New York: Random House, 2008).

[15] Fergal Keane, "The Road to War," in Sarah Beck and Malcolm Downing, eds., *The Battle for Iraq: BBC News Correspondents on the War against Saddam and a New World Agenda* (London: BBC, 2003), 45.

[16] See Stephen E. Flynn, "The Neglected Home Front," *Foreign Affairs* 81, no. 5 (September-October 2002), http://www.foreignaffairs.org/20040901faessay83504/stephen-e-flynn/the-neglected-home-frong.html; Bruce Hoffman, "Lessons of 9/11," *CT-201* (Santa Monica, California: Rand, 2002).

[17] Michael Gordon and Bernard Trainor, *Cobra II: The Inside Story of the Invasion and Occupation of Iraq* (London: Atlantic Books, 2006), 3-4.

[18] Ibid.

[19] "The Secret Downing Street Memo," *Times Online*, May 1, 2005, http://www.timesonline.co.uk/tol/news/politics/election2005/article387390.ece.

[20] http://www.un.org/webcast/ga/57/statements/020912usaE.htm.

[21] Bill Nelson, *Congressional Record*, January 28, 2004 (Senate), S311-S312, http://www.fas.org/irp/congress/2004_cr/s012804b.html.

[22] United Nations Security Council 1441 (2002), adopted November 8, 2002, *S/RES/1441 (2002)*, http://ods-dds-ny.un.org/doc/UNDOC/GEN/N2/682/26/PDF/N0268226.pdf?OpenElement.

[23] Tommy Franks, *American Soldier* (New York: HarperCollins, 2004), 329.

[24] Roland Watson, "Rumsfeld Doctrine Gives Spoils of War to Washington's Hawks," *The Times*, April 12, 2003, 20; William

P. Hawkins, "Iraq: Heavy Forces and Decisive Warfare," *Parameters* 33, no. 3 (Autumn 2003), 61.

[25] "France's Position on Iraq," press conference of Foreign Affairs Minister Dominique de Villepin (excerpts), New York, January 20 2003, http://www.ambafrance-us.org/news/statmnts/2003/vilepin012003.asp.

[26] Adam Ingram, *House of Commons Parliamentary Debates*, February 11, 2003, vol. 399, session 2002-03, col. 772, www.publications.parliament.uk/pa/cm200203/cmhansrd/vo300211/debtext/30211-07.htm.

[27] Judy Dempsey, Robert Graham, and James Harding, "NATO is Plunged into Crisis over Blockade on Turkish Defence," *The Financial Times*, February 11, 2003, 1; Stephen Castle, Andrew Grice, and Kim Sengupta, "NATO Wounded in Crossfire over Iraq," *The Independent*, February 11, 2003, 1; John Vinocur, "For Paris and Berlin, a Drive to Stay Important," *International Herald Tribune*, February 11, 2003, 1; Charles Bremner, "Chirac Risks All in Headlong Rush to Thwart Bush," *The Times*, February 11, 2003, 12.

[28] "No Grounds for War," *The Guardian*, February 15, 2003, 23.

[29] Martin Walker, "The Worst-Case Scenario," March 5, 2003, in Martin Walker, ed., *The Iraq War: As Witnessed by the Correspondents and Photographers of United Press International* (Washington, D.C.: Brassey's Inc., 2004), 3.

[30] United Nations Security Council, 4714th Meeting, *S/PV.4714*, March 7, 2003, http://ods-dds-ny.un.org/doc/UNDOC/PRO/N0327076.pdf?OpenElement.

[31] "The Foreign Minister's statement on the withdrawal of the draft resolution by the United States, Great Britain, and Spain," Paris, March 17, 2003, http://www.info-france-usa.org/news/statmnts/2003/iraq_france031703.asp.

[32] Tim Ripley, "Assault on the Al Faw Peninsula," *Jane's International Defense Review* 37 (July 2004), 47-49.

[33] "Transcript of 3/23 CENTCOM Briefing," *Release No. 03-03-54*, March 23, 2003, www.centcom.mil/CENTCOMNews/News_Release.asp?NewsRelease=20030354.txt.

[34] Rick Atkinson, *In the Company of Soldiers: A Chronicle of Combat* (New York: Henry Holt, 2004).

[35] Jim Garamone, "Remembering the 3rd Infantry Division's Thunder Runs," *American Forces Press Service*, March 21, 2004, http://209.157.64.200/focus/f-news/1102290/posts; David Zucchinoi and Mark Bowden, *Thunder Run: The Armored Strike to Capture Baghdad* (New York: Atlantic Monthly Press, 2004).

[36] Zucchino and Bowden, *Thunder Run*.

[37] David E. Sanger, "President Says Military Phase in Iraq Has Ended," *New York Times*, May 2, 2003, 1.

[38] Suzanne Goldenberg, "White House Rethinks Iraq Plan," *The Guardian*, January 14, 2004, 17.

ABOUT THE AUTHOR

Eric Gustafson graduated from the University of Minnesota, Duluth, and the Diplomatic Academy of London. His writings have appeared in *The Economist, European Voice, The Guardian, Intelligent Living,* and *The Washington Times,* and he is the author of *A Brief History of Iraq* (2006). Mr. Gustafson is a military-intelligence analyst and a noncommissioned officer in the U.S. Army. He resides in Mannheim, Germany.